Economic Policy, Financial Markets, and Economic Growth

Published in cooperation with
the Milken Institute
for Job & Capital Formation

Economic Policy, Financial Markets, and Economic Growth

EDITED BY
Benjamin Zycher
and Lewis C. Solmon

Westview Press
BOULDER • SAN FRANCISCO • OXFORD

Copyright © 1993 by Westview Press, Inc.

Published in 1993 in the United States of America by Westview Press, Inc., 5500 Central Avenue, Boulder, Colorado 80301-2877, and in the United Kingdom by Westview Press, 36 Lonsdale Road, Summertown, Oxford OX2 7EW

Library of Congress Cataloging-in-Publication Data
Economic policy, financial markets, and economic growth / edited by
  Benjamin Zycher and Lewis C. Solmon.
      p.   cm.
  Includes bibliographical references and index.
  ISBN 0-8133-8803-1
  1. Economic policy.   2. Monetary policy.   3. Economic development.
I. Zycher, Benjamin.   II. Solmon, Lewis C.
HD75.E277   1993
338.9—dc20
                                                                                    93-5957
                                                                                    CIP

Printed and bound in the United States of America

The paper used in this publication meets the requirements
of the American National Standard for Permanence of Paper
for Printed Library Materials Z39.48-1984.

10   9   8   7   6   5   4   3   2   1

Contents

Foreword

Lowell Milken

The Foundations of the Milken Families were established in 1982 with the mission to help people help themselves and those around them to lead productive and satisfying lives. Since their inception, the Foundations have worked to advance that mission by developing both the human capital of individuals as well as what sociologist James Coleman has termed social capital—the productive capacity inherent in relations among people. As the Foundations seek to connect the benefits of these forms of capital with concrete opportunities for people to lead lives of creativity and purpose, we create and seek programs which are catalysts for human development. Our focus on the human resources with which this country is so richly endowed, moreover, is common to all the programs we initiate.

The work of the Milken Institute for Job and Capital Formation is a direct outgrowth of the Foundations' mission and reflects the Foundations' commitment to investing in the security of our people, our communities, and our country. Established with a mandate to support research into and discourse on the determinants of American economic growth, the Institute examines the policies and practices needed for meaningful employment opportunities and for an economic environment producing people qualified and prepared to respond to those opportunities.

Central to the Institute's mission is its commitment to developing and maintaining a citizenry which is literate in economics. This book presents the research reported at the first of a series of planned economic conferences. Held in October 1992, the conference focused on "Economic Policy, Financial Markets, and Economic Growth" and brought together economists, business people, and other community leaders. This volume is an important means of reaching a critical academic and policy audience with the Conference's findings.

The Milken Institute for Job and Capital Formation is growing, and as it does it participates more actively and fully in the national discussion of economic policy and policy-making. Toward this end, it has launched an ambitious program to communicate the policy implications of its economic research not only to economists and business leaders but also to the general public by such means as documentary films and opinion articles.

The Foundations are excited about the Institute's accomplishments, ideas, and programs. The Institute shares with the Foundations of the Milken Families a central belief that respect for individual need and potential is pivotal as we work to restore true security—in the form of sound education, adequate health care, and the basic constituents of human well-being to our society, our communities, and our families.

The Milken Institute
for Job and Capital Formation:
An Introduction

Lewis C. Solmon

The Milken Institute for Job and Capital Formation is a private philanthropic foundation established to support research and public discourse on the determinants of American economic growth.

Among the many factors that have been suggested as important influences upon economic growth in the United States are the quality of education and access to it; the organization and structure of businesses; access to financial capital by, and the capital structures of, American firms; the efficiency of financial institutions; federal, state, and local regulatory policies; tax and government expenditure policies; the behavior of individual leaders and entrepreneurs; support for research, technological development, and innovation; the U.S. role in the international economy; the consumption and saving behavior of individuals; and social values. Notwithstanding this broad set of dimensions, the MIJCF is a research institute with a somewhat narrower focus, originally envisioned to be "job and capital formation." But neither job formation nor capital formation is an end in itself; both are necessary for economic growth and, in a larger sense, the promotion of human well-being. Thus, economic growth can be viewed as the "dependent variable" of central interest to the MIJCF, with the many and varied factors influencing economic growth as the primary objects of our research efforts. Although the roles played by capital formation and access to capital, as well as factors influencing the creation and allocation of employment, are of particular interest, many other important factors must be held constant, and so their impacts also lie within the scope of our research interests.

As the links between economic policy and economic growth are simultaneously obvious and obscure, this volume presents the papers and discussant comments delivered at the first MIJCF conference, held October 21–23, 1992, in Santa Monica, California. As economic policy clearly affects financial markets in crucial ways, and, through that avenue, economic growth, the topics addressed by the individual papers are central to the analytic and policy focus of the MIJCF. The importance and policy relevance of the conference and of the individual sessions are well illustrated by the international renown of the presenters and discussants who participated in this first MIJCF conference.

Through in-house and commissioned research studies, periodic seminars and conferences, and publication in academic, policy, and popular journals, the resident and affiliated staff of the MIJCF hope to advance our understanding of economic growth and of the capital formation, job creation, and other factors influencing it, and to use this understanding in efforts to educate opinion shapers and policymakers, as well as the public at large. Through such educational efforts we hope to aid in the strengthening of U.S. economic performance and in the broader advance of human welfare.

PART ONE

Capital Markets, Capital Formation, Savings, and Economic Growth

Introduction

That economic growth is affected by myriad factors is a truism, and the list of relevant influences of interest to scholars and policymakers is lengthy and expanding. In particular, the importance of various government policies is recognized widely, but the relative magnitudes of their effects and their respective absolute impacts upon growth are difficult to measure. Even the direction of impact of some policies—that is, the issue of whether their net effects are positive or negative—is in dispute.

The chapters in this section, by Robert J. Barro and Jack L. Carr, illustrate divergent approaches to analysis of the economic growth effects of government policies. Using straightforward econometric techniques, Barro examines factors likely on *a priori* grounds to affect the rate at which individual incomes in poor regions or nations grow relative to those in wealthier areas. This analysis of income "convergence" yields several interesting findings, among them an empirical estimate of the long-run effect on the growth of individual incomes yielded by greater resource allocation by government. Two findings that are more surprising are the ambiguity of the effect of individual income upon the saving rate and the suggested small impact of international trade upon income convergence.

Barro's chapter raises a number of interesting questions, foremost among them the issue of why government policies affecting economic growth vary so greatly among nations. That in a real sense is a restatement of a very familiar public choice issue: Why does government behave as it does, and how can the incentives shaping government behavior be structured to encourage policy choices consistent with stronger growth in individual well-being?

Other interesting issues emerged during the course of the general discussion at this first session of the MIJCF conference. Barro includes investment (as a share of GDP) as one variable affecting the growth of individual income, but does not separate the relative impacts of private and public investment. (The chapter by William A. Niskanen in Part IV of this volume addresses that issue in part.) Another interesting comment dealt with efforts to aid the economic transition and growth processes in the former Soviet Union and Eastern Europe; what can the

West do to promote political stability and the transition to capitalism? In this context, further refinements of Barro's work perhaps ought to include some measure(s) of foreign aid, as an empirical test of the benefits often purportedly engendered by such policies. This has direct relevance to U.S. domestic policy, because federal aid to inner cities in many respects is similar to U.S. foreign aid policies, and the long-run impacts of those policies in terms of economic advancement are ambiguous at best.

In Chapter 2, Carr recognizes the substantial difficulty with which existing economic models of growth actually explain observed differences in growth, both across nations and over time, and then discusses some implications of two general hypotheses about the origins of policies affecting growth. One hypothesis is the "public interest" theory of policy: government policies are adopted in efforts to further some conception of the public interest (or to negate the adverse effects of various types of market failure). The second is the "private interest" theory: government policies are the result of competition in political "markets" for the subsidies, favors, and protection from competitors demanded by interest groups.

The problem of explaining government policy choice is crucial in the growth context because the incentives shaping the choice and implementation of economic policies ultimately determine their net effects upon growth. To the extent that market failures of various types reduce national wealth, to the extent that the reduction is significant, and to the extent that market forces inherently are unable to reduce such adverse effects, the critical question remains: Are there reasons, whether conceptual or empirical, to believe that government action can be expected to yield net improvement?

After a brief discussion outlining some reasons for skepticism about the benevolence of government policy-making, often assumed implicitly but rarely justified, Carr examines the public and private interest rationales in the context of government deposit insurance for banks. The public interest rationale stems from the social costs created by "rational" runs on banks when individual depositors cannot distinguish easily between problems affecting a given bank and those affecting the banking system. Deposit insurance would prevent such runs, thus preserving the stability of the banking system. In the private interest view, on the other hand, deposit insurance provided by government is a device with which small banks can attract deposits on the same terms as large banks, despite the greater inherent riskiness of the former. Deposit insurance in this view, therefore, is an implicit subsidy scheme emanating from interest group competition, and so is likely to reduce national wealth by distorting the allocation of resources—in this case, financial capital.

Carr concludes that the histories of deposit insurance adoption in Canada and the United States are consistent with the private interest model of government behavior. This finding is important: if consistent with findings derived from empirical examinations of other policies, it suggests that government policies in general, whatever their respective rationales, systematically may yield effects upon economic growth that are negative on net.

Carr points out that deposit insurance provides incentives for excessive risk taking and other adverse behavior. One interesting point raised in the general session discussion concerned efforts by government to limit such ensuing adverse effects; an example noted by Carr is the legal limit on interest paid on insured deposits. The discussion centered upon efforts by government to reduce such negative ancillary effects of policies, and whether these efforts inherently are self-limiting or endlessly expansionary. In order to regulate, can the government focus be narrow, or must it expand continually as markets respond behaviorally to existing rules? That question has not been answered, but it is central to the examination of government and its effects upon economic growth.

1

Economic Growth, Convergence, and Government Policies

Robert J. Barro

A key issue in economic development is whether economies that start out behind tend to grow faster in per capita terms and thereby converge toward those that began ahead. This convergence property seems to apply empirically for economies that have similar underlying structures, such as the regions of the major developed countries or among the OECD countries but not for a heterogeneous collection of countries that includes the poor nations of Africa, South Asia, and Latin America. One reason for the failure of convergence in this broad context is that countries are effectively heading toward different long-run targets for per capita income. These targets depend on government policies in areas such as taxation, protection of property rights, and provision of infrastructure services and education. The targets can also vary because of factors that governments cannot readily influence, such as underlying attitudes about saving, work effort, and fertility, and the availability of natural resources. For a given long-run target—determined by government policies and other factors—the convergence tendency depends on the speed with which an economy approaches this target. This speed turns out empirically to be similar across economies, such as a broad cross-section of countries, that differ greatly in other respects. Conceptually, the speed of convergence depends on such issues as diminishing returns to capital, the behavior of saving, the mobility of capital and labor, and the diffusion of technology from leaders to followers.

I begin this chapter with a discussion of some empirical evidence on economic growth, especially as it pertains to the convergence question. Then I relate these facts to theories of economic growth and make inferences for the role of government policies.

Some Empirical Evidence on Convergence

Regional Data

Figures 1.1 through 1.4 relate to regional economies, the U.S. states and the regions of some major countries in Western Europe. Figure 1.1, which applies to 47 continental U.S. states, plots the average annual growth rate of per capita personal income (exclusive of transfer payments) from 1880 to 1988 against the logarithm of per capita personal income in 1880. The figure shows a striking inverse relationship—that is, the places that were poorer in 1880 grew significantly faster in per capita terms over the subsequent 108 years. Thus, the behavior of growth rates across the U.S. states is consistent with convergence, in the sense of the poor places growing faster than the rich ones.

Part of the story that underlies Figure 1.1 is the catch-up of the southern states to the initially richer eastern and western states. But the convergence pattern applies equally well within regions as across regions; for example, the initially poor eastern states, such as Maine and Vermont, tended to grow faster than the initially rich eastern states, such as Massachusetts and New York.

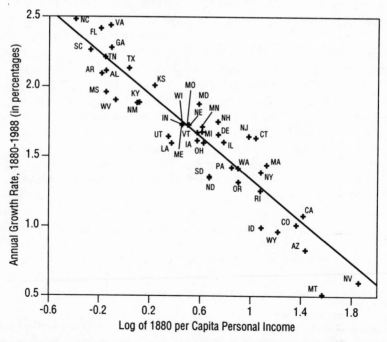

FIGURE 1.1 Convergence of Personal Income across U.S. States: 1880 Income and Income Growth from 1880 to 1988. *Note:* Data for Oklahoma are unavailable because 1880 preceded the Oklahoma land rush.

The data shown in Figure 1.1 effectively imply that the rate of convergence is roughly 2% per year (see Barro and Sala-i-Martin, 1991, for the details). In other words, about 2% of the gap between a rich and a poor economy tends to be eliminated in one year. This rate of convergence implies a half-life of about 35 years; that is, it takes 35 years on average for half of an initial spread to vanish. Furthermore, it takes 70 and 115 years, respectively, to eliminate three-quarters and 90% of the gap. These numbers accord with the period of roughly a century after 1880 that it took for the per capita income of the typical southern state to come close to that in the typical northern state.

Figure 1.2 shows a measure of the dispersion of per capita income (the standard deviation of the logarithm of per capita personal income) across the U.S. states from 1880 to 1988. (Personal income is measured exclusive of transfer payments until 1929 and is shown with and without transfers thereafter.) The dispersion declined steadily from 1880 until 1920, then rose in the 1920s because of the sharp fall in real incomes originating in agriculture. The effect of the agricultural shock was pronounced because the agricultural states had lower-than-average levels of per capita income prior to the shock. The dispersion declined from the 1930s until the late 1970s, but increased during the 1980s back to the levels of the early 1960s.

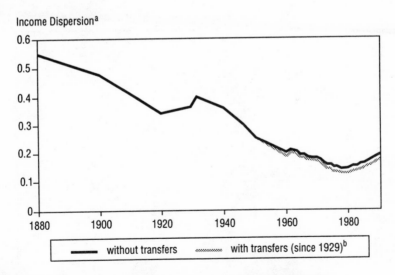

FIGURE 1.2 Dispersion of Personal Income across U.S. States, 1880-1988
[a] Income dispersion is measured by the unweighted cross-sectional standard deviation of the log of per capita personal income.
[b] Data on the dispersion of per capita personal income inclusive of government transfer payments are included since 1929, although the effect of including transfer payments is negligible before 1950.

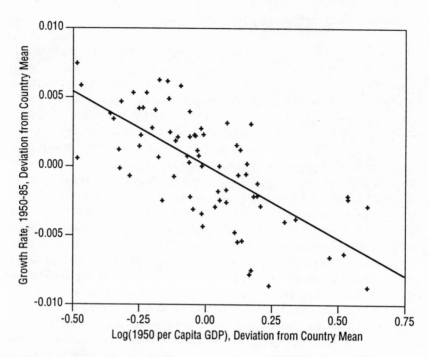

FIGURE 1.3 Growth Rate versus Initial Level of per Capita GDP for 73 European Regions

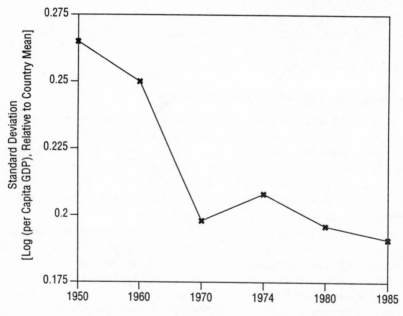

FIGURE 1.4 Dispersion of per Capita GDP across 63 Regions of Four Major European Countries

In the early 1980s, the rise in dispersion reflected the oil shock of 1979–80, an effect that was pronounced because the oil states already had above-average levels of per capita income. The behavior of oil prices does not seem, however, to account for the continuing rise in dispersion in the late 1980s. This recent behavior resembles the pattern for measures of inequality for the incomes of individuals and families. The rise in dispersion at the state level may therefore reflect elements that have been cited in studies of the increased income inequality for families: the changing technological mix and the increased returns to education.

Figures 1.3 and 1.4 describe the behavior of per capita gross domestic product (GDP) from 1950 to 1985 for 73 regions of seven European countries (11 in Germany, 11 in the United Kingdom, 20 in Italy, 21 in France, 4 in the Netherlands, 3 in Belgium, and 3 in Denmark). Figure 1.3 plots the regional growth rate of per capita GDP from 1950 to 1985 (expressed relative to the mean growth rate for the respective country) versus the logarithm of per capita GDP in 1950 (again measured relative to the mean for each country).[1] Although the relation is less striking than that shown in Figure 1.1, the inverse association between the initial position and the subsequent growth rate is statistically highly significant. The results turn out quantitatively to imply a speed of convergence that is again about 2% per year (see Barro and Sala-i-Martin, 1991). Similar behavior also shows up for the provinces of Japan, although in this case, the estimated rate of convergence is about 3% per year.

Figure 1.4 shows the dispersion across the 63 European regions from the four larger countries: Germany, the United Kingdom, Italy, and France. The dispersion of per capita GDP declined from 1950 to 1970, but then changed little on net from 1970 to 1985.

Evidence from a Broad Sample of Countries

Figures 1.5 and 1.6 provide information about convergence for 114 countries, roughly all of the significant countries that exist except for the formerly centrally planned economies. Figure 1.5 plots the average growth rate of real per capita GDP from 1960 to 1985 against the logarithm of real per capita GDP in 1960.[2] In contrast to the clear inverse relationships that showed up in Figures 1.1 and 1.3, the growth rate and initial level are essentially uncorrelated in Figure 1.5; the association is actually slightly positive. The cross-country data therefore do not reveal convergence: the poor countries did not tend to grow faster per capita than the rich, and hence, the typical poor country did not tend to catch up to the typical rich country.

The convergence behavior found for regions in Figures 1.1 and 1.3 shows up across countries if the sample is restricted to a relatively

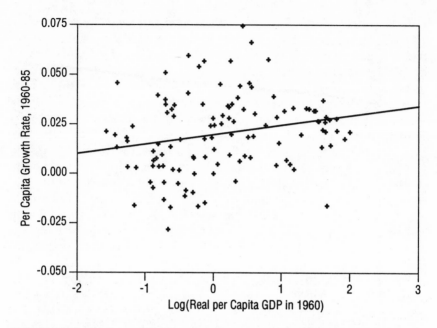

FIGURE 1.5 Growth versus Initial Level of Real per Capita GDP for 114 Countries

homogeneous group of well-off places. If one looks, for example, at the 20 countries that were members of the OECD in 1960, then the initially poorer countries tended to grow faster per capita. The estimated rate of convergence in this sample turns out, however, to be only about 1% per year.

Figure 1.6 shows the time path from 1960 to 1985 for the dispersion of per capita real GDP for the 114 countries. (The data are plotted at five-year intervals.) The dispersion rose moderately but steadily over the sample. Figure 1.7 shows that this pattern also applied since 1950 for the 60 countries that have the earlier data.

Theoretical Perspectives on the Empirical Evidence

One framework for studying convergence is the growth model developed by Solow (1956) and other economists. In this model, the force toward convergence involves the accumulation of capital through domestic savings in a context of diminishing returns. As an economy accumulates capital and thereby develops, the falling rate of return on capital tends to reduce the rate of growth. Thus, poor countries tend to grow faster because they have a higher rate of return on capital.

If different economies—say, countries or regions of countries—have the same underlying technologies, preferences, and government policies, then

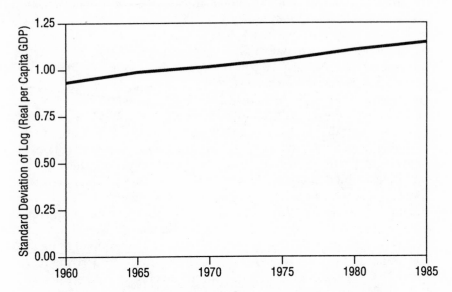

FIGURE 1.6 Dispersion of Logarithm of Real per Capita GDP for 114 Countries

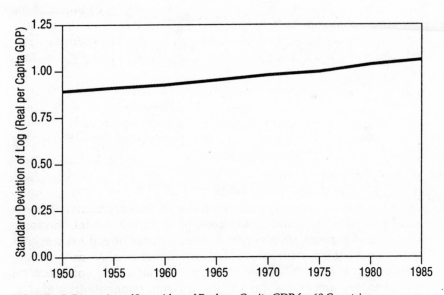

FIGURE 1.7 Dispersion of Logarithm of Real per Capita GDP for 60 Countries

the standard growth model predicts an *absolute* form of convergence. Economies with lower starting levels of income and product per person tend to grow faster in per capita terms because the smaller level of per capita product translates into a higher productivity of capital. This prediction accords with the regional data considered in Figures 1.1 and 1.3.

Quantitatively, the empirical estimate that regional convergence occurs at about 2% per year turns out to accord with the underlying growth model only if the diminishing returns to capital—the source of convergence in that model—set in slowly. We have to take a broad view of capital to include human capital—educational attainment, work experience, and health—so that the rate of return on capital does not fall rapidly as capital is accumulated. To fit the empirical estimate of the convergence rate, the share of capital income in total income has to be roughly three-quarters. This high capital share is reasonable, however, if we include human capital as part of the total capital stock.

If we try to apply the theory to the heterogeneous group of more than 100 countries, then we have to allow for differences in underlying conditions. These elements include not only the level of technology and attitudes about saving, work, and fertility, but also government policies in regard to taxation, maintenance of property rights, and provision of infrastructure services. Economies may differ substantially in some of these respects and may accordingly be converging to different long-run paths of per capita income. Let y_i be the current level of per capita income for economy i and y_i^* be the long-run target that the economy is approaching. If economies have different long-run values, y_i^*, then the standard growth model predicts a *conditional* form of convergence. An economy grows faster if its starting level of per capita income, y_i, is further away from its own long-run value, y_i^*. This conclusion follows because the private return from investment—net of taxation and risk of expropriation—depends inversely on the gap between y_i and y_i^*.

The results for the broad sample of countries shown in Figure 1.5 can fit with the standard growth model if the countries vary substantially in their target values, y_i^*. These variations could plausibly be large because of differences in government policies that affect the incentives to invest and operate efficiently: the countries differ in their openness to international trade and domestic competition, in effective tax rates on market activity, and in political stability and other factors that influence property rights. As the sample comprises considerable heterogeneity with regard to cultural histories, the countries may also vary significantly in respect to their underlying preferences about saving, fertility, and work effort.

The interpretation offered by the standard growth theory is therefore that the variations across the 114 countries in per capita GDP, y_i, reflect mainly the variations in the long-run targets, y_i^*, and are accordingly essentially uncorrelated with the gaps from the targets, $y_i - y_i^*$. Since the underlying theory predicts an inverse relation between the growth rate and this gap, this interpretation is consistent with the absence of a significant relation between the growth rate and the initial level, y_i. In contrast, for the U.S. states and regions of European countries and Japan, the interpretation was that the y_i^* were roughly equal and, hence, that the variations in y_i reflected mainly differences in the gaps, $y_i - y_i^*$. The growth rate was therefore inversely related to the initial level in these samples.

In a recent study (Barro, 1991) and in ongoing research, I have attempted to isolate observable variables that proxy for the long-run targets, y_i^*. If these targets can satisfactorily be held constant, then the theory predicts that an inverse relation between a country's growth rate and its starting position, y_i, would emerge. This result does, in fact, obtain if one holds constant such variables as the share of government consumption in GDP, measures of openness to international trade (such as tariff rates and the black-market premium on foreign exchange), indicators of political stability (such as the frequency of revolutions and coups), and measures of initial human capital (such as the values at the start of the sample of educational attainment and life expectancy).[3] If these kinds of variables are held constant, then the estimated rate of convergence for real per capita GDP turns out to be statistically highly significant and of a magnitude, about 1.5% per year, that is only slightly below that found for the U.S. states and the regions of Europe and Japan. These results are therefore consistent with the conditional convergence predicted by the standard growth model. In particular, the typical country is converging to its own long-run target at nearly the same rate at which the typical U.S. state or region of Europe and Japan is converging to its target.

Table 1.1 contains a sample of this empirical research from an ongoing project on economic growth in which I am participating at the World Bank. The table shows regression equations for the growth rate of real per capita GDP. (The data on GDP are the values adjusted for differences in purchasing power by Summers and Heston, 1988.) The estimates apply to a panel data set for 73 countries—those with a full set of data—over five-year periods from 1960 to 1985. There are 365 observations in total, five observation periods for 73 countries. The independent variables include the logarithm of real per capita GDP at the start of each period, a number of variables including government policies that can be

TABLE 1.1
Panel Regressions for Growth Rate of Real per Capita GDP,
Five-Year Intervals from 1960 to 1985

Independent Variable	Estimated Coefficients (Standard Errors)			
log(Initial GDP)	−.0167	−.0196	—.0202	−.0217
	(.0027)	(.0024)	(.0026)	(.0023)
log(School)	.0232	.0109	.0193	.0092
	(.0041)	(.0041)	(.0039)	(.0038)
(G/Y)	−.140	−.159	−.074	−.091
	(.031)	(.027)	(.031)	(.027)
Openness*log(1 + Tariff Rate)	−.201	−.050	−.239	−.145
	(.101)	(.085)	(.091)	(.078)
log(1 + Black-Market Premium)	−.0226	−.0208	−.0246	−.0235
	(.0054)	(.0049)	(.0051)	(.0047)
Frequency of revolutions and coups	−.0147	−.0107	−.0127	−.0092
	(.0074)	(.0062)	(.0066)	(.0055)
I/Y	—	.120	—	.121
		(.021)		(.019)
FERT	—	−.0037	—	−.0019
		(.0012)		(.0011)
Sub-Saharan Africa	—	—	−.0310	−.0265
			(.0055)	(.0047)
Latin America	—	—	−.0124	−.0066
			(.0039)	(.0033)
R^2, individual periods	.05, .38,	.07, .52,	.19, .33,	.24, .45,
	.22, .31,	.26, .44,	.28, .43,	.33, .52,
	.08	.22	.21	.25

Note: Data presented here are discussed in detail in Barro and Lee (1992). The dependent variable is the annual growth rate of real per capita GDP over each period (1960–65, 1965–70, 1970–75, 1975–80, 1980–85). These data are from Summers and Heston (1988). There are 365 observations (73 countries and five time periods). Coefficients are estimated by seemingly unrelated (SUR) technique, which allows a country's error term to be correlated over time. Separate constants are estimated for each time period. Other coefficients are constrained to be the same for all periods.

Initial GDP is real per capita GDP at the start of each five-year interval.

School is 1 plus the average number of years of educational attainment of the population aged 25 and over at the start of each five-year period.

G/Y is the period average of the ratio of real government consumption, exclusive of education and defense, to real GDP.

Openness is an estimate of "natural" openness, based on area and distance measures. This variable is a constant for each country.

Tariff rate is an average of official tariff rates on capital imports and intermediates, weighted by shares in imports. Only one observation per country was available for the tariff rate.

(continues)

interpreted as determinants of a country's target position, y_i^*, and a measure of educational attainment. See the notes to Table 1.1 for details.

For given values of the other variables, the estimated coefficient on the logarithm of initial per capita GDP in the first regression of Table 1.1 is –.017, standard error (s.e.) = .003. Thus, this coefficient differs significantly from zero, and the magnitude indicates a rate of convergence to the long-run target of about 1.7% per year.

I included the variable G/Y, the ratio to GDP of government consumption purchases—total purchases exclusive of public investment, educational spending, and defense outlays. This government spending variable has a significantly negative effect on the growth rate; the estimated coefficient in the first regression of Table 1.1 is –.14, s.e. = .03. The items included in this portion of government expenditure would not contribute significantly to productivity and tend to distort private decisions because of the required public finance.

Some parts of the expenditures, such as those aimed at the enforcement of regulations, would also have a direct negative effect on productivity. Ongoing research by other economists, such as William Easterly and Sergio Rebelo for the World Bank project, is aimed at pinpointing the effects from detailed aspects of the government's taxes and spending, such as marginal tax rates on capital income and outlays on public investment.

Two variables that reflect distortions of international trade have adverse effects on the growth rate. One variable is a measure of average tariff rates—the estimated coefficient on this variable in the first regression of Table 1.1 is –.20, s.e. = .10.[4] I attempted to include an index of nontariff barriers generated by the United Nations, but the available data are poor and the variable that I used did not have a significant effect on growth rates. The other trade variable included in the regressions in Table 1.1 is the black-market premium on foreign exchange. This variable is a general proxy for distortions of foreign trade, but may also proxy more broadly for other distortionary policies and for macroeconomic

---

TABLE 1.1 *(continued)*

Black-market premium is the period average of the black-market premium on foreign exchange.
Frequency of revolutions and coups is the number of revolutions and coups per year, averaged over the full sample, 1960-85.
I/Y is the ratio of real gross domestic investment to real GDP, averaged over each period.
FERT is the total fertility rate, averaged over each period.
Sub-Saharan Africa is a dummy for countries in sub-Saharan Africa.
Latin America is a dummy for countries in Latin America.

instability. In any event, the estimated coefficient in the first regression of Table 1.1 is negative and highly significant: –.023, s.e. = .005.

I included the frequency of revolutions and coups as a proxy for political stability. The estimated coefficient in the first regression is significantly negative, –.015, s.e. = .007, but may also reflect a reverse influence from bad economic times to political instability. I also looked at measures of political freedom and civil liberties generated by Gastil (1987). But these measures did not have a significant effect on growth rates once the other variables listed in Table 1.1 were held constant. In any event, the overall message from the policy variables included in the regressions is that more interference with markets and political instability have adverse effects on economic growth.

The educational attainment variable is entered in the regressions as log(1 + total years of schooling for the adult population), where the years of attainment apply to the start of each period. The parameter 1 in this expression can be viewed as the effective number of years of education obtained without formal schooling. The estimated coefficient on the schooling variable in the first regression, .0232, s.e. = .0041, is positive and highly significant. Thus, for a given value of initial per capita GDP and the other variables, countries grew faster if they began each period with a greater amount of educational attainment. As a quantitative example, if average educational attainment begins at 2 years—the average value prevailing in sub-Saharan Africa in 1980—then an increase by 0.3 years would raise the quantity, 1 + years of attainment, by 10% and thereby increase the predicted growth rate by 0.2 percentage points per year.

The second regression shown in Table 1.1 adds I/Y, the ratio of real gross domestic investment to real GDP, and the total fertility rate. (These variables are measured as averages over each period.) In the Solow growth model, the investment ratio (or the saving rate) and the fertility rate (or the growth rate of population) are exogenous variables. These variables do not influence the long-run growth rate, but do affect the long-run level of per capita output, y_i^*. An increase in I/Y raises y_i^*, whereas a rise in fertility lowers y_i^*. Therefore, for a given value of initial per capita GDP, an increase in I/Y would raise the growth rate, whereas an increase in the fertility rate would lower the growth rate. The second regression in Table 1.1 shows that the estimated coefficient of I/Y is positive and highly significant (.120, s.e. = .021), whereas that for fertility is negative and significant (–.0037, s.e. = .0012). These results are consistent with the Solow model of economic growth. An interesting finding from this regression is that the inclusion of the investment ratio and the fertility rate roughly halves the estimated coefficient on the schooling variable: the estimated value is now .0109, s.e. = .0041. This result indicates that a good deal of the effect of initial human capital on the growth rate works through its positive effect on investment and negative effect on fertility. Similarly, the estimated influences of some of the policy variables—especially the tariff rate and political instability—are reduced when the investment ratio and the fertility rate are held constant.

The third and fourth regressions shown in Table 1.1 include dummy variables for sub-Saharan Africa and Latin America. Both continent dummies are significantly negative, substantially so for sub-Saharan Africa. The main inference from these results is that the independent variables that I have been able to measure and hold constant are insufficient to explain all of the poor growth performances in these regions. One possibility is that the measure of educational attainment in sub-Saharan Africa, although low, does not fully capture the low levels of human capital in this region. Other researchers in the World Bank project are examining other influences on the growth process. For example, Bob King and Ross Levine have been studying the effects from development of the financial system. They find that a more developed system of *private* credit has positive effects on growth for given values of the kinds of variables that I include in Table 1.1. Paul Romer (1990) has been examining the impact of foreign investment, and he finds that this investment has been an important source of technological progress in some cases, although the broader impact of foreign investment is not yet clear.

It should be stressed that the findings on convergence from the cross-country sample in Table 1.1 do not mean that the typical poor country in Africa, South Asia, or Latin America will tend to catch up to the richer countries in the world. The poor countries have long-run target positions, y_i^*, that are as low on average as their current positions, y_i, and therefore do not tend to grow especially quickly. Convergence toward the rich countries would be predicted only if the underlying determinants of y_i^*—such as openness to trade, political stability, and additional determinants that I was unable to measure directly—were improved, and the standard growth model provides no basis for predicting these improvements in underlying policies.

Additional Determinants of the Rate of Convergence

The Saving Rate

Extensions of the Solow growth model by Cass (1965) and Koopmans (1965) built on the earlier work of Ramsey (1928) to determine the saving rate through consumer optimization. As an economy develops, the saving rate need not remain constant (as Solow had assumed), but may instead fall or rise. If the saving rate were high at low levels of per capita income but then declined as an economy developed, then the convergence rate would be higher: poor countries would grow rapidly partly because the rate of return on capital was high and partly because they saved a lot. In contrast, if the saving rate were low initially and then increased with development, then the convergence rate would be reduced: the high rate of return on capital in poor economies would have to fight against the limited supply of savings.

Although the extensions of the neoclassical growth model allow for a formal analysis of the determinants of saving, the end result is that the relation of the saving rate to the level of economic development is ambiguous. The behavior of the rate of return—high when the stock of capital is small and declining as capital is accumulated—suggests that the saving rate would fall as an economy grows. The permanent-income hypothesis provides an opposing force: poor countries (that are converging toward high long-run levels of income) have a large positive gap between permanent and current income and tend accordingly to consume a lot and save little. This force attenuates as the economy develops; hence, the saving rate would increase.

The offset of the two forces—the substitution effect from the rate of return and the income effect caused by the gap between current and permanent income—leads to an ambiguous pattern for the saving rate. In fact, a more detailed analysis of the consumer's optimization problem suggests that the saving rate could plausibly remain roughly stable as an economy develops. This pattern also accords with some limited empirical evidence about the transitional behavior of saving rates for the large sample of countries mentioned before. The bottom line, therefore, is that the effect of economic development on the saving rate does not seem to be an important element in the observed patterns of convergence.

Capital Mobility

The theoretical framework considered thus far assumes a closed economy: goods do not move across borders and the residents or government of one economy cannot borrow from or lend to those in another economy. This assumption is unrealistic for countries, but is especially troubling for the regions of the United States, the Western European countries, and Japan.

The introduction of international trade in goods and assets has two types of effects in the context of the standard growth model. First, the long-run target, y_i^*, can be affected. The gains from trade and the benefits from specialization suggest that y_i^* would rise when the economy was opened. The exposure to foreign competition can also promote domestic efficiency; for example, Tornell and Velasco (1992) show that the potential for "capital flight" (including the brain drain for human capital) from a country with poorly defined property rights provides competitive pressure that generates an improvement in property rights and, hence, in the incentives to invest domestically. Thus, capital flight can lead indirectly to a higher growth rate.[5]

A second effect is that the potential to borrow and use foreign capital speeds up the adjustment process. Economies with low ratios of capital to labor—in relation to their steady-state values—would tend to become international borrowers, whereas those with high ratios would tend to become lenders. In the simplest situation of a perfect international credit market and no adjustment costs for capital accumulation, a small economy with a low starting ratio of capital to labor would adjust instantaneously to its long-run values of capital, production, and wage rates. (The economy's capital income and domestically owned assets tend, however, to converge slowly or not at all to those prevailing elsewhere.)

More realistically, a substantial fraction of the capital stock—especially human capital—cannot be financed by foreign borrowing or direct foreign investment. This kind of capital accumulation therefore requires a substantial element of domestic savings. Moreover, the adjustment costs for expanding the stock of human capital are large; that is, the process of expanding human capital cannot be accelerated greatly without encountering a rapid falloff in the rate of return on investment. These considerations suggest that the speed of convergence for an open economy may not be that much greater than that for a closed economy.

This conclusion is supported by some fragments of empirical evidence. First, the rate of conditional convergence across countries is only slightly less than that for regions of countries, although the mobility of capital would be much greater across the regions. Second, the speed of convergence for measures of production across the U.S. states (based on data for gross state product) is similar to that for measures of income (based on statistics for personal income). If the mobility of capital were a key element, then the rate of convergence would be greater for production (and the stock of productive capital) than for income (and the stock of domestic assets).

The Migration of Persons

Another force that influences convergence is the mobility of labor and persons across economies. Labor, responding to wage-rate differentials, tends to move toward economies that have high ratios of capital to labor (in relation to their steady-state ratios) and to places with high steady-state ratios of capital to labor (because a high steady-state value reflects elements such as low tax rates and a high intrinsic level of productivity).[6] The migration of labor toward economies that have high capital/labor ratios moves the ratios toward their steady-state values and thereby tends to speed up the process of convergence.

Barro and Sala-i-Martin (1991) have shown that migration across the U.S. states from 1900 to 1987 occurred in the anticipated manner—people moved on net toward places with higher per capita personal income after holding constant some measures of amenities and population density. (The results are similar if only the labor compensation part of personal income is used.) Although the estimated effect of per capita income on net migration was positive and highly statistically significant, the magnitude of the effect was not large: a 10% increase in a state's per capita income was estimated to raise net in-migration only by enough to raise the state's rate of population growth by about one-quarter percentage point per year. The interpretation is that the costs attached to moving are high even for migration across states within the United States.

The small magnitude of response of migration to income differentials led to the conclusion that internal migration contributed little to the speed of convergence for state averages of personal income. That is, the estimates suggest that the rate of convergence of per capita personal income across the U.S. states—about 2% per year—would have been about the same if internal migration had not been possible. Ongoing research on within-country migration for the regions of Western European countries generates similar findings. Migration has occurred in the expected direction—toward the richer regions—but this process has not been a major contributor to the estimated speed of convergence of per capita gross domestic product across the regions.

The Diffusion of Technology

The most interesting aspect of recent theories of economic growth, represented by Romer (1990) and Grossman and Helpman (1991, chaps. 3-4), concerns theories of technological progress in the leading economies. In these models, a technological advance shows up either as the discovery of a new type of product (a new kind of productive input or a new variety of final good) or as an improvement in the quality or productivity of an existing product. These advances require purposive research effort, although the output from the research sector may involve random elements.

The incentive to commit resources to research requires a reward for success. In the models, the rewards take the form of monopoly rentals on product innovations. That is, a successful innovator's monopoly position lasts for a while because of first-mover advantages, secrecy, and possibly formal patent protection.[7]

Growth can be sustained in these models if diminishing returns do not apply, that is, if the returns from new discoveries do not decline in relation to the costs of making the discoveries. One reason diminishing returns may not apply is that the potential supply of new ideas and products is effectively unlimited.

For a single economy, the technological progress generated in recent theoretical models substitutes for the exogenous technological progress that is assumed in the standard growth model. For studying convergence across economies, the interesting application of the new theories is to the process of adaptation or imitation by followers of the innovations that were made by leaders. The cost of imitation for a follower can be modeled as similar to the cost of discovery for a leader, except that the cost of imitation is likely to be smaller and subject to less uncertainty. These considerations suggest that a follower would grow faster than a leader and thereby tend to catch up to the leader. This conclusion may not hold, however, if the follower country's environment is hostile to investment (in the form here of expenses for technological adaptation) because of poorly defined property rights, high rates of taxation, and so on.

Although innovation in the world economy may not be subject to diminishing returns, the process of imitation by a single country would encounter diminishing returns as it exhausts the pool of innovations from abroad that are readily adaptable to the domestic context. This consideration leads to the usual convergence property: a follower country tends to grow faster the larger the stock of potential imitations and, hence, the further its per capita income is from that of the leaders. The convergence result is again conditional on aspects of the domestic economy—such as government policies, attitudes about saving, and intrinsic levels of productivity—that affect the returns from technological adaptation.

Direct foreign investment can serve as a substitute for domestic expenditures on technological adaptation and imitation. This foreign activity is likely to have some advantages over local imitation: first, the foreign producer who is familiar with a new technology may have lower costs for adapting the technology to another location; second, direct foreign investment may get around the credit-market problems associated with loans to less developed countries (if the collateral represented by the direct investment is better than that embodied in a loan); and third, the incentive to innovate in the first place is appropriately greater if the inventor has foreign rights and is therefore not subject to uncompensated imitation.

Foreign investment of this type has been described as important to the process of economic growth in case studies, such as the one for Singapore by Young (1992). Young also observes that imitation of technology was central to the development of Hong Kong, and many researchers have argued that Japan and other Pacific Rim countries have thrived on the adaptation of ideas that were discovered elsewhere. I do not know of any studies that have systematically assessed the effects of technological diffusion and foreign investment on economic growth and convergence for a broad cross section of countries.

Concluding Observations

A number of forces tend to raise an economy's per capita growth rate when its level of per capita income is further below its long-run target. These forces include diminishing returns to capital, the mobility of capital and labor, and the diffusion of technology from leader to follower economies. This type of conditional convergence does not necessarily imply absolute convergence—that is, a systematic tendency for poor economies to grow faster than rich ones—because the long-run targets can differ. These differences can reflect variations in attitudes toward saving, fertility, and work effort, but the main source of divergence is likely to be government policies that affect the incentives to invest and to operate efficiently.

The existence of absolute convergence—poor economies tending to catch up to rich ones—depends on whether the convergence property applies to government policies and to the other determinants of long-run target positions. Is there some tendency for policies that hinder economic growth to be replaced by favorable policies, or, at least, is there some tendency for all policies to revert to some kind of mean behavior? The standard growth theory or other economic models considered in this chapter provide no basis for predicting this kind of convergence for government policies. This broader question of convergence has to be analyzed through methods of political economy (although, of course, the best political scientists now rely mainly on economic reasoning).

In recent years, most of the centrally planned economies have moved away from socialism and toward free markets, whereas the United States has tended to increase its degree of socialism (especially after the departure of President Reagan). Similarly, some of the most poorly managed economies in Latin America—such as Argentina and Mexico in recent years and Chile some time ago—have become heroes. The dispersion in the extent of socialism seems therefore to be narrowing. Perhaps the empirical lesson is that countries have a tendency to converge toward policies that are neither too harmful nor too favorable to economic well-being. I am unsure, however, whether a sound theory of political economy would generate this answer.

Notes

1. The relation shown in Figure 1.3 turns out to be similar if the values are not filtered for the country means. That is, for the seven countries considered here, convergence appears as much across countries as within countries.

2. The data are the values adjusted for differences in purchasing power by Summers and Heston (1988).

3. The role for the stock of initial human capital is hard to explain within the standard growth model, but can be interpreted within extensions of this model. This initial stock can measure imbalances between human and physical capital: a model with two types of capital goods implies that growth rates would be rapid when human capital is high in relation to physical capital, as in the recovery from a war that destroyed mostly physical capital. Theories of the diffusion of technology also suggest that a large stock of human capital can assist in the rapid adoption of leading technologies and lead thereby to high rates of growth.

4. The tariff rate enters as an interaction with an estimate of "natural openness," the country's ratio of imports to GDP that would have occurred in the absence of trade distortions. This openness was estimated to be a negative function of the country's area and its weighted-average distance from major markets. The idea is that distortions caused by tariffs have a larger adverse influence on growth for countries that are naturally more open (small countries and countries that are close to major potential trading partners). See Lee (1992) for a discussion.

5. Another effect of openness on y_i^* arises if the domestic economy's willingness to save differs from that for the world. The opening of an economy to international credit markets would raise y_i^* if the domestic residents were relatively impatient.

6. Openness to migration may also affect an economy's steady-state position. This openness may, for example, allow for a better match between persons and an economy's natural resources and may provide for competitive pressures that influence domestic policies. The latter argument parallels Tornell and Velasco's (1992) discussion about the beneficial effects of capital mobility. There may also be scale effects (positive or negative) if constant returns to scale are not a reasonable approximation.

7. I am focusing on the role of these models as positive theories of economic growth and not on the often contradictory inferences that have been drawn for desirable government policies. The policy implications derive from positive or negative gaps between social and private rates of return. Positive gaps can reflect uncompensated spillover benefits in research and production, the consequences of monopoly pricing of the existing goods, and the disincentive effects of taxation. Negative gaps can come from the seeking of existing monopoly rentals by new entrants or from congestion effects (negative spillovers from economic activity).

References

Barro, R. J. (1991). "Economic Growth in a Cross Section of Countries." *Quarterly Journal of Economics, 106,* 407–443.

Barro, R. J., and Lee, J. (1992). "Economic Growth in a Panel of Countries." Unpublished manuscript, Harvard University.

Barro, R. J., and Sala-i-Martin, X. (1991). "Convergence across States and Regions." *Brookings Papers on Economic Activity, 1*, 107–158.

Cass, D. (1965). "Optimum Growth in an Aggregate Model of Capital Accumulation." *Review of Economic Studies, 32*, 233–240.

Gastil, R. D. (1987). *Freedom in the World*. Westport, CT: Greenwood.

Grossman, G. M., and Helpman, E. (1991). *Innovation and Growth in the Global Economy*. Cambridge: MIT Press.

Koopmans, T. C. (1965). "On the Concept of Optimal Economic Growth." In Pontifica Academia Scientiarum (Ed.), *The Econometric Approach to Development Planning*. Amsterdam: North Holland.

Lee, J. (1992). "International Trade, Distortions, and Long-Run Economic Growth." Unpublished manuscript, Harvard University.

Ramsey, F. P. (1928). "A Mathematical Theory of Saving." *Economic Journal, 38*, 69–75.

Romer, P. M. (1990). "Endogenous Technological Change." *Journal of Political Economy, 98*, (supplement), S71–S102.

Solow, R. M. (1956). "A Contribution to the Theory of Economic Growth." *Quarterly Journal of Economics, 70*, 65–94.

Summers, R., and Heston, A., (1988). "A New Set of International Comparisons of Real Product and Price Levels: Estimates for 130 Countries, 1950–1985." *Review of Income and Wealth, 34*, 1–25.

Tornell, A., and Velasco, A. (1992). "The Tragedy of the Commons and Economic Growth: Why Does Capital Flow from Poor to Rich Countries?" Unpublished manuscript, New York University.

Young, A. (1992). "A Tale of Two Cities: Factor Accumulation and Technical Change in Hong Kong and Singapore." In *NBER Macroeconomics Annual* (Vol. 7). Cambridge: MIT Press.

2

Deposit Insurance, Savings, and Economic Growth

Jack L. Carr

Sustained economic growth is the solution to many of the problems currently facing world economies. Economic growth, rather than government redistributive policies, has been the greatest alleviator of poverty. Wealth creation is clearly superior to wealth redistribution in providing long-term solutions to pressing economic problems. The greater the rate of growth of output, the greater will be the creation of new jobs. The determination of appropriate policy to enable economic growth to take place is crucial for a research organization such as the Milken Institute, which is interested in job and capital formation. In fact, understanding the growth process is a fundamental question for economics.

For a long time, economists concentrated on static rather than dynamic models, and there was inadequate research in the study of growth. Fortunately, the past 5 to 10 years have seen a major research effort devoted to growth.[1] This new research is promising, but it is still in the embryonic stage. Unfortunately, at the present time, economics still cannot answer the fundamental question of why some countries grow rapidly and others grow slowly. Why were Spain and Portugal major economic powers in the sixteenth century but relatively underdeveloped economies in the twentieth century? Why did Argentina have per capita income levels comparable to Canada at the end of the 1800s but now has substantially less per capita income than Canada? Why is per capita income in the United States between 20 and 40 times the level in India? Why did economic growth take off in both Canada and the United States in the period immediately after World War II but slow down in both countries in the mid-1970s?

Currently we have a number of growth models, but none is capable of explaining the cross-sectional and time-series growth data.[2] As is always the case in economics, different models lead to different policy prescriptions for government. The next section of this chapter provides a brief review of developments in the growth literature and examines some of the policy implications of the new models of growth. In the discussion of policy it becomes crucial to distinguish between a private interest theory of policy and a public interest theory. The chapter then examines one particular policy and its effect on economic growth, the enactment of compulsory deposit insurance in both Canada and the United States. Data are presented that support a private interest theory of deposit insurance. Because deposit insurance has a major impact on the operation of the banking sector, I argue that deposit insurance has affected the efficient allocation of savings and the growth rate. The final section of the chapter presents the main conclusions of this study.

Review of Growth Theory

Adam Smith and the Classical Theory of Growth[3]

As with most subjects in economics, serious research in growth theory began with Adam Smith. *An Inquiry into the Nature and Causes of the Wealth of Nations* (1776/1937) is in fact a study into the factors leading to high per capita incomes and high per capita growth rates. For the classical economists the question of economic growth was the fundamental question in economics. To Smith, the wealth of a nation was unrelated to the amount of money in a nation. Wealth depended upon the level of factor endowments: land, labor, and capital. Leaving individuals to pursue their own self-interest resulted in the accumulation of capital (in order to allow for the division of labor), the efficient allocation of resources, increases in output per worker, and economic growth. For Adam Smith, growth was a natural outcome of letting individuals pursue their own self-interest (i.e., allowing economic agents to maximize their respective objective functions).

> The uniform, constant and uninterrupted effort of every man to better his condition, the principle from which public and national, as well as private opulence is originally derived, is frequently powerful enough to maintain the natural progress of things towards improvement, in spite both of the extravagance of government and of the greatest errors of administration. Like the unknown principles of animal life, it frequently restores health and vigour to the constitution, in spite not only of the disease but of the absurd prescriptions of the doctor (Smith, 1776/1937, p. 326).

For Smith, economic growth could be robust even in the face of many misdirected government policies, but "absurd" government policy could in fact significantly reduce economic growth rates. In considering the situation of China, where economic growth seemed to be nonexistent,[4] Smith argues:

> A country which neglects or despises foreign commerce and which admits the vessels of foreign nations into one or two of its ports only, cannot transact the same quantity of business which it might do with different laws and institutions. In a country too, where, though the rich or owners of large capital enjoy a good deal of security, the poor or owners of small capital enjoy scarce any, but are liable, under the pretense of justice, to be pillaged and plundered at any time by the inferior mandarins, the quantity of stock *employed* in all of the different branches of business transacted within it, can never be equal to what the nature and extent of that business might admit. (p. 95, emphasis added)

Smith gives examples of other government policies that will lower economic growth:

> A defect in the law may sometimes raise the rate of interest considerably above what the condition of the country, as to wealth or poverty, would require. When the law does not enforce the performance of contracts, it puts all borrowers nearly upon the same footing with bankrupts or people of doubtful credit in better regulated countries. The uncertainty of receiving his money makes the lender exact the same usurious interest which is usually required from bankrupts. (p. 95)

He goes on:

> When the law prohibits interest altogether, it does not prevent it. Many people must borrow and nobody will lend without such a consideration for the use of the money as is suitable, not only to what can be made by the use of it, but to the difficulty and danger of eroding the law. (p. 96)

In summary, Adam Smith believed that the operation of free, unfettered markets would lead to efficient resource allocation and maximum economic wealth creation. Capital accumulation and growth would take place naturally. The role of government was to ensure peace, define property rights, and enforce contracts. Government policies, such as trade restrictions enacted to advance private local interests, had the potential of reducing aggregate economic wealth and growth rates. For Adam Smith, what was crucial for the growth process was providing economic agents with the correct incentives. Free and unfettered markets provided these agents with "correct" incentives. Government policy had the ability to distort incentives, misallocate resources, and reduce aggregate wealth and growth. Adam Smith concentrated on the working of markets and on the microeconomic issues of facing economic agents with appropriate relative prices. For Smith, having economies establish correct relative prices was of fundamental importance for wealth creation and growth.

Solow and Denison and the Neoclassical Theory of Growth

The neoclassical theory of growth (see Denison, 1961; Solow, 1956) moved away from the microeconomic emphasis of Smith on the operation of markets and concentrated instead on the macroeconomic aspects of growth. The neoclassical theory postulated an aggregate production function for the economy as a whole. Aggregate output depended upon the aggregate stock of labor and capital and on the state of technology.[5] In the simplest form of the neoclassical theory, economic agents maximize a utility function that depends on a per capita consumption stream. The rate of growth of per capita output is proportional to the exogenously given rate of technological change. Hence, technological change is the key factor in explaining growth. With exogenous technological change, however, this model could not explain variations in growth.

The neoclassical model changed the emphasis in growth theory from an examination of individual markets and efficient allocation of resources to an examination of aggregate magnitudes such as aggregate capital/output rates and aggregate levels of capital. The neoclassical model stresses the difference between level effects and growth rate effects. For example, an implication of the neoclassical model is that a change in the saving rate will *not* affect the balanced growth rate. A higher savings rate would be associated with higher output levels along the balanced growth path. The balanced growth rates would be identical in two economies with different savings rates. Similarly, it is argued that government policies that result in inefficient resource allocation affect the level of output and not its rate of growth. Lucas (1988) argues that, for example, the removal of trade barriers "that reduced output by five percent (an enormous effect) spread out over ten years is simply a one-half of one percent annual growth rate stimulus" (p. 12).[6]

I would argue that if the elimination of one inefficient government policy raised growth rates of output per capita from 2% to 2.5% for a 10-year period, this represents a significant and important effect on growth. "Simply a one-half of one percent annual growth rate stimulus" is a very significant stimulus. Also, governments enact many different types of laws that interfere with the operation of free markets and misallocate resources. If a government were to enact distorting tax laws, labor laws, pay and employment "equity" schemes, protective tariffs, and laws establishing marketing boards, wage and price controls, and numerous other forms of economic regulation, this would not only misallocate resources but cause a waste of society's resources through the encouragement of rent-seeking activities.[7] If government were to fail to protect property rights, this also would lead to lower levels of output.[8] If government were to enact a large number of policies that distort incentives over a number of years, these actions would be capable of affecting growth rates over long periods of time.[9] The distinction between level and growth effects is an important one. However, this distinction should not cause us to look solely at aggregate magnitudes in examining growth rates. Economics is about incentives. Policies that continually distort incentives will affect growth rates. The lessons from the neoclassical growth model should not cause us to forget the major result of the classical growth model. Inefficient and distorting government policies can and do have significant effects on both the level and rate of growth of output over sustained periods of time.[10]

There is one other development from the neoclassical tradition that I would like to discuss. The neoclassical model itself was designed by Solow (1956) and Denison (1961) to explain U.S. growth in the first half of the twentieth century. This model was not designed to explain cross-country growth rates. However, from the neoclassical tradition, growth accounting developed to explain cross-country differences. Assuming common technology, cross-country growth differences could be explained by differences in either population growth or capital accumulation[11] and differences in growth in output per capita could be explained by differences in growth in capital per capita.

One implication from the growth accounting literature is that the growth process could be speeded up in underdeveloped countries by giving aid to these countries in the form of physical capital—for example, railways, dams, and steel plants. These policies were tried, and a significant number of the projects failed.[12] One reason for the failure of these projects was that they concentrated on the macroeconomic variable of aggregate capital and ignored the microeconomic issue of whether, for instance, capital-intensive steel plants were optimal in a country with a low price for labor. What is optimal for the developed country is not necessarily optimal for the underdeveloped country. Stressing the accumulation of capital rather than the efficient use of capital will not result in increased economic growth.[13] The evidence from actual development policies underscores the importance of looking at the efficient allocation of resources in attempting to improve economic growth rates.

The "New" Endogenous Growth Literature

The "new" endogenous growth literature builds on the neoclassical growth models of Solow and Denison. In the neoclassical model, growth is determined by exogenous factors such as the rate of growth of disembodied technology. The new growth literature views growth as an endogenous outcome of the operation of a market economy. The key question in these models is what acts as the "engine of growth." Accumulation of physical capital is ruled out as the source of continuous growth in per capita output in all these models because of diminishing marginal productivity. Following the pioneering work of Schultz (1961), a number of researchers use human capital accumulation as the prime engine of growth (for example see Becker, Murphy, and Tamura, 1990).

The main insight of Paul Romer (1986) is that when capital investment takes place under conditions of increasing returns to scale, it is no longer necessary to have the marginal product of capital continually fall until it equals the discount rate. With increasing returns to scale, capital can accumulate without bounds and continual growth in per capita output can be maintained. However, increasing returns due to internal economies of scale is inconsistent with the competitive model. As a consequence, these models have external economies in production as the source of the increasing returns to scale. One of the main sources of these spillover effects is the accumulation of knowledge. Some models postulate that increases in the human capital of fellow workers increase one's own individual productivity (see Lucas, 1990). Other models postulate spillover effects from R&D investment (see Romer, 1990).

Debate on Economic Policies to Promote Growth

Because of the interest here in policy, let us first consider the policy implications of an endogenous growth model where spillover effects in knowledge-based activities provide for the main engine of growth.[14] The existence of spillover effects in some endogenous growth models can lead to a role for government policy in the growth process. For illustrative purposes, let us consider the specific model with knowledge spillovers of Grossman and Helpman (1990). In this model there are two sectors. Output depends on land and labor and "knowledge" (a public input).

$$X^i = K\, F^i(T^i, L^i) \qquad\qquad i = 1, 2$$

where K represents the stock of knowledge, T the amount of land, and L the amount of labor. Knowledge accumulates as a result of the manufacturing process in Sector 1. Hence, there are learning-by-doing benefits in Sector 1 that are external to the firms that generate them and that increase productivity in both sectors.

$$\dot{K} = bX^1.$$

With a small open economy, protection in the Sector 1 industry is welfare improving. Protection of the sector with the learning-by-doing benefits increases economic growth by shifting resources into the knowledge-creating activity.[15]

Spillover effects in endogenous growth models allows for the possibility of trade policy or an industrial strategy to increase economic growth. This policy result of some of the endogenous growth models comes into direct conflict with the policy results of the classical model of growth of Adam Smith. To Adam Smith, free trade was crucial in providing for satisfactory economic growth, and growth was a natural process unless interfered with by government policies that disturbed incentives or failed to enforce or defend property rights. In particular, Smith argued that protectionist trade policies retard growth. Smith believed that industry would spend considerable resources (i.e., in rent-seeking activity) to lobby governments to eliminate competition, and that trade protection was enacted invariably to subsidize private interests. In endogenous growth models with spillover effects, governments are acting in the public interest essentially to overcome market failure.[16]

It is of crucial importance to distinguish between the private interest theory and public interest theory for any given government policy. Incorrect policy causes economic growth to move in the opposite direction to that intended. There is no doubt that economists can build models that will make any government policy welfare improving. The arguments concerning spillover effects and market failure are not new. These arguments have always been used to justify government intervention in the operation of the markets. The current models are now more mathematically sophisticated than the "old" growth models, but the crucial issues are still the same. How empirically significant are the modeled externalities? If the externalities are significant, has the market not found ways to internalize them? If externalities and market failures exist, are government policies welfare improving? Does the cost of government intervention outweigh any potential benefits of reducing market failure?

If higher human capital of fellow workers in a firm increases the productivity of coworkers, why is this externality not internalized through labor contracts within the firm? If higher human capital of workers in one firm increases the productivity of workers in other firms, it is easier to see how these externalities are not internalized but it is more difficult to comprehend the exact nature of these externalities. It is easy to postulate externalities; it is much more difficult to document that these externalities actually exist.[17]

Even if externalities that are not fully internalized exist, this still does not justify government intervention. One needs a model of government. Most growth models lack such a model of government, or they have a very naive view of government. As Krueger (1990) argues in evaluating development models, "Implicitly, it was assumed that the government would behave as a benevolent social guardian, in Fabian Socialist tradition. Economists would serve in government, calculating shadow prices and formulating planning models. Selfless bureaucrats would then carry out the plans. Co-ordination and administration of public sector activity was implicitly assumed to be costless" (p. 12).

Information and knowledge were assumed to be costly in the private sector but costless in the public sector. Private individuals were assumed to act in their own self-interest, but public officials were assumed to act selflessly in the pursuit of the public interest. Also, the actions of potential gainers or losers from a particular government policy were not modeled. It was assumed that no resources were used by potential beneficiaries or potential losers in affecting government policy. Clearly, the cost of government intervention may outweigh any potential benefits of reducing market failure. The effects of government failure may be much worse than the effects of market failure!

Before the policy implications of any endogenous growth models with spillover effects can be seriously considered, these models must be rigorously tested. These models ultimately must be capable of explaining the available cross-sectional and time-series data. In the absence of a complete test of the model, tests of the implications of the various government policies can be conducted. For example, if the public interest argument for protection of an industry with learning by doing is correct, this policy benefits all industry and hence should be supported by all industry. Analysis of voting records (in democratic countries) can be undertaken to see if the voting record is consistent with the public or private interest theory.

In the next section, I propose to examine in detail the public interest and private interest theories of one government policy: compulsory non-risk-rated deposit insurance. I have chosen this particular policy because deposit insurance fundamentally affects the operation of the banking system and is capable of affecting the efficient allocation of savings and, as a consequence, economic growth rates.

Deposit Insurance: Public or Private Interest?

In the growth literature reviewed in the previous section, investment by firms in physical capital or in new technologies is crucial to the growth process. A well-functioning financial system is a key element of the investment process in allocating savings to investing firms (for evidence on this point, see De Long, 1990). The financial system is crucial in the transformation of savings into firm capital. The accumulation of savings and physical capital is not as important to growth as the effective use of the savings. A well-functioning financial system ensures that savings are allocated to those firms that can utilize them most effectively. Because of the key role of the financial system in the growth process, I propose to examine one particular government policy, non-risk-rated deposit insurance, which has had a profound effect on the operation of financial markets (and hence on the allocation of savings for individual firm capital formation).[18]

One of the earliest arguments advanced for publicly provided deposit insurance was made by Friedman and Schwartz (1963), who viewed deposit insurance as "the most important structural change in the banking system to result from the 1933 panic and indeed, in our view the structural change most conducive to monetary stability" (p. 434). Friedman and Schwartz realized that this was intrusive government policy, but that deposit insurance was needed to guarantee the stability of the banking system and to prevent bank runs.[19] Because of the "first come, first served" rule in settling bank claims (prior to bankruptcy), there were runs on banks that were rumored to have problems. Because of costly information, if depositors could not differentiate between firm-specific and industrywide shocks, there would be a contagion effect from a bank failure and banking panics could result. Hence, there were negative externalities in bank failures. The argument was that public-provided deposit insurance could eliminate bank runs by eliminating the threat to depositors' funds. According to this argument, deposit insurance is in the public interest: it prevents bank runs, provides for a stable banking system, and allows economic agents to have confidence in the safety of their savings in banks. The past 10 years have seen the development of a number of elegant models characterized by imperfect information that led to rational bank runs. The models of Diamond and Dybvig (1983), Jacklin and Bhattacharya (1988), Postlewaite and Vives (1987), and Smith (1988) are all in the Friedman and Schwartz tradition and offer a public interest explanation for government-provided deposit insurance. However, I believe these models are incapable of explaining the actual evolution of deposit insurance schemes in Canada and the United States.

Government-provided non-risk-rated deposit insurance is a major intervention by government in the operation of the banking system. In a banking system without government interference, risky small banks would have a difficult time competing with safe larger banks. Small banks would either be unable to attract deposits or would have to pay a risk premium. A non-risk-rated deposit insurance scheme allows riskier banks to attract deposits on the same terms as safer banks. This scheme protects and subsidizes riskier banks at the expense of safe banks. I contend that deposit insurance was enacted in the private interest of high-risk (small) banks. I also argue that such a scheme ultimately destabilizes the banking system; it results in a misallocation of deposit savings to high-risk institutions, an inappropriately high level of risky investments, and, as a consequence, a higher level of bankruptcies among financial intermediaries. These effects result in a lower level of income and a lower level of growth. There are additional negative effects of such a scheme on growth. The initial lobbying by the beneficiaries of the scheme (the small banks) and the continual lobbying to maintain the scheme absorb resources and reduce income. In addition, when increased bankruptcies occur, general taxpayers are called upon to help finance the scheme; the resulting higher taxes imposed on productive sectors of the economy will reduce the incentive to produce, and this too results in a decrease in income. One additional effect of the rent seeking to maintain this scheme is that talented people are attracted to rent-seeking activities and away from entrepreneurial activities. This movement of talented people away from productive activities results in lower income levels and lower rates of growth (this argument is made by Murphy et al., 1991).

As in the example of the relationship between growth and government intervention discussed above, there are two plausible explanations for major government intervention in the banking sector. If the public interest explanation is correct, deposit insurance prevents bank runs and provides for a stable banking system, which is of fundamental importance in providing for transformation of savings into capital formation and providing for economic growth. If the private interest explanation is correct, publicly provided non-risk-rated deposit insurance is a major government intervention in the operation of financial markets to protect the private interest of small risky banks. Such intervention misallocates savings, destabilizes the financial system, and retards capital formation and economic growth. It is of crucial importance to differentiate between these two explanations of deposit insurance. I propose to examine the evolution of deposit insurance in Canada and the United States in order to test these two hypotheses.

Deposit Insurance in Canada

Deposit insurance was introduced in Canada in 1967. Until 1967, banking in Canada consisted of a small number of large national banks (with an extended network of branches) and entry barriers into national banking. Small regional banks existed, but they technically were known as "trust and loan" companies.[20] Small regional banks did not become important until after World War II. The banking system in Canada before 1967 was very stable. The last bank to fail before 1967 was the Home Bank in 1923. Canada went through the Great Depression without deposit insurance and without a single bank failure. The Canadian banking system was *not* subject to bank runs.

In 1966 some local trust and loan companies were experiencing difficulties. With increased financial volatility (primarily in interest rates) beginning in the mid-1960s, local trust and loan companies (i.e., small banks), with their undiversified regional portfolios, were institutions at risk. Depositors withdrew money from the small banks and placed it with the large national banks. This was not a bank run in any meaningful sense of the term. No disintermediation took place—depositors were simply switching deposits from what they perceived to be risky institutions to safer institutions. This transfer did not take place because of imperfect information. In fact, depositors switched from small to large banks because of relatively accurate information on the increased riskiness of small banks.

The small trust companies lobbied government for protection of their deposit base, and in 1967 the federal government enacted non-risk-rated deposit insurance. I believe that the facts of the introduction of deposit insurance in Canada do not fit the public interest theory:

1. Deposit insurance in Canada was enacted when the banking system was stable.
2. The Canadian banking system had been stable for a long time. No Canadian bank failed during the Great Depression. This should dispel the myth that deposit insurance is necessary to maintain bank stability.
3. The large national banks opposed the introduction of deposit insurance. If deposit insurance is in the public interest, *all* banks should have welcomed its introduction. A more stable financial system would be beneficial to all banks.
4. When deposit insurance was introduced, it was compulsory for the large national banks and optional for the smaller provincially incorporated trust and loan companies. The public interest argument would dictate that all banks should be compelled to join.

This provision is consistent with the private interest theory that deposit insurance subsidized the small risky banks and taxed the large safer banks. The large safer banks would have to be compelled to join. No bank would freely volunteer to be taxed. It should be noted that *all* provincially incorporated trust and loan companies voluntarily joined the deposit insurance scheme. This is further evidence that these small banks were the main beneficiaries of this scheme.

The data from the post-deposit insurance era in Canada are also supportive of the private interest theory. If deposit insurance subsidized small banks, it should encourage the entry of new small banks. From 1949 to 1966, 37 new trust and loan companies entered the industry,[21] resulting in a net entry of 12 new firms in the period prior to deposit insurance. From 1968 to 1985, 62 new trust and loan companies entered the industry, resulting in a net entry of 31 companies.[22] Of the 91 loan and trust companies that existed in 1985, 62 entered after 1967.

This evidence on entry is reinforced by a standard index of concentration, the Herfindahl index. From 1949 to 1967, the Herfindahl index declined by 0.4% annually; after 1967, it declined by a significantly larger downward trend of 1.3% annually.

The private interest theory claims that deposit insurance subsidizes small risky banks and taxes large safer banks and hence results in an inefficiently high level of risk in the portfolios of banks. This higher level of risk taking should lead to an increase in bank failures. From 1949 to 1966 there were no failures among national banks or trust and loan companies in Canada. From 1968 to 1987, 14 Ontario or federal trust and loan companies failed, of which 11 were incorporated after 1967, and 3 national banks failed, all of which were incorporated after 1967.

Trust and loan company failures, which were uncommon prior to 1967, became commonplace after the introduction of deposit insurance. Bank failures, which were unheard of prior to 1967, occurred for the first time in the post-deposit insurance era. Deposit insurance in Canada has clearly weakened the stability of the banking system. The introduction of deposit insurance resulted in the inefficient allocation of savings to high-risk activities. Inappropriate levels of risk were assumed by financial intermediaries. Financial institutions became insolvent, with the resulting loss of resources caused by "bankruptcy costs." Deposit insurance has been very costly for Canada.

The Canadian evidence strongly supports a private interest rather than public interest explanation of deposit insurance and points to large dead-weight costs of this government intervention in the financial system.

Deposit Insurance in the United States

Early forms of deposit insurance in the United States go back to 1829, when a "deposit guaranty" law was passed in the state of New York. Under such a law, the state collects non-risk-rated premiums from the banks and uses this fund to guarantee deposits. If the fund itself is inadequate to meet the claims of insolvent banks, the member banks themselves are liable for any deficiency. In 1837 the New York Guaranty Fund became insolvent and the law was abolished in 1842. A few other eastern states had similar experiences.

From 1907 to 1917, eight state governments enacted bank guaranty laws (for discussion of this period, see Calomiris, 1990; White, 1983).[23] All these states had relatively large numbers of country banks, and all these state schemes failed. Consider, for example, the situation in South Dakota. Prior to the enactment of the state scheme, on average, about 13 banks failed per year (there were about 500 state banks in South Dakota). After the introduction of the guaranty laws, the failure rate increased dramatically, and by 1926, 50% of state banks in South Dakota had become insolvent.

The state schemes failed for two primary reasons. In the first place, non-risk-rated compulsory insurance subsidized risky activity, and as a result encouraged risky behavior on the part of the banks. Second, large state banks opposed the scheme. They opposed being taxed (via flat insurance premiums) to subsidize their small riskier competitors. These large banks could leave the state guaranty system if they became national banks, and this is exactly what they did. Large banks left the system, leaving for the most part only small risky banks.

I contend that with the failure of the state schemes, and with the banking crises of 1930-33 resulting in the failure of the unit banking rule in protecting small country banks,[24] small banks throughout the country pressured Congress to enact deposit insurance. A national scheme would not allow the better risks to opt out. By 1932, 16 bills were introduced in Congress to enact deposit insurance—13 in the House of Representatives and 3 in the Senate.[25] In 1933, the National Bank Guaranty Fund was set up, and in 1935 it was turned into a true system of deposit insurance.

The 1935 bill compelled all member banks of the Federal Reserve System to have deposit insurance. This provision compelled the good risks to stay in the system. Nonmember banks had the option of obtaining deposit insurance. The 1935 law expressly stated that there could be no discrimination between member and nonmember banks, or large and small banks, and there was none. It would seem that this provision dictated flat-rate premiums, so that small and large banks were levied the same premium per dollar of deposit. This provision is consistent with the private interest theory.

It should be noted that when the state bank guaranty funds were set up from 1907 to 1917, restrictions were placed on the rate of interest that could be paid on insured deposits. Similarly, usury restrictions were adopted when national deposit insurance was enacted in the Bank Act of 1933. The same Bank Act of 1933 that enacted deposit insurance also prohibited interest payments on demand deposits in Federal Reserve member banks and empowered the Board of Governors of the Federal Reserve System to impose maximum rates that could be paid by member banks on time deposits. The Bank Act of 1935 also prohibited interest on demand deposits in other insured banks and allowed interest rate ceilings on time deposits to be set by the FDIC on insured nonmember banks.

The general interpretation of these usury restrictions, advanced by Friedman and Schwartz (1963), has been that these restrictions were a government-enforced price-fixing agreement. The interpretation I advance is that the government understood the moral hazards inherent in any deposit insurance scheme,[26] and the usury restrictions were placed to limit these problems. With deposit insurance, risky institutions have an incentive to obtain large amounts of deposits by paying premiums above the going rate of interest on deposits. These deposits are then invested in risky assets. Insured depositors have an incentive to place their deposits in those institutions paying the highest rates on deposits, regardless of the riskiness of the investing institutions' portfolios. Restricting the interest paid on insured deposits limits the ability of risky institutions to attract new funds. The strongest evidence that supports this moral hazard interpretation of interest rate regulations is that the regulations were enacted as part of a comprehensive system of deposit insurance. In addition, the restrictions applied to *all* banks that had deposit insurance. Given the existence of deposit insurance, the interest rate regulations, by limiting the effects of moral hazard, were in all likelihood welfare improving. I will return to this point shortly.

An examination of the timing of the enactment of deposit insurance schemes in the United States can shed light on the private versus public interest debate. In fact, the whole North American experience provides a useful test of the two hypotheses. When Congress created the national banking system in 1863, it intended to phase out state banks. It never realized this intention, however. From 1891 to 1920 state-chartered banks increased from 3,100 to 22,000 (while national banks increased from 3,600 to 8,000) (see Barnett, 1911). With their increasing numbers, state banks increased their political strength, and from 1907 to 1917 they were able to obtain state guaranty systems in eight rural states. These systems enabled the small state banks to compete more effectively with the large (national) banks. When the state schemes failed because the better risks left the systems, the small state banks lobbied for a national system (where the better risks would be compelled to remain in the system). Such a national scheme was enacted in 1933.

In Canada between 1901 and 1923, nine banks failed (see Beckhart, 1929, pp. 334–337). These failures caused the government to consider deposit insurance explicitly during the revisions of the Bank Act in 1914 and 1923, with the U.S. state schemes as the model. Canada rejected deposit insurance. I contend that this was because in Canada, there were only a few small and risky banks. After World War II, there was substantial growth in regional trust and loan companies, and it was only with this growth that there developed a significant political lobby to pressure the government to enact deposit insurance in 1967.

The differences in the Canadian and U.S. experiences can be explained by the private interest theory. It is only with the growth of small local banks that a private interest group becomes viable to lobby for deposit insurance. The public interest theory is incapable of explaining why Canada and the United States enacted deposit insurance at different times. If deposit insurance was beneficial to the United States in the 1920s and 1930s, it should also have been beneficial to Canada. Why did Canada not enact deposit insurance at that time?

Let us now consider the post-national deposit insurance era in the United States. Private interest theory would predict increased entry of risky banks and, as a consequence, an increase in bank failures. This did occur in the United States, but with an implausibly long time lag. "From 1921 to 1933, each year requires at least three digits to record the number of banks that suspended; from 1934 on two digits suffice and from 1943 through 1960, one digit for both insured and noninsured banks" (Friedman and Schwartz, 1963, p. 437). This low failure rate continued until the beginning of the 1980s. By the middle of the 1980s the failure rate of banks was substantial, and once again three digits were required to record the number of suspended banks. Why this long time lag?

The answer lies in an argument made by Keeley (1990), who asserts that banks were protected, by a number of arrangements, from competition: "In the 1950's and even early 1960's banks partially were protected from competition by a variety of regulatory barriers. For example, chartering was very restrictive until the mid 1960's . . . . Moreover, some banks were protected by various state laws that limited or prohibited branching, multibank holding company, and interstate bank expansion" (p. 1185). These entry barriers made bank charters valuable, and the valuable bank charters constituted a bond whose value disappeared in bankruptcy. This bond substantially eliminated any moral hazard problem.

With the elimination of these entry barriers in the 1970s and 1980s, competition increased, the value of the bond disappeared, and the expected
moral hazard problem became operative.[27]

The moral hazard problem worsened in the 1980s for another reason:
interest rate controls on deposits were eliminated. This deposit interest
rate deregulation allowed risky institutions to obtain a greater share of
deposit funds, resulting in increased growth of these risky institutions,
which in turn contributed to the high rate of bank failures in the 1980s.

This episode illustrates that deregulation, with continued deposit
insurance, can have harmful effects. Deposit insurance, with its attendant moral hazard problems, requires substantial government regulation to make the system manageable. Deregulation of financial markets
in the 1980s, and increased moral hazard from deposit insurance
imposed substantial costs on the U.S. economy. The solution is not the
abandonment of deregulation; rather, consideration should be given to
the abandonment of deposit insurance. Half measures, in this case, may
be worse than no measures. The lessons of the 1980s indicate that deregulation cannot be considered complete until there is a solution to the
deposit insurance problem. Reform of the deposit insurance system may
not be able to correct its fundamental deficiency (for an analysis of various proposals to reform deposit insurance, see Kane, 1985). Deposit
insurance has existed for so long that it is generally assumed that the
banking system cannot operate efficiently in its absence. The Canadian
example prior to 1967 shows that a stable banking system can be operated in the absence of government-run deposit insurance.

In summary, the U.S. evidence on the timing and introduction of
deposit insurance is consistent with the private interest explanation,
although at first it appears somewhat puzzling because of the long time
lag between enactment of deposit insurance and the eventual increase in
bank failures resulting from that enactment. This lag is explained by the
existence of entry barriers in the banking sector. Failures did occur, but
only after substantial deregulation of the financial system.

The Canadian and U.S. evidence provides strong support for the private interest theory of deposit insurance.

Summary and Conclusions

The Canadian evidence clearly demonstrates that a stable financial
system can exist without government-run deposit insurance. Canada
endured the Great Depression without a single bank failure. From the
end of World War II to 1967, the date of the introduction of deposit
insurance, there were no bank failures in Canada. The Canadian experience demonstrates that a U.S. banking system without deposit insurance

and without restrictions on entry and growth can indeed be a stable system. The worst of all worlds may be a system of government-run deposit insurance with substantial deregulation.

The evidence in both the Canadian and U.S. cases supports my argument for the private interest explanation of deposit insurance. Deposit insurance was enacted to support the private interest of small local banks (why small local banks command the power they do is still an open question). The enactment of deposit insurance has not been without its costs. Deposit insurance has subsidized risky ventures on the part of banks and has resulted in too much of the savings of both Canada and the United States being directed to risky ventures. This increase in risk has led to increased instability and increased failure of financial institutions. This failure occurred in Canada rather quickly after the introduction of deposit insurance. In fact, in Canada after the introduction of deposit insurance, bank entry restrictions were substantially eased. In the United States, the failure occurred after a long lag following the introduction of deposit insurance. The U.S. failure rate increased after substantial deregulation of the U.S. system.

Although failures occurred later in the U.S. system than in the Canadian system, when they did occur they were much more severe and threatened the stability of the domestic financial system. The public liability for commercial bank failures in the United States is estimated to be between $30 billion and $40 billion (Mishkin, 1992), and the corresponding liability for savings and loan failures is estimated to be $300–$400 billion (Romer and Weingast, 1990). Losses of this magnitude and threats to the stability of the financial system reduce job and capital formation in the United States and result in lower economic growth rates. Losses of this magnitude ultimately result in higher taxes imposed on the productive sector, and this also results in lower economic growth.

Both Canada and the United States have experienced slowed economic growth since the mid-1970s. From 1960 to 1973, growth in per capita output in Canada averaged 3.1% per annum; in the United States it averaged 2.7% per annum. From 1973 to 1988, economic growth in Canada averaged 2.3% per annum; in the United States it averaged 1.7% per annum (Summers and Heston, 1991). Some researchers would argue that the period from just after World War II until the 1970s was anomalous. It represents a time of spectacular economic growth. The period since 1975 has merely reestablished the growth rates that existed from 1913 to 1950. This may all be true, but it does not explain why growth started to slow down in the mid 1970s.

Some researchers believe that the dramatic rise in oil prices following the oil crisis of 1973 explains the slowdown in growth. This may explain some of the slowdown in the U.S. growth rate, but it cannot explain the

Canadian data. Canada is a net energy exporter. A rise in energy prices is beneficial to Canada and should lead to increased, not decreased, growth.

Other researchers would argue that the fall in the growth rate in the mid-1970s occurred in almost all OECD countries, and hence it is useless to look for country-specific causes. The problem with this approach is that ignoring country-specific explanations leaves very few ways to account for the observed phenomena. In addition, with a world closely linked by trade, a fall in North American growth rates would certainly influence OECD growth rates.

I would argue that the financial system instability in both Canada and the United States resulting from their systems of deposit insurance has contributed to the slower economic growth rates of the last 15 years. The stability of the financial system is crucial to the growth process. Deposit insurance is just one of many examples of government interference that has occurred that is capable of affecting the growth process. Government bailouts of failing firms, government wage and price controls, government employment or pay equity regulations, government agricultural regulations, government industrial strategies—all represent interference in the operation of free markets, and all are capable of reducing economic growth rates.

The lessons of development economics teach us that savings and additions to capital are not enough to ensure economic growth. In many developing countries savings rates rose substantially from the 1950s to the 1970s, and yet growth rates either remained constant or fell. Krueger (1990) gives the example of the savings rate in India, which rose from 14% of GNP in 1960 to 22% in 1987, with growth rates not changing at all. The key to growth does not lie in the accumulation of capital and savings but in the efficient utilization of resources. Government interference in the operation of markets disturbs incentives and results in resource misallocation. Government-run compulsory deposit insurance does not affect the volume of savings but does affect the efficient use of savings. Deposit insurance results in too much savings being directed to risky activity. The misallocation of savings will certainly retard economic growth.

If government interference prevents entrepreneurs from starting firms and keeping the profit from these endeavors then talented individuals will be discouraged from becoming entrepreneurs. Murphy et al. (1991) argue that when this happens economic growth slows down. To support this argument they give the examples of Mandarin China, Medieval Europe, and many African countries today, where government interference in the operation of free markets dramatically slowed down growth. When there is little government interference, as was the case in Great Britain at the time of the Industrial Revolution, in the United

States in late nineteenth and early twentieth centuries, and in some Asian countries today, economic growth is robust.

Proponents of government interference in the operation of markets will always claim that the government action is taken in the public interest and is needed to prevent market failure. It should be incumbent on those recommending government interference to demonstrate empirically the existence of economically significant externalities that the market is incapable of internalizing and that the benefits from government action will outweigh the costs. The debate over appropriate government action will almost invariably revolve around the correctness of the public interest versus private interest explanation.

The new growth literature has made an admirable beginning in the investigation of the growth process by refocusing the interest of economists on the crucial problems of economic growth. This new literature should not cause us to forget the lessons of Adam Smith, however. Whatever new factors in the growth process the new literature draws our attention to, whether it be learning by doing or human capital formation, we should not forget the crucial role incentives play in economic growth. Through promotion of private interests, government has the ability to distort incentives and retard economic growth. There is an appropriate role for government in the growth process: government is needed for the definition and enforcement of property rights, and to provide both internal and external order. Despite the criticism of Karl Marx, wars are not conducive to economic growth in the capitalist system.[28] Political stability and peace are necessary for economic growth.

If my thesis in this chapter—that deposit insurance was enacted to promote the private interest of small local banks and not to promote the public interest—is correct, then deposit insurance is not required to ensure the stability of a financial system. The Canadian evidence clearly indicates that a financial system can be stable without government-run deposit insurance. Correcting the fundamental deficiencies of deposit insurance may not be possible. If this is the case, the optimal policy is to eliminate deposit insurance and deregulate the financial system. The experience of the 1980s has indicated that a policy of deregulation alone, without elimination of deposit insurance, may be the worst of all worlds.

Elimination of government interference in financial markets through deregulation and elimination of deposit insurance will ensure a stable financial system and an efficient allocation of savings; will ensure that savings are efficiently converted to firm capital, promoting optimal capital formation; and will remove a major impediment to economic growth, and hence will promote a higher rate of economic growth and a higher rate of job formation.

Notes

1. The new interest in growth started with the work of Romer (1986) and Lucas (1988).

2. The "growth" in new growth models has certainly been matched by growth in empirical studies. These studies invariably include a large number of regressors. In fact, more than 50 variables have been found to be significantly correlated with growth. However, correlation does not imply causation. Levine and Renelt (1992) have found that almost all of the cross-sectional studies are not robust with respect to small changes in the conditioning information set. The fragility of the empirical results means that one cannot have much confidence in the findings of these studies.

3. This brief summary discusses only the views of Smith. A more thorough summary would also examine the Ricardian model of growth.

4. Smith looks at the Chinese situation because he asks whether there is a limit to capital accumulation (i.e., whether the long-run equilibrium growth rate is zero). Smith does not rule out such a situation from a theoretical point of view, although he claims "perhaps no country has ever yet arrived at this degree of opulence" (p. 95).

5. Earlier work in growth theory by Harrod (1948) and Domar (1957) also emphasized the macroeconomic aspects of growth. In fact, Solow viewed his work as an extension of the Harrod-Domar model, where capital-labor substitution in his model replaced the assumption of fixed proportions of the Harrod-Domar model. In the Harrod-Domar model the natural rate of growth of output equals the savings rate divided by the optimal capital/output ratio. Technology was assumed to be exogenous in the neoclassical world.

6. Lucas (1988) argues that "inefficiencies are important and their removal certainly desirable, but the familiar ones are level effects, not growth effects. This is exactly why it is not paradoxical that centrally planned economies, with allocative inefficiencies of legendary proportions, grow about as fast as market economies" (p. 12). I wonder if Lucas had written his article in 1992 instead of 1988, would he still have made the above statement? It seems that growth rates in centrally planned economies were maintained through creative accounting and the running down of the capital stock. It is now evident that correctly measured equilibrium growth rates in the centrally planned economies were substantially less than those in market economies.

7. Rent-seeking activities can reduce economic growth for number of reasons. For analysis of the effects of rent seeking on growth, see Murphy, Schleifer, and Vishny (1991). Rent-seeking activities not only absorb resources but also result in a tax on the productive sector that reduces the incentive to produce and results in the most talented members of society becoming rent seekers rather than productive entrepreneurs.

8. It should be noted that government bureaucrats may not be interested in well-defined property rights. Ill-defined property rights can result in government officials collecting a greater payment from rent seekers.

9. Fischer (1991) argues that the level/growth distinctions are largely irrelevant for most of the empirical growth literature, given the limited time series that exists for a large number of countries.

10. Barro (1991) finds that a higher share of government consumption expenditure, ill-defined property rights (as measured by political instability), and market distortion all have negative impact on economic growth.

11. With common technology and preferences and factor mobility, the neoclassical model predicts a convergence of all countries in levels of income and rates of growth. The lack of convergence in the cross-country data is an important empirical phenomenon that is inconsistent with the prediction of the neoclassical model. For evidence on convergence, see Baumol (1986).

12. Pranab Bardham (1990), in summarizing the literature on the role of the state and economic development, states that "the literature in development economics has now turned full circle from the unquestioning dirigism of the early 1950's to the gory neoclassical accounts in recent years of failure and disasters of regulatory interventionist states" (p. 3). Also see Krueger (1990) for a discussion of government failures in development policy.

13. De Long and Summers (1991) believe in the importance of machinery and equipment capital, but nevertheless stress that "a growth strategy based on equipment investment must be market conforming, not market replacing" (p. 485).

14. It should be noted that different endogenous growth models have different policy implications. This particular one was chosen for illustrative purposes only; it is not meant to be representative of "typical" endogenous models.

15. It should be noted that this argument for protection is similar to the infant industry argument. The main difference is that the infant industry argument is for short-run protection, whereas this example argues for permanent protection. The case of the infant industry argument can be illustrative for the case considered here. According to Krueger (1990), many infant industry tariffs had a "scope and height of protection that was far greater than could be defended on infant industry grounds" (p. 14). For example, in Turkey, effective rates of protection were 200% some 20 years after the birth of the infant industries. Generally, the existence of these tariffs spawns industry pressure groups that lobby government to maintain the protection indefinitely. This illustrates that in the dynamics of policymaking, the equilibrium policy may be completely different from the policy that was initially promised.

16. There have been a number of empirical studies to examine the effects of government on economic growth. These studies almost all include as a measure of government the level of government expenditures. In the example of trade protection, a major government interference, there is no government expenditure. In fact, such a policy may result in increased government revenue. This example shows the inappropriateness of measuring the role of government simply by examining government expenditures. Barro (1991) tries to correct this problem by looking at measures of market distortion as a measure of government activity.

17. Much of the evidence of knowledge spillover effects and externalities is anecdotal. An exception to this is the work of Jaffe (1986), who found circumstantial

evidence of spillovers from R&D. In an econometric analysis, Jaffe found that "firms whose research is in areas where there is much research by other firms have, on average, more patents per dollar of R&D" (p. 998).

18. The discussion of the rationale for deposit insurance and deposit insurance in Canada is based on joint research I conducted with Frank Mathewson (see Carr and Mathewson, 1992). The discussion of deposit insurance in the United States is based on a joint research program with Frank Mathewson and Neil Quigley.

19. Although Friedman and Schwartz recommended deposit insurance, this was not their first best policy; the first best policy was 100% reserves.

20. In 1966 the average size of Ontario and federal trust and loan companies was $59.6 million, compared with an average size of national banks of $3.4 billion (in assets).

21. The sample includes Ontario trust and loan companies and all federally incorporated trust and loan companies.

22. The explanation for this increased entry does not lie with an economy that was growing faster. From 1949 to 1966 GNP grew in Canada by 5.2% per annum; from 1968 to 1985, it grew at 4.0% per annum.

23. The states that enacted these laws were Oklahoma (1908), Kansas (1909), Texas (1909), Nebraska (1909), Mississippi (1914), South Dakota (1915), North Dakota (1917), and Washington (1917).

24. I am in the process of collecting data to show that during the three banking crises of the early 1930s depositors did have information on the riskiness of banks and transferred funds from small risky banks to larger secure banks.

25. I am in the process of collecting congressional voting records to ascertain the regional support for these bills.

26. The government had this knowledge because of the experience with the earlier state deposit insurance schemes. In addition, the large banks stressed these adverse moral hazard effects as one of the prime reasons not to adopt deposit insurance.

27. Keeley also claims that technological change increased the competition that banks faced from nonbank financial firms such as investment companies, brokerage firms, and insurance companies. Such changes also decreased the value of bank charters.

28. An examination of economic growth in Yugoslavia today would provide support for the thesis that war retards growth.

References

Bardham, P. (1990). "Symposium on the State and Economic Development." *Journal of Economic Perspectives, 4*, 3–7.

Barnett, G. E. (1911). *State Banks and Trust Companies*. Washington, DC: National Monetary Commission.

Barro, R. J. (1991). "Economic Growth in a Cross Section of Countries." *Quarterly Journal of Economics, 106*, 407–443.

Baumol, W. J. (1986). "Productivity Growth, Convergence, and Welfare: What the Long-Run Data Show." *American Economic Review, 76*, 1072–1085.

Becker, G. S., Murphy, K. M., and Tamura, R. (1990). "Human Capital, Fertility and Economic Growth." *Journal of Political Economy, 98*, 12–37.

Beckhart, B. H. (1929). "The Banking System of Canada." In H. P. Willis and B. H. Beckhart (Eds.), *Foreign Banking Systems*. New York: Holt.

Calomiris, C. W. (1990). "Is Deposit Insurance Necessary? A Historical Perspective." *Journal of Economic History, 50*, 283–295.

Carr, J., and Mathewson, F. (1992). "The Effect of Deposit Insurance in Financial Institutions." Unpublished manuscript.

De Long, J. B. (1990). "Did J. P. Morgan's Men Add Value? An Economist's Perspective on Financial Capitalism." NBER Working Paper 3426.

De Long, J. B., and Summers, L. H. (1991). "Equipment Investment and Economic Growth." *Quarterly Journal of Economics, 106*, 445–502.

Denison, E. F. (1961). *The Sources of Economic Growth in the United States*. Washington, DC: Committee on Economic Development.

Diamond, D., and Dybvig, P. (1983). "Bank Runs, Deposit Insurance and Liquidity." *Journal of Political Economy, 91*, 401–419.

Domar, E. (1957). *Essays in the Theory of Economic Growth*. Oxford: Oxford University Press.

Fischer, S. (1991). "Growth, Macroeconomics and Development." In *NBER Macroeconomics Annual* (Vol. 6). Cambridge: MIT Press.

Friedman, M., and Schwartz, A. (1963). *A Monetary History of the United States, 1867–1960*. Princeton, NJ: Princeton University Press.

Grossman, G. M., and Helpman, E. (1990). "Trade, Innovation and Growth." *American Economic Review, 80*, 86–91.

Harrod, R. F. (1948). *Towards a Dynamic Economics*. London: Macmillan.

Jacklin, C., and Bhattacharya, S. (1988). "Distinguishing Panics and Information-Based Bank Runs." *Journal of Political Economy, 96*, 569–592.

Jaffe, A. B. (1986). "Technological Opportunity and Spillovers of R&D: Evidence from Firms, Patents, Profits and Market Value." *American Economic Review, 76*, 984–1001.

Kane, E. J. (1985). *The Gathering Crisis in Federal Deposit Insurance*. Cambridge: MIT Press.

Keeley, M. (1990). "Deposit Insurance, Risk and Market Power." *American Economic Review, 80*, 1183–1200.

Krueger, A. O. (1990). "Government Failures in Development." *Journal of Economic Perspectives, 4*, 9–24.

Levine, R., and Renelt, D. (1992). "A Sensitivity Analysis of Cross-Country Growth Regressions." *American Economic Review, 82*, 942-963.

Lucas, R. E., Jr. (1988). "On the Mechanics of Economic Development." *Journal of Monetary Economics, 22*, 3–42

Lucas, R. E., Jr. (1990). "Why Doesn't Capital Flow from Rich to Poor Countries?" *American Economic Review, 80*, 92–96

Mishkin, F. S. (1992). "An Evaluation of the Treasury Plan for Banking Reform." *Journal of Economic Perspectives, 6*, 133–153.

Murphy, K., Schleifer, A., and Vishny, R. W. (1991). "The Allocation of Talent: Implications for Growth." *Quarterly Journal of Economics, 106,* 501–530.

Postlewaite, A., and Vives, X. (1987). "Bank Runs as an Equilibrium Phenomenon." *Journal of Political Economy, 95,* 485–491.

Romer, P. M. (1986). "Increasing Returns and Long-Run Growth." *Journal of Political Economy, 94,* 1002–1037.

Romer, P. M. (1990). "Endogenous Technological Change." *Journal of Political Economy, 98* (supplement), S71–S102.

Romer, T., and Weingast, B. R. (1990). "Political Foundations of the Thrift Debacle." Hoover Institution Working Paper E 90 22.

Schultz, T. W. (1961). "Investment in Human Capital." *American Economic Review, 51,* 1–17.

Smith, A. (1937). *An Inquiry into the Nature and Causes of the Wealth of Nations.* New York: Modern Library. (Original work published 1776).

Smith, B. (1988). "Bank Panics, Suspensions and Geography: Some Notes on the Contagion of Fear in Banking." Rochester Center for Economic Growth.

Solow, R. M. (1956). "A Contribution to the Theory of Economic Growth." *Quarterly Journal of Economics, 70,* 65–94.

Summers, R., and Heston, A. (1991). "The Penn World Table Mach 5: An Expanded Set of International Comparisons, 1950–1988." *Quarterly Journal of Economics, 106,* 327-368.

White, E. N. (1983). *The Regulation and Reform of the American Banking System, 1900–1929.* Princeton, NJ: Princeton University Press.

Comment

Reuven Brenner

Barro opens his chapter, his latest work in a sequence of studies on growth, with this observation: "A key issue in economic development is whether economies that start out behind tend to grow faster in per capita terms and thereby converge toward those that began ahead." This is a startling beginning.

Every economist who is interested in economic development knows— or should know, if he or she examines stretches of 100 years—about the rise and decline of regions, cities, nations, and empires. The decline is at times relative, at times absolute. Here is an observation made 2,500 years ago by Herodotus in his *Histories* (Book 1):

> For most cities which were great once are small today; and those which used to be small were great in my own time. Knowing, therefore, that human prosperity never abides long in the same place, I shall pay attention to both alike. (as quoted in Bauer, 1984, p. 176)

There is plenty of evidence that societies leapfrogged one another not only in Ancient Greece and Rome, but in many other parts of the world. *Leapfrogging* means that societies that were far behind not only caught up with those who were ahead, but outdid them. Of course, this also means that societies that were ahead fell behind, implying that poor places grew faster than richer ones. Rome, Byzantium, Spain and Portugal, the Italian city-states, the Arab countries, the Ottoman Empire, the Netherlands, England, China, the South American countries—all rose and also declined, not only in relative terms, but, at times, in absolute terms.[1]

So I do not quite understand why one would even raise the issue of "*whether* economies that start out behind tend to grow faster." Everybody knows the answer: some societies not only catch up, but outdo others, whereas other societies fall behind and do not catch up for decades or centuries. Thus, the key issue to which Barro refers has been answered for a long time. The debated, key questions are the following: Why does leapfrogging occur? How does it occur? How long does it take to catch up? Can the neoclassical models of growth explain why some societies fall behind not only relatively, but even in absolute terms? For a number of different reasons, I do not think that Barro's framework and sequence of studies—including the one presented here—is capable of handling either these questions or many of the problems to which it claims to give answers. I also have great difficulty understanding his methods, though to some of his numbers, which are more reliable, I can give an interpretation—however, that interpretation has nothing to do with the model he is testing.

The transitional growth process on which Barro relies draws on Solow-type neoclassical models, within which the important questions cannot be addressed. Within them, there is substitution between physical and human capital, and investment depends on relative returns. If there is a scarce resource, innovations will overcome the problem. Thus, although growth rates may vary, in terms of the model's postulates themselves, the possibility that there will be no growth just does not exist. The model makes one prediction: that a country's per capita growth rate tends to be inversely related to its starting level of per capita income. The convergence between poor and rich countries is brought about, under certain conditions, through the adjustment of capital-labor ratios. Barro claims to falsify this prediction both for the United States and for a sample of countries around the world. I think he fails to do so.

How Can One Interpret Barro's Statistical Results?

As noted above, economic historians are aware of the fact that there are many societies and regions that have suffered not just short-term, cyclical, declines, but declines over very long periods of time. Barro's international sample even makes additions to this list. Given that Barro's model itself excludes such a possibility, is not such evidence sufficient to invalidate it? The usual defenses that generalizations are necessary and that the appropriate method for judging the relevance of a theory is to examine whether the statements are valid in a statistical sense are not applicable in this case. Yes, generalizations are necessary in science, but for only one reason: to discover exceptions to the rule. In this case, however, the exceptions have already been discovered. So why not discard the model?[2]

In Barro's initial model, used only for the United States, each state was viewed as a small, closed economy, producing identical goods. The government appears as just one of the nine standard sectors in each state, but it has no special role in having an effect on incentives. Barro had to make this assumption about government to be consistent with the neoclassical, Solow-type model, whose implications he tested. Maybe this was not a very important assumption for comparing the 50 states, since they had similar laws, regulations, and institutions, and thus people living within their borders had similar incentives. But from the variables included in the present study, it is clear that Barro no longer has the initial model in mind.

In the present work under consideration, the variables explaining convergence are, among others, government consumption (exclusive of education and defense—although Barro does not explain why defense should be excluded),[3] tariff rates, black-market premium, and frequency of revolution. Thus, Barro tests here a model in which convergence of incomes is no longer a matter of adjustment of capital-labor ratios (as in the U.S. study), but of what one intuitively—but superficially—thinks of as "incentives." The variables affecting incentives determine the economies' long-term targets.[4] The variations in incomes across 114 countries in one study, 73 here, reflect variations in the long-term targets.

Although Barro does not present any model that would show how to link growth, violence, and black markets with the simple, neoclassical growth model, he makes a strong statement. He argues that a combined model is being tested here, and that, when holding the targets constant, he also obtains the inverse relationship between a country's growth rate and its starting position—both as predicted by the neoclassical model and as he obtained for the United States. The twin results are not a miracle, but they show that if one is ingenious and patient enough to mine a body of aggregate data with a statistical reliability in mind, but without relevance to the source, meaning, or significance of the data, one will be able to get pretty much whatever statistical result one wants.

Before discussing a few straightforward and a few more complicated problems with the data and the empirical examinations, I want to make it clear that I have no doubt that societies with similar institutions and incentive structures eventually converge—I shall explain below how I interpret this convergence. Already Baumol (1986) has found such convergence for 16 advanced countries, but not for the less developed countries. I do not find this statistical result either useful or interesting, however, if one wants to say something about growth. For thousands of years people have known that this happens. Also, the models on which the tests are based beg all the interesting questions about why incentives differ, and how one can explain prolonged decline within the same model that explains growth. Briefly, models that cannot explain leapfrogging, and within which institutions and the incentive structure (broadly understood)—which lead to "the emergence of novelty" (Usher, 1949)—do not play central roles, are sterile exercises and do not tell us anything about the engines of growth.

The Numbers

How can one interpret Barro's numbers? There are 73 countries in the present sample, but I do not know which ones, each with five observations. If they are more or less the same countries as in Barro's 1991 study, about a quarter of them are African countries notorious for their unreliable statistics, be they about demography or aggregates.

Here are two examples of this unreliability. In 1992, it was widely publicized that Nigeria does not have a population of 100 million, as previously claimed, but only 80 million. In Cameroon, nobody knows what has happened to life expectancy or fertility: the last published census was done in the mid-1970s. The numbers that appear in official statistics currently are based on projections from that time. This was also the method used to get Nigeria's—now discarded—population figure of 100 million. Looking at aggregate data coming from countries getting international aid, I am always reminded of the numbers that came out of an area in China in two enumerations. In one, the population was 28 million. Five years later, it was 105 million. The reason for the difference: the first census was done for tax and military purposes, the second for famine relief (see Huff, 1954, p. 134). What if all the sub-Saharan African data—for which Barro uses a dummy—and other data as well suffer from such problems?

One of the explanatory variables in the statistical analysis is the black-market premium. But if there was a black market in foreign exchange, I would like to know how many other goods and services were traded in black markets, and whether or not they were captured by the national statistics. In recent years, a large literature has appeared about the extent of black markets in South American, African, Asian and even European countries (Greece, Spain, and Italy having the largest estimated shares), not counted in national statistics. Italy acknowledged this explicitly when in 1987 it significantly revised its aggregate statistics: that year its GNP jumped by 18%.[5]

In addition to the areas raised above, there are other problems with the international comparison. The number of children in a family in rural areas has for a long time been far greater than in urban ones, one reason being that the opportunity cost of raising kids on a farm is lower than that of raising them in the city. Thus, a lower per capita income in rural areas exaggerates poverty: income per capita, correctly calculated, could be similar. When this situation applies, I do not know how much of the differences in average incomes among and within states and countries in Barro's examinations were no more than statistical artifacts, and part of the convergence a statistical illusion. There is a vast literature on the subject of comparing cost of living between urban and rural settings when there are differences and changes in life expectancy or other demographic variables and when there is a relative decline of small-scale agriculture in the course of economic development.[6] Barro does not raise or discuss any of these topics. Rather, he uses the official figures, known for their unreliability (and there is no reason to assume that the errors are constant).[7]

Still, significant as the above discussion has shown them to be, all of these problems with aggregate numbers could be overcome, though I do not think it would be worth the effort if one's goal is to say something about growth. The next section sketches an alternative way of examining questions linked with growth, based on my own fumbling, and gives a completely different interpretation to Barro's data and results.

The U.S. Results: What Do They Tell Us about Growth?

As noted above, Barro's initial research for the United States viewed the states as small, isolated, closed economies, producing identical goods—as required by the Solow-type growth models. The catching up of the poorer states was then interpreted as being to a large extent a matter of adjustment of capital-labor ratios. But that is not the story I read when looking at the numbers, and at prosperity either in the United States or elsewhere in the world, now or in the past. What I read are two main stories. One, which I explain in this section, is general; the other, to which I shall turn later, is more specific (though linked with the more general one).

The general story implies that once a certain incentive structure is in place across regions, growth comes about through specialization, diversity, division of labor—all consequences of entrepreneurship and innovations.[8] The specialization and diversity happen as consequences of the persisting search for markets by entrepreneurs, and their eventual discovery, either by entrepreneurs or by innovators.

The increased division of labor does not imply that growth per capita must necessarily be associated with population growth: innovations can be secured even if the population remains stationary.[9] The story is the following: as income in the city grows and diversity and specialization increase, income increases, which affects more distant areas. As buying power in these more distant areas increases, markets grow even if population does not. If the new centers of growth attract people, the process is reinforced and leads to additional specialization and urbanization.[10] In the concluding section of this chapter I shall explain quickly how this view of the engine of growth can be linked with both prosperity *and* declines over long stretches of human history, and how it can be linked with leapfrogging. But first let us go back to the United States data, and see how it can be read through these prisms.

Barro tests his views on very aggregate levels, so to evaluate his results through these prisms, let us take the rate of urbanization as a proxy for division of labor and diversity of occupations in the United States (but not in countries with a different incentive regime).[11] Across the United States, the urban population grew at an annual rate of roughly 2.8% between 1900 and 1930, and 2.0% over the next 30 years, whereas Barro's convergence rate is about 2% (meaning that 2% of the gap between a rich region and a poor region tends to be eliminated in one year, on average). One would expect that if growth rates and per capita incomes were not too inaccurately measured, Barro's "convergence coefficient" would reflect—approximately—the differential annual rate of urban population growth both across states and within them. One would expect to find that the same measured convergence occurs in places where similar shifts take place, and that, after a certain level is reached, less urbanized areas will be more quickly urbanized than those that already are, will show increased specialization, and will grow faster. Table 1 shows sample calculations I have made for the various states to give an idea of the magnitudes and variations in urbanization rates. If the aforementioned process of increased specialization is the main story that Barro's U.S. numbers capture, the measured convergence between and within states reflects increased specialization and increased division of labor, and has nothing to do with the aggregate, homogeneous neoclassical growth models.[12]

Here are some additional numbers for the period 1960–90, referring now to the international sample. In the industrialized world, 61% of the population lived in cities in 1960, and 73% in 1990. For the poorest countries, the proportions were, respectively, 16% and 28%; for those with "medium human development," 25% and 42%; and for the more developed Asian and South American countries, 52% and 75% (United Nations, 1991).[13] For the industrialized world, the annual rate of increase in urban population was 1.4%, which is very close to Barro's convergence number. For the relatively developed Asian and South American countries, it was about 3.6%—Barro's estimated rate of convergence for Japan is 3% per year. For what the United Nations (1991) calls countries with "medium human development," the number rose to an annual 4.2%, and it was the largest for the less developed countries, standing at 5.3%. However, there is no reason to expect convergence of these poorer countries even if their urbanization rates are higher, because frequently their populations had no diversified skills or their governments did not allow them to experiment and diversify.

TABLE 1
Urban Population Growth, 1900-1960, Total United States and Selected States

Year	Urban Population	Rural Population	Total Population	Urban as % of Total	Annual Growth Rate %
US					
1900	30.16	45.8	75.96	39.7	
1930	68.9	53.8	122.7	56.2	2.8
1960	124.7	53.7	178.4	69.9	2.0
Illinois					
1900	2.6	2.2	4.8	54.2	
1930	5.6	1.99	7.59	73.8	2.6
1960	8.14	1.94	10.08	80.8	1.3
Mississippi					
1900	0.12	1.4	1.52	7.9	
1930	0.34	1.6	1.94	17.5	3.5
1960	0.82	1.3	2.12	38.7	3.0
Vermont					
1900	0.076	0.27	0.346	22.0	
1930	0.12	0.24	0.36	33.3	1.5
1960	0.15	0.24	0.39	38.5	0.8
New York					
1900	5.3	1.9	7.2	73.6	
1930	10.5	2	12.5	84.0	2.3
1960	14.3	2.45	16.75	85.4	1.0

Source: U.S. Department of Commerce, Bureau of the Census (1976).

Growth and Employment: Specific Trends

In his comments on Barro's U.S. investigation, Blanchard (1991) also criticizes Barro's findings, though on very different grounds. The following reflects his main point, and leads to my next main one:

> In light of [Barro's] model, the reader may conclude that the *main* fact about regional growth in the United States has been the convergence of personal income per capita, presumably caused by the adjustment of capital-labor ratios. This conclusion would be wrong. Surely, an equally important fact is the amazing range of employment growth rates across states. . . . over the last 40 years average annual employment growth rates have ranged from close to 0 percent for West Virginia to above 5 percent for Nevada, Arizona, and Florida. The challenge is to reconcile this range of growth rates with the authors' fact of convergence in incomes per capita. (p. 160)

What are the additional lessons for growth theory when one takes this information into account? The story seems simple: it is the emergence of state-specific novelties—keeping in mind that we are talking not about people in different countries, but about people making decisions under similar institutions, and thus similar incentives.

The story of Nevada's novelty is different from those of the rest of the states, and the lesson it holds for growth theory is indirect. The innovation was that Nevada legalized the gambling industry when other states outlawed it (see Brenner and Brenner, 1990). The southern states' link with an innovation—air-conditioning—is more interesting. I would like to present it in some detail because it both tells something general about growth and raises additional doubts about the interpretation of Barro's statistical results and the policy implications he derives from them.

Heat and humidity at one time prevented some industries from spreading, but nice and dry weather attracted others. Initially, two of southern California's biggest industries—entertainment and aerospace—located there for the latter reasons. However, textile mills, for example, could not be built in humid places. They demanded solutions for controlling moisture in textiles, by adding measured quantities of steam into the atmosphere. (It is this procedure that was initially called "conditioning the air" and was the origin of the term "air-condition.") A physicist, Stuart W. Cramer, presented the first scientific paper on the topic before the American Cotton Manufacturers' Association in 1907.

Printers and lithographers were the other major industrial group looking for solutions. Their problems were that fluctuations in humidity and temperature led to numerous production difficulties: paper expanded and contracted, ink flowed or dried up, colors varied between printings (see Panati, 1987, pp. 159–160).

Willis Carriér, an engineer graduating from Cornell, came up with the first commercial air-cooling system in 1902, responding to an assignment from a Brooklyn printer. But it was not until 1919 that the first air-conditioned movie house opened in Chicago. Offices and department stores installed air-conditioning during the 1930s and 1940s, and claimed that it increased productivity: employees voluntarily arrived early and left late. Because of World War II, it was not until the 1950s that air-conditioning spread throughout the United States—and that is exactly when the rapid growth in both employment and per capita income started in the warmer states or the warmer parts of states (the case of California). Between 1950 and 1988, employment grew at a rate of more than 5% a year in Florida and Arizona, whereas the United States average is between 2% and 3% (see Blanchard, 1991).

To put it in technical terms, innovations (technological as well as legislative, as in the case of gambling laws) led first to increasing returns, to changes in growth in employment rates (as when air-conditioning changed the southern states), to shifts in specializations across states, and to innovations and entrepreneurship, and they induce additional division of labor: these are the engines of growth. Adjusting labor-capital ratios has little to do with them.

Policy Implications

Political Stability

Let us turn now to the international comparison. One of Barro's conclusions is that "the overall message from the policy variables included in the regressions is that more interference with markets and political instability have adverse effects on economic growth" (p. 20). I am sure that Barro does not want us to conclude that political instability in Spain following Franco's rule, political instability in various Latin American or South American countries after one dictator or another has been thrown out, or political instability following the fall of communist regimes has been adverse to growth.[14] Also, although the current constitutional debate in Canada will never lead to a revolution, and may not be captured by Barro's political instability variable, there is no doubt that there is political instability there. Even if Canada does not break up, there will be a redistribution of powers from the federal government to the provinces. Does such political instability have necessarily adverse effects? Given that, in general, countries do not break up without first being politically unstable for a while, the question is, When is political instability favorable to growth and when is it not? By lumping all countries together, without examining what types of political regimes societies abandoned and toward which ones they are heading, Barro gets a statistical result, but I do not think it helps us understand growth patterns.

Here is a brief summary of historical events, which I shall later use in an additional context, to make this point clear. In a recent essay, North and Weingast (1989) show how the 1688 Glorious Revolution was a critical factor explaining England's growth. The sequence of events leading to it was as follows. Repeated fiscal crises of the Stuarts led them to engage in forced loans, to sell monopolies, and to render property rights less secure in the early seventeenth century. Parliament and the courts became engaged in the struggle against the monarchy. This led to civil war and a series of failed experiments with political institutions. Stability was regained with the Glorious Revolution, when parliamentary supremacy, controlling financial matters in particular, and independence of the judiciary led to greater insurance against monopolization of power. Thus, the long period of instability led to the establishment of those institutions that played a critical role in England's rise.

Or consider a more general and, in its implications, far more troubling example for those who want to study growth through disciplinary, narrow, technical prisms. The religious wars in Europe were terrible, but they eventually led to the separation of church and state. Societies in which the two were or are still not separate—Russia before the revolution, Islamic countries, China during long periods in its history—prospered less than others. There are historians and legal scholars who view in the lack of separation, the greater monopoly power and the diversification of ideas this power prevented—here again is a link with my general point on diversity—one of the greatest obstacles to prosperity. Yet these societies may be measured as being politically very stable for long periods of time (see Berman, 1983; Brenner, 1983, 1990; Hill, 1992).[15]

The breakup of communist regimes requires a separate discussion, though in this case too the eventual failure of the system had much to do with the fact that it diminished the incentives of learning by trial and error and severely limited the range of occupations and specialization. We are thus back, once again, to the issue of diminished diversity.

The type of statistical analysis Barro does would confirm, superficially, the negative correlation between political stability and growth rates in these countries—when they were communist. But this would be little more than a statistical artifact (with the exception of Yugoslavia). The numbers that passed for national statistics in these regimes were little more than tricks pulled out of hats. They were meaningless because outputs were exaggerated and goods were recorded at fictitious prices. The resulting aggregate numbers showed growth, but life expectancy was declining, infant mortality was rising, people had to wait increasing numbers of hours for food, and there were waits of years for phones, cars, refrigerators, furniture, and apartments—all recorded in official statistics as being available at low prices. Thus political stability in those regimes had an adverse effect on growth—never mind what was measured.[16]

The reason I bring up the case of communist countries is that in one of his works Barro makes the prediction, based on his convergence coefficient, that it would take East Germany about 35 years to catch up partially, to close half of the gap between itself and West Germany. Based on my arguments about the importance of diverse skills in explaining growth, I would make a different prediction: that it would take about 35 years for East Germany to catch up entirely. The reason is that it takes about a generation to learn the skills that political frontiers prevented East Germans from learning *during a generation*—and I am not talking here about statistically measured "human capital," to which I shall come below. I emphasize that the East Germans were only a generation behind because if it were more than a generation, I would expect that it would take much longer to catch up. The shrewdness necessary for trade is passed from one generation to the next through a variety of complex channels; formal education may advance this process by teaching ways of spotting new opportunities, but formal education is no substitute for the generational transfer of information gained by experience.

Externalities

Consider the paragraphs that immediately follow Barro's statement that "interference with markets and political instability have adverse effects on economic growth." These paragraphs show how education has a positive effect on growth, yet if there is a sector in which governments have obviously interfered with markets during recent years, it is education. This seems to me an obvious inconsistency in the text; I expected Barro to discuss it, but he does not.

I know that there are economists who have suggested that "education" is a public good, and that the sector producing it should therefore be treated differently from others, justifying government interference. Is it just a coincidence that people in the education sector write these studies? I am afraid that some of the models come perilously close to confusing promotion of knowledge with the advocacy of policy. (See Lucas, 1988; Romer, 1990.) Maybe Barro buys the externality argument, and that is why he treats education separately, in spite of the accumulating evidence all over the world, and in the United States in particular, of the failure of the public system of education on every level. Maybe he does not—it is hard to know from this or his other texts.

Maybe Barro does not buy the externality argument, but considers it separately to have a proxy for human capital, however flawed. Still, as the text stands now, with the statement that, *ceteris paribus*, a certain increase in education would increase growth by a certain amount, it implies that the provision of education is costless. This may be true if there are externalities in education or if education is subsidized from outside sources. However, for the type of worldwide analysis that Barro does, the latter cannot be the case: the resources must be transferred from some country, and there they must show up as "government interference."[17] As the text now stands, it implies that education is the exception to the general rule Barro found that government interference has adverse effects on growth.[18]

I find the argument about externalities to education troubling on other grounds as well. It is very easy to build just about any mathematical model—logical speculations, that is—showing that if a sector has external effects, one government intervention or another can bring about a magic cure. Some make this argument about education, others—such as Lawrence Summers and Bradford De Long (1992)—about just about any machinery and equipment. Summers and DeLong claim that because of big spillover effects, the return on such investments to the economy as a whole is far greater than the return to any individual firm (because of quicker diffusion of technology throughout the economy).

The only sector whose subsidy was not yet justified on similar general grounds is the capital market, though, as Carr points out in his contribution to this volume, models to justify intervention in the banking sector on such grounds abound. It can be done even on general grounds, though it would be wrong to start writing such models. North and Weingast (1989) show how, in England, once political stability was achieved, there was a rapid development of capital markets, a wide range of securities, and negotiable instruments, all of which were important in England's subsequent growth. McNeill (1974, chap. 1) shows how one of the main aspects of the Italian city-states' spectacular rise resulted from the creation of ad hoc corporations.

So what is one to conclude from all the logical speculations advocating government intervention on the basis of externalities? If all the sectors can be shown to have positive externalities and are to be subsidized, who will be taxed? And if subsidies are selective, which industries will get them? There is little reason to expect that governments would have subsidized the textile, printing, and theater industries hoping for speedier invention and diffusion of air-conditioning. And how are these conclusions compatible with the negative finding that Barro obtains concerning government interference's effect on growth? I thought that Coase (1988) already gave answers to these questions: one should worry as much about solutions as about the problems, and also consider each problem in reference to circumstances, and not in general.[19] There are no magic cures, contrary to what all these mathematical speculations based on externalities suggest.

At this point, let me link the discussion again with Carr's chapter. Carr describes the history of policies concerning deposit insurance in the United States and Canada, and suggests that the financial system would work better without this interference. He also argues that deregulation of financial institutions without simultaneous elimination of deposit insurance is a disastrous combination, as the recent savings and loan fiasco showed. He argues further that the savings rate is less important than the effective use of savings. I agree with all these points.

I have only one minor disagreement with Carr's arguments and descriptions. He should have distinguished in his analyses the circumstances that led to the intervention, and others that explain the persistence, of deposit insurance. Deposit insurance, like many other banking regulations, was introduced in the United States during the Great Depression, when, as Friedman and Schwartz (1963) have pointed out, it might have played a positive role in preventing additional panic. So it is possible that once the government committed one big mistake, an additional intervention was needed to repair the damage. The problem has been that the regulation remained in place even when the circumstances changed, and it was no longer needed. At this point it became harmful, although people invented theories—I would call them excuses—to justify its persistence. That is what many social scientists do today, a role they inherited from priests and astrologers. This is exactly the process through which harmful myths have always come into being (for discussion of how this process takes place in the sciences and at universities, see Brenner, 1991c; Colander and Brenner, 1992, chap. 1).

Thus, one should examine separately the origins of an idea, a regulation, and its persistence. To explain the origins, one should pay attention to the circumstances in which the policy emerged. To explain its persistence, once its harms become evident, one should examine features of the political process that prevent its abolition. This brief scenario also suggests the way I would approach—and have approached—the broader issue of convergence for government policies, an issue Barro mentions in his concluding comments.

How Is Adam Smith Relevant?

Carr briefly summarizes theories of growth, starting with Adam Smith. I have commented on all the theories that Carr covers, with the exception of Smith's. Smith's comments on the division of labor being limited by the extent of the market (a point Carr does not raise) make it clear that Smith did say important things about growth.[20]

Contrary to what Carr is saying, however, Smith did not think that government intervention was always bad. Whether it was or it was not depended upon the circumstances. Smith favored restrictions on foreign trade, for example, in two cases. The first one was "when some particular sort of industry is necessary for the defense of the country" (Smith, 1976, p. 485; Smith was in favor of the Navigation Act), and "the second case, in which it will generally be advantageous to lay some burden upon foreign for the encouragement of domestic industry, is, when some tax is imposed at home upon the produce of the latter. In this case, it seems reasonable that an equal tax should be imposed upon the like produce of the former" (p. 487).[21] Also, Smith was not against government intervention on other grounds:

> When a company of merchants undertake, at their own risk and expense, to establish a new trade with some remote and barbarous nation, it may not be unreasonable to incorporate them into a joint stock company, and to grant them, in case of their success, a monopoly of the trade for a certain number of years. (p. 277)

Translated to our times, this reminds one of justifications for interventions in research and development. But Smith was careful to qualify his recommendation, advocating that the intervention should be temporary.[22]

I quote Adam Smith not to suggest necessarily that he was right (though I think he was), but to show that if one wants to advance a general proposition against government intervention, Adam Smith is not the authority to rely upon. However, if one wants to get insights into the process of growth, I would recommend rereading him. There are no aggregate statistics in *The Wealth of Nations*. The statistics that appear are discussed, without exception, with their historical background. I think that more can be learned about growth from these discussions than from all the standard ahistorical macroeconomic and development literature published since. A close reading of Chapter 3, for example, on the accumulation of capital, suggests that without examining the institutional structure, one cannot even evaluate the impact of the accumulation of human capital on growth:

> The labor of some of the most respectable orders in the society is, like that of menial servants, unproductive of any value. . . . The sovereign, for example, with all the officers both of justice and war who serve under him, the whole army and navy, are unproductive laborers. . . . In the same class must be ranked, some both of the gravest and most important, and some of the most frivolous professions: churchmen, lawyers, physicians, men of letters of all kinds; players, bufoons, musicians, opera-singers, opera-dancers etc. (p. 352)

I will leave this point at that.[23]

Conclusions

Barro remarks that the long-run targets depend "on government policies in areas such as taxation, protection of property rights, and provision of infrastructure services and education. The targets can also vary because of factors that governments cannot readily influence, such as underlying attitudes about saving, work effort, and fertility, and the availability of natural resources" (p. 9). If one wants to shed light on why some places grow and others fail, one needs to examine why societies differ so much in the ways in which these targets are determined.

I promised to sketch very briefly my views about what drives historical change.[24] It is the emergence of novelty—innovations, in a very broad sense of the word. The main factor I have identified that makes novelty emerge in one place rather than another is the encounter with diversity. In concrete terms, this means coming into contact either with strangers, who bring information, or with adversity, which forces a society to bet on new ideas. Such events prevent societies from settling into routine behavior. They induce members of these societies to do things in new ways, hoping either to restore their wealth or to leapfrog their fellows. When and where this does not happen, people settle into routines.[25]

Initially, societies developed in places where geography enabled more frequent encounters among strangers. That is why, over long periods of time, ports and other places where international trade routes passed became the centers where novelty emerged. Foreigners brought information, which opened people's eyes to new opportunities. Through the process described above, these encounters led to an endogenous process of growth over broad areas.

Today, the institutional structure of the industrially advanced societies gives the option of leapfrogging, and thus encourages entrepreneurship and innovation. This process has resulted in specialization and continuous division of labor, and thus the creation of "modern" strangers. Also, technology has become so widespread that even isolated people can now be in touch with "strangers" without moving.

This institutional structure thus enables leapfrogging: that is, people can expect to outdo their fellows. This also means that there are others who fall behind. The fact that societies are forced to take into account the reactions of the latter group explains why there are obstacles inherent in the process that we call "growth." The obstacles are endogenous. Just as people in the past have at times decided to accept or reject what was foreign to them—at times reacting violently—specialization and the previously described incentive system bring similar reactions.

The reason is that novelty implies that traditional trades fall into oblivion, and new ones must be learned. Traditions must be abandoned, and new habits must be acquired. There are new centers of skill, and traditional groups break up. These consequences and resulting reactions set in motion a process that slows down the trend toward specialization and increased diversity. The danger exists that there will be societies where traditions will be reinforced, where more will be spent on the military, and where people will fall into routines. Thus, prosperity is not inevitable. Societies that either close themselves or, through a wide variety of regulations and policies, maintain rigidity can fall behind, and may become extinct. Such rigidity is reinforced by beliefs about the source of such societies' wealth, which affect their social and political structure—even if they are wrong.

The difficult task is to discard such myths and to maintain a society that is balanced between rigidity and change. This is the condition necessary for creativity, for the emergence of novelty.

The above is a bit of a caricature of human history in a few paragraphs.[26] I believe that there are grains of truth in it. In any case, it is simply a device to bring to the fore my main arguments.

To conclude: if the goal is to learn something about growth, and to draw conclusions about policies, there is not much reason to make aggregate statistical analyses. Instead, economists should pay attention to the incentive structure, derived from a detailed examination of laws, regulations, traditions, and institutions. My suspicion is that economists avoid doing such examinations because the models they build stand in the way of their viewing the emergence of novelty as the central part of the story (this point is made in various contexts by Coase, 1988; Colander and Brenner, 1992; Schultz, 1990; Young, 1928). Also, they are comfortable making statistical analyses of aggregates, even if they do not know much about either the ways they are calculated or how innovations alter their meaning (see Brenner, 1992; Wriston, 1992). Because national governments and administrative areas produce aggregate statistics and make decisions on policies, economists tend to look upon them when examining growth. I have tried to argue here that this outlook is misleading. To learn about prosperity, economists should focus their examinations on features of centers of skill that either radiate influences through "innovations" or fall into oblivion. They should stop focusing on nations, or on administrative units that create statistics.[27]

Notes

1. There is extensive literature on this subject by historians, anthropologists, and economists. See Gibbon (1990), Cipolla (1970), Olson (1982), Brenner (1983), Kennedy (1987), and Tainter (1988).

2. It seems to me that the field of theories of economic development is falling today for the same type of sterile exercises it fell for in the 1960s and 1970s, when the large majority of the practitioners in this field wrote models upon models about the pervasiveness of vicious circles. Though those who criticized the models mentioned Hong Kong, Taiwan, South Korea, and a few other countries as counterexamples, they were dismissed with the statement that generalizations cannot be dismissed with counterexamples, and the appropriate method of testing is validity in a statistical sense. See discussion in Bauer (1984, chap. 9).

3. Though he does not say, I guess that Barro's reason for excluding education is that he does not want to double-count it, as it is captured implicitly in the schooling variable.

4. Maybe Barro relies on Romer's model. That model is intellectually somewhat more satisfying than the simplistic Solow-type ones because there is an

implicit incentive structure that drives it. Still, that model cannot account for disinvestment either, not to speak of anything linked with military, violence, black markets, and so on.

5. For details on how the figure of 18% was chosen, when the estimates are that the black market varies between 25% to 40%, see Brenner (1992, chap. 1).

6. See Kuznets (1942), Usher (1968), and Bauer (1984, chap. 9) for references, calculations, and discussion. Usher shows how biases, which do not remain constant over time, amount for less developed countries to several hundred percent.

7. I do not want to imply that correctly calculated, average income per capita in the U.S. regions was the same every year, and that the convergence is just a statistical artifact, though I suspect that frequently that is the case when regions under one political system are being compared over longer periods of time, so that the effects of state-specific innovations are eliminated.

8. The nature of the incentive structure is implicit in the model of human behavior presented most accurately in Brenner and Brenner (1990, app. 1). It explains the meaning of leapfrogging for individuals.

9. Also, diversity does not refer just to sectors, but to specialization within each, as well as the various professions. See Schultz (1990, chap. 17).

10. This is the way I interpret Adam Smith's statement on the "division of labor being limited by the extent of the market." Coase (1988) calls this process "contracting out," which in his view too leads to specialization. Others view it as being linked to increasing returns. For a number of reasons, which will become clearer in the next section, I prefer to view it as an innovation.

11. The dispersion of measured occupations does not even get close to what diversity means (for instance, see Schultz's, 1990, description of the range of specialized occupations in pig production and in growing hybrid corn, which in official statistics just pass for farmers).

12. This same model can also explain why some societies could decline, even if their population is growing, if the population growth is not accompanied by an institutional change that favors diversity. See Brenner (1983, 1989).

13. These numbers must be interpreted cautiously because of the existence of a number of what one could call city-states: Singapore, Hong Kong, Qatar, Bahrain. See United Nations (1991, p. 176, tab. 20).

14. Obviously, growth must be measured over lengths of time of more than 5 or 10 years, and some economic historians claim that only periods of 30 years or more are meaningful (see Lane, 1966).

15. Consider the politically extremely stable "primitive" societies which did not grow at all. See Brenner (1983, chap. 2) for a discussion of the evidence.

16. For discussion on the meaning of statistics in the communist bloc, see Brenner (1990, 1991a, 1991b, 1992).

17. Maybe Barro has a more complicated model in mind, where the transfer from a richer to a poorer country prevents migration, or increased political instability, in which case we are dealing with one additional form of externality. This is not an abstract argument: West Germany agreed to pay money to the former Soviet Union and to build apartments in its territory, so as to get rid of the Red Army more quickly.

18. Whatever the case, Barro should add explanations and qualifications to the text. Or maybe he should compare the contribution of the education sector when it was privately offered relative to times and countries when and where it was not. Or maybe he should refer to existing research suggesting that there is no positive correlation between growth rates and expenditures on education per capita in the industrialized countries.

19. These observations should not be taken to imply that economists cannot make generalizations about historical changes, and must try to examine the portions of general theories that are relevant. Rather, my point is that to use economic and statistical analyses effectively, it is not enough to know their principles. The principles of mechanics and electricity are the same for every machine and electric circuit, but this knowledge will not help the engineer or technician repair anything unless he or she knows the type of machine to be repaired.

20. It is important to bear in mind, however, that Smith himself was anything but specialized. He wrote about history, music, poetry, law, and a whole theory of moral sentiments, which was considered his masterpiece before *The Wealth of Nations.*

21. The defense argument can be abused dangerously; see Brenner (1987, chap. 7).

22. Apparently in Japan many firms that were initially subsidized or owned by the government were privatized within a few years (see Brenner, 1987, chap. 7).

23. See Brenner (1991c) and the chapters in Colander and Brenner (1992) on the lack of productivity, or even counterproductivity, of professions with very high statistical human capital.

24. The evidence and discussion can be found in my books and articles. A historian whose views I share, and who reached his conclusions by looking at a set of evidence very different from that I used, is William McNeill. See the way he summarizes his lifetime work in his 1986 book.

25. The evidence suggests that knowledge does not advance if one interacts with people who have "human capital." Their capital must be very different.

26. It also explains why some places rose, and others declined (see details in Brenner, 1983, 1987, 1989).

27. Within the cities of the United States there are pockets of growth and pockets of decline. More can be learned by examining them than by looking at any aggregates.

References

Barro, R. J. (1991). "Economic Growth in a Cross Section of Countries." *Quarterly Journal of Economics, 106,* 407–443.

Barro, R. J., and Sala-i-Martin, X. (1991). "Convergence across States and Regions." *Brookings Papers on Economic Activity, 1,* 107–158.

Bauer, P. T. (1984). *Reality and Rhetoric: Studies in the Economics of Development.* Cambridge, MA: Harvard University Press.

Baumol, W. J. (1986). "Productivity Growth, Convergence, and Welfare: What the Long-Run Data Show." *American Economic Review, 76,* 1072–1085.

Berman, H., (1983). *Law and Revolution.* Cambridge, MA: Harvard University Press.

Blanchard, O. J. (1991). "Comments and Discussion." *Brookings Papers on Economic Activity, 1,* 159–177.

Brenner, R. (1983). *History: The Human Gamble.* Chicago: University of Chicago Press.

Brenner, R. (1987). *Rivalry.* Cambridge: Cambridge University Press.

Brenner, R. (1989). *Betting on Ideas: Wars, Invention, Inflation.* Chicago: University of Chicago Press.

Brenner, R. (1990). "The Long Road from Serfdom and How to Shorten It." *Canadian Business Law Journal, 17,* 195–226.

Brenner, R. (1991a). "From Envy and Distrust to Trust and Ambition." *Rivista di Politica Economica, 81,* 31–59.

Brenner, R. (1991b). "Legal Reforms in the Eastern Bloc: A Precondition to Monetary and Fiscal Policies." In E. M. Claassen (Ed.), *Exchange Rate Policies of the Less Developed Market and Socialist Economies* (pp. 151–174). San Francisco: International Center for Economic Growth.

Brenner, R. (1991c). "Extracting Sunbeams Out of Cucumbers: Or, What Is Bad Social Science, and Why Is It Practiced?" *Queen's Quarterly, 99,* 519–554.

Brenner, R. (1992). "The End of Economic Myths." Unpublished manuscript, McGill University.

Brenner, R., and Brenner, G. A. (1990). *Gambling and Speculation: A Theory, a History and a Future of Some Human Decisions.* Cambridge: Cambridge University Press.

Cipolla, C. (Ed.). (1970). *The Economic Decline of Empires.* London: Methuen.

Coase, R. (1988). *The Firm, the Market and the Law.* Chicago: University of Chicago Press.

Colander, D., and Brenner, R. (Eds.). (1992). *Educating Economists.* Ann Arbor: University of Michigan Press.

Friedman, M., and Schwartz, A. (1963). *A Monetary History of the United States, 1867–1960.* Princeton, NJ: Princeton University Press.

Gibbon, E. (1990). *Decline and Fall of the Roman Empire.* New York: Fawcett Premier.

Hill, C. (1992, August). "The Integration of the Middle East into the World Economy." Paper presented at the meeting of the Mont Pélerin Society, Vancouver.

Huff, D. (1954). *How to Lie with Statistics.* New York: W. W. Norton.

Kennedy, P. (1987). *The Rise and Fall of the Great Powers.* New York: Random House.

Kuznets, S. (1942). *National Income and Its Composition* (Vol. 2). Cambridge, MA: National Bureau of Economic Research.

Lane, F. C. (1966). *Venice and History.* Baltimore: Johns Hopkins University Press.

Lucas, R. E., Jr. (1988). "On the Mechanics of Economic Development." *Journal of Monetary Economics, 22,* 3–42.

McNeill, W. H. (1974). *Venice: The Hinge of Europe 1081–1797.* Chicago: University of Chicago Press.

McNeill, W. H. (1986). *Mythistory and Other Essays*. Chicago: University of Chicago Press.

North, D. C. (1990). *Institutions, Institutional Change and Economic Performance*. Cambridge: Cambridge University Press.

North, D. C., and Weingast, B. W. (1989). "The Evolution of Institutions Governing Public Choice in 17th Century England." *Journal of Economic History, 49*, 803–832.

Olson, M. (1982). *The Rise and Decline of Nations*. New Haven, CT: Yale University Press.

Panati, C. (1987). *Extraordinary Origins of Everyday Things*. New York: Harper & Row.

Romer, P. M. (1990). "Endogenous Technological Change." *Journal of Political Economy, 98* (supplement), S71–S102.

Schultz, T. W. (1990). *Restoring Economic Equilibrium*. Oxford: Basil Blackwell.

Smith, A. (1976). *The Wealth of Nations*. Chicago: University of Chicago Press.

Solow, R. M. (1956). "A Contribution to the Economic Theory of Growth." *Quarterly Journal of Economics, 70*, 65–94.

Summers, L. H., and DeLong, J. B. (1992, September 12). "American Meets Europe in Wyoming." *The Economist*.

Tainter, J. A. (1988). *The Collapse of Complex Societies*. Cambridge: Cambridge University Press.

United Nations. (1991). *Rapport Mondial sur le Développement Humain*. Paris: Economica.

U.S. Department of Commerce, Bureau of the Census. (1976). *Historical Statistics of the United States from Colonial Times to 1970*. Washington, DC: Government Printing Office.

Usher, D. (1968). *The Price Mechanism and the Meaning of Income Statistics*. Oxford: Oxford University Press.

Usher, P. A. (1949). "The Significance of Modern Empiricism for History and Economics." *Journal of Economic History, 9*, 137-155.

Wriston, W. B. (1992). *The Twilight of Sovereignty*. New York: Charles Scribner's Sons.

Young, A. A. (1928). "Increasing Returns and Economic Progress." *Economic Journal, 38*, 527–542.

Comment

Michael R. Darby

It is a great pleasure to take part in this important conference and particularly to contribute to this section, because it gives me the opportunity to study the excellent work of Robert Barro and Jack Carr. I fear that I have a reputation for not pulling punches as a discussant, but the preceding chapters challenge even me to find things to criticize. I do have a few quibbles, which I shall attend to, but mostly these comments will be in the nature of supplementary exposition of some of the points that I think are important implications of this research.

I shall start with the chapter by Barro which is a report on aspects of a larger effort by Barro and his colleagues that I believe has been extraordinarily fruitful. My primary concern here is to develop further the implications of the investment in human capital in terms of the long-run level of per capita income that Barro calls y_i^* or target income. I fear that *target income*—like *permanent income*, to which it is related—may be a misleading term because target income changes over time in ways that are both predictable and crucial to understanding growth.

The regressions in Table 1.1, which I presume were estimated with constant terms not reported here, can be interpreted as saying that a constant fraction of the percentage difference between current and target income is eliminated each period. This discussion will be familiar to readers who have worked much in the area of money demand functions. With constant terms, the regression can also be interpreted as allowing for normal growth, with the current-target gap leading to variations around that normal growth. In the money demand literature, much work has been devoted to details of the dynamics that may be impossible to infer from the data Barro presents.

I would have preferred it if Barro had expressed the coefficient estimates other than those for initial log GDP in terms of their implied values for the log y_i^* equation. We can infer these magnitudes by dividing by the adjustment coefficient, which is equivalent here to multiplying the estimates by a factor of 50 or 60. It may be easier to think in terms of Barro's example of raising education in sub-Saharan Africa by 10% in terms of its long-run or target income effect of about 10%, given that the adjustment coefficient and impact coefficient are approximately equal. It is intuitive, if we have a good measure of human capital, that in the long run output should increase by X% if human capital increases by X%.

If we think along these lines, we see that in Table 1.1 the schooling variable is the only one besides log GDP with a plausible continuing trend, and that trend will ultimately determine the growth rate of per capita output. Step changes in the other variables are more likely, and those would change the level of target income but not its growth rate looking forward. Of course, during the adjustment period actual per capita output would grow faster or slower than target income, and those effects are far from trivial.

In his subsequent work, I hope that Barro will consider whether he really believes that the rate of adjustment is the same for different causes of deviations between target and actual income and, if not, how he would model that. Jack Carr and I did some such thinking for money demand models, so this will serve as my segue from Barro's excellent chapter to Carr's.

Carr has actually written two chapters and I am not sure they fit well together. One is a review of the literature on economic growth and the second is a cross-border comparison of U.S. and Canadian experience with deposit insurance and some implications of that experience for growth.

My main concern with the literature review is that it buys the "new growth" theorists' claims about the inadequacies of neoclassical growth theory. The claims I have in mind all focus on the most primitive of the neoclassical growth models, in which labor grew only through population growth and omitted human capital investment as a form of labor growth.

More sophisticated models incorporated growth in human capital as a form of labor augmentation, which would account for persistent differences among nations in the levels and growth rates of output per worker. Some models even allowed for imperfect substitution between raw labor and human capital. Admittedly, the growth literature of the 1960s and 1970s was not too exciting, but it did a much better job of explaining the world than the recent literature credits it with.

Indeed, Barro's chapter can be motivated entirely by reference to neoclassical growth models with exogenous human capital growth. It illustrates that variations in the levels and rates of growth are accounted for primarily by factors that explain the level and growth of labor input, the aggregate production function, and physical capital investment. Technological change is taken as constant across time and countries.

Recent literature—and Robert Barro follows this approach in interpreting his results—takes human and nonhuman capital formation as pretty much the same rather than seeing raw labor growth and human capital investment as equivalent ways of increasing labor. I suspect that the latter is more nearly correct, and using that approach makes interpreting the empirical evidence easier. The substantive point is that we do not need the externalities of the new growth models to understand growth around the world, so maybe we do not need their peculiar policy implications.

Barro's work also provides evidence that the differences in how societies are ordered and regulated really do make a big difference, as argued by Jack Carr and Adam Smith. These effects would show up in the three main factors of the neoclassical growth model: the aggregate production function, the labor input growth path, and the investment/output ratio. Regulation and distortions certainly can affect the aggregate production function, which is a behavioral rather than purely technical relation. Taxation, property rights, and rent-seeking activities will also affect the quantity of labor supplied, given the endowment, choices between quality and quantity of children, and how much capital relative to output is accumulated.

Let us turn to the second of Carr's subjects—deposit insurance. In this part of his chapter, Carr takes a radical turn from the Friedman-Schwartz argument of deposit insurance as an engine of macroeconomic stability. He instead argues that deposit insurance will lead banks to make riskier loans, so that investment is less efficient in producing capital stock than otherwise. This is an interesting hypothesis, but we cannot be sure of the direction of the effect, and I am skeptical of its magnitude. If banks make riskier investments, we can conclude that more banks will go bankrupt, but not that bank-financed investments as a whole will be less productive. With risk aversions, large payoffs are discounted or underweighted in evaluating investment opportunities relative to a simple output criterion. By reducing risk aversion, deposit insurance can lead to an increased output from bank-financed investments. Is this likely to be a significant factor? I doubt it, but I doubt that the principal-agent arguments stressed by Carr really account for a lot of GDP, either.

While I am skeptical that Carr and his associates have really identified a major determinant of economic growth in deposit insurance, I am much more persuaded that they are correct that existing deposit insurance schemes are overall output-reducing cross-transfers from efficient to inefficient producers of banking services and that there are less costly ways to achieve macroeconomic stability. That accomplishment may be enough for one research program.

PART TWO

Financial Markets
and Economic Regulation

Introduction

Whatever the central driving force behind the implementation of given regulatory initiatives, and whatever the degree to which good intentions underlie them, it is nonetheless the case that ensuing consequences can be both unforeseen and unpleasing. Whether intended or not, regulation, like all government policy, engenders allocational effects and so inexorably creates winners and losers—and regulation of financial markets is no exception.

The U.S. system of deposit insurance, combined with the necessary loosening in the 1970s and 1980s of restrictions on interest rates payable on insured deposits, creates incentives for excessive risk taking on the part of depository institutions. Combined with such other regulatory restrictions as the geographic limits on branching that increase further the riskiness of depository operations, the deposit insurance system was the central source of the savings and loan implosion. The substantial costs yielded by that debacle led to the adoption of numerous regulations, both formal and informal, intended at least ostensibly to reduce risk taking on the part of insured commercial and savings banks.

Thus was the U.S. banking system led to a new realm of unintended consequences. The chapters in this section, by Glenn Yago and Benjamin Zycher, discuss these regulatory effects in the context of the supply of financial capital. Yago argues that the 1990–91 recession, and the ensuing period of slow growth, resulted not from traditional macroeconomic factors, but instead from institutional and regulatory rigidities affecting certain sectors in particular. Yago reviews several past economic downturns similar to the recent one in terms of the role played by capital markets and reduced capital availability, and argues that reduced access to capital played a central role in all. Moreover, increased regulation has led "to a fundamental departure of banks from their historic role as providers of credit to growth businesses." Yago goes on to argue as well that regulatory constraints imposed upon the use of high-yield ("junk") debt have created a structural barrier for small and medium-sized firms in terms of access to financial capital, and that this condition has harmed employment creation for the entire U.S. economy.

Although both Yago and Zycher conclude that regulatory constraints have reduced the supply of capital for important economic sectors, Zycher, unlike Yago, argues that the 1990–91 recession indeed was different from earlier ones, and that the conventional wisdom on the existence of a generalized "credit crunch," endorsed by Yago, is incorrect. Zycher argues that the recent recession was different in that it was more heavily structural (as opposed to cyclical) than earlier ones, and that the emergence of the "leverage ratio" and "risk-based" regulatory capitalization standards for banks has led to a major shift in the composition of bank assets away from lending to small and medium-sized commercial and industrial firms.

Because the "credit crunch" did not afflict the entire economy, much less so in a proportional sense, Zycher argues that "credit crunch" is an unfortunate term; the Fed supplied substantial new reserves to the banking system, and those reserves were not left idle. A better term perhaps is "sectoral crunch," indicating the disproportional effect of the regulations upon particular sectors. In any event, Zycher illustrates the important differences in bank lending behavior during the latest business cycle relative to that during the 1979–82 cycle; the upshot of the statistical analysis is that the decline in bank assets and the substantial shift toward government securities in bank asset portfolios resulted from the capitalization regulations rather than from aggregate economic conditions. Zycher then provides theoretical and empirical arguments supporting Yago's conclusion that the regulations have disproportionally adverse impacts upon the supply of capital to small and medium-sized businesses.

Some interesting arguments were made during the discussion following the presentation of the papers appearing in the section, particularly in an international context. One point was that the "credit crunch" seems to be a multinational phenomenon in the context of real estate loans, a fact suggesting not a "credit crunch" but instead a disinflationary process making real estate investments riskier from the viewpoint of lenders operating under very different regulatory regimes. Another comment was made to the effect that "credit crunches," however defined, are less likely to occur as capital markets become more open internationally. Finally, the point was made that bank capital ratios in the days before deposit insurance were a good deal higher than is the case under the new capitalization standards. That observation raises the intriguing possibility that the new capitalization standards still are too low, and that bank lending to small and medium-sized businesses actually may be too high!

3

Financial Repression and the Capital Crunch Recession: Political and Regulatory Barriers to Growth Economics

Glenn Yago

The objective of this chapter is to explore historical, theoretical, and empirical issues that can inform our understanding of institutional processes that destabilize and create barriers to economic growth. I will review and attempt to synthesize diverse research findings on financial innovations and their impacts on capital markets and regulatory and financial policies, and resulting measurable and monitorable impacts of these factors on economic growth.

Throughout the current political season, policy pundits across the left-right spectrum fiddle at the margins of macroeconomic policy levers that appear unhinged from a lackluster economy that makes the boundary between recession and recovery increasingly obscure. The events of the past decade were not kind to the presumptions of conventional macroeconomic theory and policy. Standard relationships connecting money growth to income growth, economic expansion, or price inflation collapsed. Anticipated effects of government spending not only failed to materialize, but often distorted market demand and failed to reverse downturns in nonfinancial economic activity during both recessions of the early 1980s and 1990s.

In this context, this political season's policy course orbits predictably around tax cuts (for whom?), interest rate manipulations (how far?), and public spending increases (for what?). Long-established patterns of income and wealth polarization continue. Within the restrictive macroeconomic boundaries of existing policy debates, trade-offs between equity and growth are considered inherent, rather than mutually supportive dynamic elements of an expanding economy.

In this chapter I attempt to synthesize lessons from diverse experiences and fields in order to link issues and questions in such a way as to resolve the existing conundrum forcing choices between equity and growth that produce neither. The United States has been unique in the history of the development of capitalism in developing social, political, and financial institutions based on advancing and expanding participation (Moore, 1966). U.S. capitalist development was specifically entrepreneurial—that is, based upon the expansion and proliferation of entrepreneurial units, as opposed to more state-sponsored business development. This main tendency has, by no means, been continuous. Political business cycles have periodically resulted in rigidities in market development that fostered bureaucratic over entrepreneurial growth, entrance barriers over access, economic concentration over competition, restrictions over flexibility, and regulation over incentives (Chandler, 1968; Chandler and Daems, 1974).

In attempting to shed some light on the current economic wheel spinning that may be observed in indicators of this cyclical "recovery," I will also review the institutional factors that produced this capital crunch recession. In the range of business cycles, this recession and sputtering recovery are different, but not unprecedented, from earlier downturns (1887, 1914, 1931, 1974) that were produced by shifts and constrictions in capital flow. I will present evidence of why this recession is not cyclical and macroeconomic, but structural and institutional—the result of rigidities that artificially inhibit business and financial innovation through restrictive government regulation and financial institutional behavior.

Specifically, this chapter is organized to review the following:

- historical themes in capital access, financial institutional development, and political regulation
- theoretical background in economic theory regarding institutional changes and investment
- current evidence of the impacts of political regulation on economic growth

Historical Review: Ownership, Access, and Repressive Regulation of Capital

The broad sweep of American history demonstrates continuity toward expanded economic participation commensurate with political participation. The process of economic enfranchisement, of which capital access is a critical element, encompassed debates surrounding economic and regulatory policy affecting capital access that centers on technical considerations of financial, accounting, and economic measurement. In this discussion, an explicit linkage needs to be made between capital access and capital ownership as requisite economic underpinnings for the successful realization of political democracy in the American republic.

Defining the American Dream: Entrepreneurial Ownership and Capital Access

The desired economic goal to "be an owner" has deep historical antecedents in U.S. history and popular culture. Moreover, it has become a theme in recent contests for corporate control and the shareholder rights movement, where the transition from passive to active investors has occurred in efforts to introduce democratic principles into corporate governance practice (e.g., the United Shareholders Association and proposed changes in SEC proxy voting rules). According to survey data, nearly a fifth of those in the U.S. labor force have owned their own businesses or been self-employed at some point in their working careers—more than in any other contemporary democracy (Lipset, 1977). Nearly half of all Americans aspire to business ownership. Self-employment has been the fastest-growing occupational category of the past decade.

This all points toward a long-standing tradition and aspiration in our political culture of seeking economic independence—not through inherited wealth or government entitlement, but through property ownership. The capacity of our capital markets and financial institutions to support those popular aspirations of Jeffersonian democracy that have survived industrialization and technological changes in the nation's economic base are crucial.

The historical origins of this sentiment are long-standing, as many historians have shown (Goodwyn, 1976; Greider, 1987; Lasch, 1991; Schlesinger, 1945). Freedom and liberty in the nineteenth century were rooted in the notion of a broad distribution of property ownership and property rights and their link to political rights. From Jefferson to Jackson and including the formative stages of the Republican party, the themes of capital ownership are given common voice. The Industrial Revolution and growth of wage labor challenged the assumption of expanded ownership. But as Lasch (1991) notes:

> Even when Americans finally came to accept the wage system as an indispensable feature of capitalism, they continued to comfort themselves with the thought that no one had to occupy the condition of a wage earner indefinitely—that each successive wave of immigrants, starting at the bottom, would eventually climb the ladder of success into the proprietary class. . . . permanent status as wage workers . . . simply could not be reconciled with the American Dream as it was conventionally understood. (p. 276)

Capital, through property ownership and personal independence, was considered a precondition of citizenship. The origins of this particularly American root of economic democracy go back to revolutionary Philadelphia and the trading of merchant credits to capitalize businesses in the face of British currency restrictions on the colonies (Foner, 1976). After the American Revolution, the homestead movement inspired efforts to provide access to capital ownership through land and home ownership. The former was furthered by President Lincoln in the Homestead Act of 1862, the latter through the proliferation of building and loan (later savings and loan) associations from the 1830s onward culminating in enabling financial institutional legislation and federal subsidization in the twentieth century.

The homestead movement was the last capital participation policy furthered by the federal government until the system of federal mortgage subsidization in the 1930s. Both landownership grants and mortgage risk subsidization were hugely successful economic policies for the United States as a developing nation. The westward movement, commercial expansion and creation of a national market, and movement toward majority home ownership became popular and widespread. Legislation enabling employee stock ownership in the 1970s enabled ownership change and corporate restructuring as well.

In more recent years, in the absence of capital ownership policy, a variety of substantive and symbolic programs and policies through redistribution took the place of democracy's proprietary dimension. As Lasch (1991) notes in his assessment derived from an abundance of research on the welfare, foreign, and economic policies of the twentieth-century United States:

> Attempts to achieve redistribution of income, to equalize opportunity in various ways, to incorporate the working classes into a society of consumers, or to foster economic growth and overseas expansion as a substitute for social reform can all be considered as twentieth century substitutes for property ownership. (p. 206)

Capital ownership requires capital access. In the absence of aristocratic traditions of inherited wealth and granting of seignorial rights, access to capital credit or equity markets became key to expanding economic growth and ownership in the United States. Capital access, as the late Louis Kelso was fond of saying, is "democracy's missing link" (see, e.g., Kelso and Kelso, 1986).

The current capital crunch that torpedoed economic growth has historical precedents during earlier periods of American history. The extension of ownership rights and creation of national markets to enable ownership participation and change have been central in the ability to finance economic growth. The Jackson-Biddle battles over the Bank of the United States in the 1830s led to an expansion of decentralized, state banking, transportation, urban development, and the westward movement. Government equity sponsorship of landownership (in the Homestead Act) later extended to credit sponsorship for home ownership. As Greider (1987) relates, "If the control of credit (and money creation) was concentrated in the hands of a few, then all the variety of individual enterprise would be held in thrall by them" (p. 256).

Repressive Regulation and Capital Access, 1890s

An early example of attempts to establish institutional flexibility and financial innovation are to be found in the historical movement toward growth economics occurring at the end of the nineteenth century, when price deflation and inflexible monetary policies led to continuous economic contractions (1873–77, 1882–85, and 1893–97). C. W. MacCune, not unlike later financial theorists/practitioners, authored the Farmer's Alliance's comprehensive program of economic reforms to expand capital access and thereby lessen agricultural producers' dependence upon bankers and suppliers.

Some distorted elements of this program later appeared in the legislation establishing the Federal Reserve Bank of 1914. In the 1890s, still informed by the popular agenda of capital access, MacCune's program worked as follows. The U.S. Treasury would establish federal warehouses and grain elevators in agricultural areas. Farmers depositing crops would be able to borrow against their crops at a 1% or 2% rate, sell the crops at prevailing market prices, or borrow on the value of their land. Farmers would be paid in current or negotiable certificates of deposit. This monetized and expanded the credit system because it was based not on an obligation to the past, but on a contract with the future—a concept common to modern financial theory and practice and later popularized in the high-yield bond market and other financial innovations of the 1980s.

1914

In 1914, an industrial capital crunch emerged with the prospect of world war, as stock dumping became widespread as investors fled to liquidity and the safety of gold. Both London and New York exchanges shut down and bank runs followed. The federal government issued "emergency currency," but businesses were unable to get credit or to sell securities in the absence of an aftermarket. The infusion of gold payments through war-related orders into the currency stream and the sprouting of renegade securities markets enabled the stock market to reopen. Credit and capital rationing had created conditions for economic crisis (Bordo, Rappoport, and Schwartz, 1992). However, the resurgence of capital markets leading to the reopening of the New York Stock Exchange averted a more severe downturn.

1930–33

Similar restrictions in capital access were coincident with adverse developments in the macroeconomy during the 1930–33 period. Problems in the financial system tended to lead to output declines as there was a sharp contraction in lending to less creditworthy borrowers. As Bernanke (1983) has demonstrated, the effects of a credit squeeze on aggregate demand helped convert the severe but not unprecedented economic downturn of 1929–30 into a severe and protracted depression. Not entirely unlike the current credit crunch, the shrinkage of commercial loans during 1930 reflected the business recession; however, during 1931 and the first half of 1932, loan restrictions represented pressure by banks on customers for repayment of loans and refusal by banks to grant new loans. The pressure exerted by banks on customers for repayment of loans and their reluctance to make new loans to all but large corporations contributed to the depression. Small and medium-sized businesses faced extended difficulty in securing operating funds, which impeded any recovery. This was particularly true for households, farmers, unincorporated businesses, and small corporations, which had the highest reliance on bank credit.

Precisely at the time when the costs of financial intermediation needed to be reduced to spur growth, investors were discouraged from supporting financial institutions and borrowers were discouraged by new regulations and related difficulties. Equity and bond markets collapsed for banks as bank bashing became common in Washington, delaying economic recovery.

This delayed a number of financial innovations that had expanded capital credit access during the 1920s, when innovators like A. P. Giannini redefined the terms and conditions of mortgage and business credit for working people at the early Bank of America, which became a model for commercial banking innovation and later credit expansion through federal mortgage programs as well in the 1930s (Dana, 1947). The same credit access model was applied to small business and higher educational finance during the post-World War II period. Recent financial innovations in securitization also reflect the expansion of capital access as a mechanism for financing aggregate economic growth and change.

1974

Similarly, the evolution of financial innovation, accompanied by enhanced regulation and restriction, occurred in the credit crunch of 1974 and its aftermath. Small and medium-sized companies found it difficult to raise capital. A sharp increase in oil prices sent inflation and interest rates soaring in 1974. As yields in the open market rose above interest rate ceilings on bank deposits, deposited funds flowed out of the banking system. Deteriorating bank capital positions and declining real estate and stock market values led banks to curtail lending to all but the largest and highest-rated companies. Commercial bank loans shrunk by $16 billion, or 10%, the largest single-year decline in 25 years. As the credit crunch spread, job losses increased, security prices of sound companies declined, and defaults increased in real estate and retailing.

By the end of the 1970s, patterns of corporate concentration, conglomerate diversification strategies, and global competition had led the U.S. economy into long-term economic stagnation. Paradoxically, the companies with the highest returns on capital, fastest rates of market share and employment growth, and greatest contributions to technological and new product innovation had the least access to capital. Advances in corporate finance, designing capital structures that would minimize firms' costs of capital, developed in the high-yield bond market, coupled with an active equity market, provided flexible, fixed-rate, long-term financing (Yago, 1991). The raising of new capital through the high-yield bond market as well as through common stock and other equity-related securities enabled companies to achieve lower overall mixed costs of capital.

Financial Repression: Redlining American Business

Macroeconomic analysis regarding investment finance usually focuses upon the relationship between national savings and investment aggregates. Keynes, however, has demonstrated that in order for entrepreneurs to invest, they must obtain sufficient short-term finance during the period of producing the investment and be reasonably satisfied that they can eventually fund short-term obligations by a long-term issue on satisfactory conditions. For both aspects of this twofold nature of investment to occur, it makes "no difference to the amount of 'finance' which has to be found by the market as a whole, but only to the channel through which it reaches the entrepreneur" (in Glahe, 1991, p. 166). The institutional, noneconomic processes that can cauterize the flow of capital through financial channels are of key importance in any assessment of the impacts of public policy and have been widely disregarded in national policy debates.

A good deal of literature on development economics has described how financial institutions and channels can suffer from *financial repression* through government strategies of low interest rate ceilings and selective credit policies that inhibit saving by deliberately maintaining interest rates below their market levels and despite investment opportunities, forcing economic growth below its potential (McKinnon, 1973; Shaw, 1973). More broadly, financial repression results in the rationing of scarce saving. When associated with government deficits, it reduces the availability of scarce resources to the private sector, leaving savings and investment to be unproductively allocated on a nonprice basis by shortsighted bureaucracy (Fry, 1989). This type of capital squeeze, most often associated with developing economies, appears a familiar situation in the United States, where we have banks now lending more funds to government than to business.

In developed economies, where credit-based financial systems have been increasingly replaced by capital market-based financial systems, another form of financial repression appears, based not upon macropolicies per se, but upon regulatory restrictions on both financial institutions and capital markets that constrict capital flow channels and thereby inhibit growth. Even with financial liberalization, without substantial development and continued innovation within the securities market (inhibited by regulatory restrictions and the chilling effects of excessive litigation), risk avoidance by investors and entrepreneurs, along with credit rationing and adverse selection problems, becomes apparent in the economy (Stiglitz and Weiss, 1981). The outcome is repression of the financial sector caused by government's increasing its own access to capital through existing credit channels and taxation. This phenomenon of regulatory repression of the financial sector (a) reduces the efficiency of the financial sector, (b) increases the costs of intermediation, (c) reduces the amount of investment, and (d) reduces growth rates in the economy.

In general theoretical terms, this describes the process that has been under way in the current regulatory recession. By now, it is clear that this recession has not followed previous cyclical patterns—the severity of the recession itself and the paucity of strong recovery signs suggest that we must look beyond business-cycle and macroeconomic factors to understand the institutional and political conditions that gave rise to current economic conditions. As the banking system in the United States evolved into the rather comfortable role of provider of intermediary short-term finance and the capital credit markets provided an increasingly larger role in the credit allocation process, both became vulnerable to regulatory reversals of financial liberalization by 1989. Similarly, equity markets, although strong throughout this period, were unable to pick up the slack in capital access. Equity markets by the beginning of the

1990s played increasingly the role of supporting existing companies rather than recharging the economy with new ones (Yago, Tanenbaum, and Cometta-Berndt, 1989).

Causes and Effects of the Regulatory Recession, 1989–92

Increasing evidence suggests that a capital crunch has prevented economic recovery. According to the Federal Reserve's Flow of Funds data, net new commercial bank loans to non-financial corporations fell to $2 billion in 1990 from $33.1 billion in 1989. Over the same period, proceeds raised in the high-yield bond market dropped to $1.4 billion from $27.6 billion. Venture capital, initial public offerings of equity, and other entrepreneurial sources of investment capital contracted to $91 billion in 1990 from $287 billion at their peak in 1987. These patterns have persisted for small and medium-sized companies in recent fiscal quarters.

As argued above, this recession is therefore different, but not unprecedented, from those in other periods when there were restrictions in the channels of capital flow that prevented capital access for entrepreneurial capitalism (1897, 1914, 1931, 1974). In each of these earlier periods there is evidence of how political/institutional forces worsened business cycles through regulations and restrictions on lending and investment practices. In each period as well, financial innovations stimulated capital markets and enabled recovery.

The economy's current lackluster performance has been persistent and resistant to fiscal and monetary stimulative policies. This suggests that institutional limitations in our financial institutions and markets have created barriers to change. In the aftermath of the 1974 credit crunch and related business cycle, the late 1970s witnessed massive changes in capital markets. Financial innovations, credit liberalization, and a focus on strategic financing through lower cost of capital unleashed massive levels of corporate change and innovation that had really only begun to filter through the economy before being abruptly terminated by 1989.

Prior to the 1980s, the largest companies with access to the capital markets (about 5% of the public corporations) had slower and often negative growth, an aversion to creating or inability to create new products and services, spotty return on capital both internally and for equity investors, and negative job formation.

In an increasingly globally competitive economy, these companies had high credit ratings and little debt, which, given the market conditions of the time, resulted in higher costs of capital than those faced by international competitors. This led to accounting hurdle rates that precluded modernizing investments (National Research Council, 1988).

TABLE 3.1
Recent Trends in Financing: Nonfinancial Corporations (in billions of dollars)

	1985	1986	1987	1988	1989	1990
All debt instruments[a]	134.5	209.7	123.7	184.6	159.5	97.6
corporate bonds	73.5	126.8	79.4	102.9	73.7	61.5
bank loans	32.0	49.9	4.1	32.8	33.1	2.0
commercial paper	9.7	20.4	11.9	2.3	-9.3	14.6
other loans	9.5	23.7	23.4	25.8	26.9	23.9
Memo Items						
bank loans to nonfarm,						
noncorporate businesses	6.2	11.7	10.7	8.1	4.2	0.1
mortgages to nonfarm,						
noncorporate businesses	111.0	76.3	50.0	39.5	35.6	0.4

Source: Flow of Funds, Federal Reserve Board.
[a] Components do not add to total; excludes tax-exempt debt and mortgages.

Trends in financing of nonfinancial corporations reflect the larger role capital markets played relative to banks as a source of growth capital (see Table 3.1). Government-forced and -inspired liquidations in the noninvestment grade market and mounting regulatory pressures upon banks were events that conspired to create the current capital crunch. Net extensions of mortgages and bank loans fell sharply to the nonfarm sector and have continued to fall for each quarter since 1990 (*Federal Reserve Bulletin,* September 1992). Though the movement toward nonbank channels of finance increased overall capital availability, allocation problems appeared to arise as the result of market and government barriers.

In short, an examination of the composition, pattern, and costs of new issues in both equity and debt markets, patterns of bank lending evidenced by the Federal Reserve Flow of Funds and survey of senior loan officers, and contraction of other sources of entrepreneurial finance suggests that by the late 1980s it became unfashionable to lend to American business. Not only the constriction of capital flow channels but also the policy-induced rigidity in corporate capital structures resulted in the wholesale destruction of values in the capital markets, furthering panic selling and creating new barriers to capital access for newcomers in the capital marketplace.

Regulating Change by Repressing Growth Finance: Capital Sectors and the Impacts of Regulation

This section examines patterns of regulation that have inhibited change and growth in the economy, through restrictions on changing capital ownership, on commercial bank lending, on savings and loan lending, and on insurance companies' lending; through contraction in mutual funds; and through discouragement of investments by pension funds. Additionally, changes in tax codes and other regulations introduced rigidities both in corporate capital structures and in capital markets, further inhibiting the adaptive capacity of corporations both to finance expansion and to adjust to downturns (see Table 3.2). In all cases, sometimes disparate and at other times related policy initiatives converged to create barriers to new capital ownership and capital access.

TABLE 3.2
Legislative/Regulatory Chronology:
Measures Inducing Rigidity in Capital Structures and Markets

Date	Event
1985	U.S. Congress makes a series of decisions on tender offers, lockups, contracts, and poison pills. Further, Congress takes action on such issues as taxes, junk bonds, antitrust, tender offer rules, and disclosure requirements, all of which affect M&A activity.
1986 (January)	Federal Reserve Board votes to apply the margin rules of Regulation G to junk bond-financed takeovers by shell corporations. The Fed specifically exempts two types of situations: (1) when the shell and the target will merge, and (2) when an operating company issues or guarantees the junk bond.
1986	In the 100th U.S. Congress stricter regulations and new legislation are proposed (31 pieces of legislation) to check excessive speculation in securities markets, inasmuch as such speculation is damaging to corporations and converts too much equity into debt. Although the U.S. market system can tolerate many types of transactions, concern is expressed that economic and corporate behavior must be delineated from tolerating today's runaway speculation.
1986	The Tax Reform Act of 1986 limits interest expense deductions. Tax treatment of interest deductions in leveraged redemptions involves (1) the so-called trade or business interest, (2) investment interest, (3) portfolio interest, (4) passive activity interest, and (5) personal interest. Initial public offerings and leveraged buyouts are affected by the tax changes. The tax changes increase overall corporate taxes by lowering tax rates while expanding the tax base. If inflation is ignored, the cost of debt is greater as the tax rate declines.
1986	National Association of Insurance Commissioners (NAIC) approves annual statement that requires all insurers to report the bonds they own categorized by investment grade and quality as determined by the NAIC Securities Valuation Office.
1987	U.S. congressional hearings detail the buildup of corporate debt and the impact of overnight restructuring, and should result in a call for stricter federal controls in four areas: (1) greenmail, (2) tender offers mechanics, (3) defense tactics, and (4) junk bonds.

(continues)

TABLE 3.2 *(continued)*

Date	Event
1987	The role of thrifts in the junk bond market and the role of junk bonds in corporate takeovers are addressed by the Senate Banking Committee. As legislation is developed, the focus is on the social and economic benefits of corporate takeovers as well as the role of savings and loans.
1987	Long-standing congressional prohibition against a binding vote that would modify any core term—such as principal amount, interest rate, and maturity date—of a bond indenture should be repealed and replaced with a simple and flexible standard, implemented by the SEC rule making, that would prohibit fraud and distortion in bond recapitalizations.
1987	A proposal in the Revenue Act of 1987 curbs the use of pension funds as a source of financing for real estate.
1989	Proposed federal legislation to curb excessive use of debt in LBOs could include partial deductibility of interest and dividends, increased disclosure requirements from managers seeking LBOs, and new limits on participation in LBOs by investment bankers.
1989	From a tax law perspective, concerns voiced about LBOs focus on the fact that there is a tax incentive for corporations to use debt rather than equity. To help rectify this situation, the Joint Committee on Taxation considers the integration of corporate and individual tax systems. The problem with any form of integration, however, is that the federal government cannot afford it. Another option discussed by the Joint Committee is limiting the deductibility of corporate interest expenses.
1989	The Financial Institutions Reform, Recovery, and Enforcement Act (FIRREA) limits the percentage of assets that can be held by thrifts in junk bonds and also requires that these high-yield bonds be marked to market for regulatory accounting.
1989 (August)	U.S. Congress gives S&Ls five years to get rid of their junk bonds; mark to market thrift accounting rules require immediate divestment.
1989	The Revenue Reconciliation Act of 1989 (RRA) is a large piece of legislation containing a separate title of specifically targeted revisions to the Internal Revenue Code (IRC) and lacks any coherent overall tax policy. Some of the provisions reflect an antitakeover mood, whereas others attempt to close loopholes. The addition of special rules for original issue discount (OID) on certain high-yield obligations results from congressional concern about junk bonds.
1989	Tax legislation is proposed that would remove the tax advantages of two categories of junk: high-yield zero-coupon bonds and pay-in-kind bonds. An amendment to the savings and loan association bailout bill is also introduced to prohibit thrifts from purchasing or holding junk bonds.
1989	U. S. Congress reduces the tax shields related to M&As—a part of the latest tax revision legislation approved by Congress in this session. Restraints are placed on the deduction of interest on the riskiest types of debt securities

(continues)

TABLE 3.2 *(continued)*

Date	Event
	with deferred interest payments and on tax refunds for portions of net operating losses caused by leveraged transactions, including recapitalizations and acquisitions. The new law does not affect the tax benefits for the ESOP as an acquisition vehicle, but it could have significant effects on the establishment of defensive ESOPs.
1990 (February)	SEC decision may force additional disclosure rules for junk bond issuers.
1990 (March)	New York State begins regulation. Currently only two states have regulations governing high-risk insurance company securities holdings, but a substantial number of states may issue some sort of directive by 1991. New York State limits an insurance company's holdings of junk bonds to 20% of total assets as of 1987. Arizona limits junk bonds to 20% of an insurer's assets or 200% of its net worth. New Jersey and Illinois are considering regulations similar to New York's.
1990	Although the junk bond era is over, politicians are still passing antitakeover legislation. The states' latest antitakeover laws typically prevent holders of more than 20% of a local firm's shares from voting on a merger or takeover. In effect, the laws deprive those with the largest ownership interest of a vote.
1990	NAIC moves to accelerate the rate of accumulation of reserves for insurers holding junk bonds and other high-yield securities. The NAIC sees the need to accelerate the rate of reserving because of concern that the accumulation periods were set 30 years ago, when there were no new junk bonds.
1990	NAIC's loss reserve regulation requires most property-casualty insurers to have an actuary, or a loss reserve specialist, approved by an insurance commissioner, certify the adequacy of loss reserves reported in annual statements. Insurers must begin complying with the regulation in their 1990 annual statements.
1990	NAIC examines proposals concerning whether or not to use reserve requirements to curb the amount of noninvestment-grade debt that an insurance company could carry in the future. Also, the reserve requirements would be cut in half, from 2% to 1%, or debt rated AAA, AA or A. The NAIC also considers three industry proposals concerning the transition period and proposes a six-tier system that more closely parallels the brackets used by the rating agencies.
1990	Congress ends the tax break on lending to employee stock ownership plans, but allows ESOPs to issue debt in public markets.
1990	Congress, in an extreme departure from years of established judicial principles and administrative rulings, enacts legislation on 10/27/90 that determines the cancellation of indebtedness income and original issue discount consequences in debt-for-debt exchanges by comparing the old debt to the current value of the new debt, without regard to the new debt's face amount.

(continues)

TABLE 3.2 *(continued)*

Date	Event
1990	Tax liability is incurred on the preferred stock issued in the transactions—these shares carry a redemption price that is greater than the issue price. The new tax legislation opts to treat such shares the way original-issue discount bonds are treated, in that the difference will be amortized over the life of the issue and taxed annually as a dividend. A troubled company that exchanges old debt for new debt or stock now will have to pay tax on "discharge of indebtedness," computed as the difference between the face value of the old debt and the issue price of the new security. Another change outlaws the use of tax refunds for loss carrybacks as a source of equity in an LBO.
1990 (November)	Proposed New York State amendment to junk bond regulation reflects a rating system instituted by the NAIC in June 1990, in which bond quality was divided into six categories, with Category 1 representing the highest-grade bonds and Category 6 the lowest grade, those in or near default. Category 3 bonds were assigned a description of medium quality. Repeatedly, speakers at the hearing testify that Category 3 bonds should not be included with Category 4, 5, and 6 bonds (i.e., a small firm that has demonstrated reliability and that has a sound credit history may not be investment grade, but should not be considered junk from an investment standpoint).
1990	Minnesota Task Force recommends that state regulators have more authority to scrutinize insurers' finances and to take quicker action against financing ailing insurers.
1990	Tax provisions of new congressional budget package mandate that a debtor who exchanges new debt for existing debt generates cancellation-of-indebtedness (COD) income to the extent that the principal amount of the retired debt exceeds the issue price of the new.

Restrictions on Changes in Capital Ownership and Impacts

Ownership change has long been a source of managerial innovation and strategic redirection for corporations (Chandler and Daems, 1974). Moreover, substantial evidence emerged from the deconglomeration wave of ownership changes that occurred during the 1980s of the salutary effect of new ownership on corporate strategic focus (Comment and Jarrell, 1991), investor returns (Jensen, 1989; Lehn and Poulsen, 1988), reductions in overhead costs (Lichtenberg and Siegel, 1980), productivity yields (Yago, Lichtenberg, and Siegel, 1989), and long-term employment stability and growth (Brown and Medoff, 1987; Yago, 1991).

Nevertheless, one of the more significant moves to restrict corporate restructuring activity and economic change came in the form of anti-takeover legislation designed to protect existing managers of public companies. From 1985 to 1989, antitakeover sentiments swept through state legislatures as part of the regulatory wave against high-yield bonds, buyouts, and changes in corporate control. In all, 36 states now offer statutory protection from takeovers. No shareholder vote is required for in-state companies to be protected under these statutes.

In every state, local corporations threatened by ownership change sponsored and promoted antitakeover legislation (see Table 3.3). The organization of private power to mold public policy on this issue is reflected in the activities of the Business Roundtable and specific corporations. Subsequently, numerous studies demonstrated the negative impacts of these regulations upon stock values and shareholder losses (Mitchell and Netter, 1988). With the imposition of these regulations, takeovers became restricted only to larger corporations. By the 1990s, we began to witness takeover activity more reminiscent of the unsuccessful conglomeration wave of the 1960s and 1970s that sparked declines in corporate competitiveness internationally rather than the movement of deconglomeration, deconcentration, and corporate focus that had largely characterized merger and acquisition activity for most of the 1980s.

TABLE 3.3
Antitakeover Chronology

State	Type of Statute	Prompted By [a]	Introduced	Passed By Legislature	Signed By Governor
Ohio	1	Marathon Oil ($USX)	01/07/82	11/17/82	11/18/82
Michigan	3	supported by the Chamber of Commerce	11/03/83	05/09/84	05/25/84
Pennsylvania	2	Scott Paper Co. ($) (drafted by the Pennsylvania Chamber of Commerce)	11/16/83	12/13/83	12/23/83
Maryland	3	Martin Marietta ($), McCormick, PHH Group, Foremost-McKesson		04/03/83 (originally vetoed 05/26/83)	06/21/83
Wisconsin	3		06/09/83	03/22/84	04/18/84
Connecticut	3	Aetna Casualty & Life ($)	02/15/84	05/07/84	06/04/84
Louisiana	3		04/30/84	06/25/84	07/13/84
Minnesota	1		03/06/84	04/18/84	04/25/84
Missouri	1	TWA ($ATL)	05/28/84	05/29/84	05/30/84
Georgia	3	amended first-generation statute	01/22/85	02/07/85	03/27/85
Mississippi	3	First MS Corporations (chemicals)	01/11/85	02/13/85	03/29/85
Hawaii	1	International Holding Capital Corporation	02/11/85	04/12/85	04/23/85

(continues)

TABLE 3.3 *(continued)*

State	Type of Statute	Prompted By [a]	Introduced	Passed By Legislature	Signed By Governor
Illinois	3	Abbott Laboratories ($)	02/28/85	06/24/85	08/24/85
Utah	2	Northwest Pipeline Co.	11/13/85	02/26/86	03/18/86
Maine	2	Great Northern Nekoosa Corp.	03/08/85	06/10/85	06/21/85
New York	4	CBS (drafted by Business Council of New York)	10/30/85 03/08/85	12/10/85 06/27/85	12/16/85
			(original bill vetoed 08/13/85)		
Indiana	1, 4	Arvin Industries	01/08/86	02/28/86	03/05/86
Kentucky	3, 4	Ashland Oil ($)	03/27/86	03/27/86	03/28/86
Missouri	4	TWA ($ATL)	02/06/86	04/22/86	06/23/86
New Jersey	4	Schering-Plough, Merck ($), Becton Dickinson, Johnson & Johnson	01/27/86	06/26/86	08/05/86
Ohio	1	Marathon Oil ($USX), Goodyear ($)	11/19/86	11/20/86	11/22/86
Virginia	3	Dan River Mills (drafted by Hutton & Williams Law firm)	01/15/85	02/21/85	03/24/85
Washington	3	Weyerhaeuser ($)	02/05/85	04/18/85	05/13/85
Wisconsin	1		02/11/86	03/26/86	04/10/86
Missouri	1, 4	—[b]	01/14/87	06/15/87	08/11/87
Florida	1, 3	Harcourt-Brace	03/03/87 04/03/87		07/02/87
			(filed with secretary of state; no signature by governor necessary)		
Oregon	1		03/09/87	06/27/87	07/18/87
North Carolina	1, 3	Burlington Industries	04/14/87	04/23/87	(no signature necessary)
			(state revised 05/01, 05/13)		
Louisiana	1, 3	—[b]	05/04/87	06/10/87	06/11/87
Nevada	1, 3		05/06/87	06/01/87	06/06/87
Utah	1	—[b]	05/20/87	05/20/87	05/29/87
Massachusetts	1	Gillette ($)	06/30/87	07/16/87	07/21/87
Minnesota	1, 4	Dayton-Hudson ($)	06/25/87	06/25/87	06/25/87
Arizona	1, 4	Greyhound ($)	07/20/87	07/21/87	07/22/87
Washington	4	Boeing ($)	08/10/87	08/10/87	08/11/87
			(proposed by Boeing 08/04/87)		
Wisconsin	4	G. Heilman	09/15/87	09/16/87	09/17/87

(continues)

TABLE 3.3 *(continued)*

State	Type of Statute	Prompted By [a]	Introduced	Passed By Legislature	Signed By Governor
New York			03/89	04/89	04/89
		(eliminated interest deductibility on acquisition-related debt and eliminated the use of net operating losses in acquisitions; eliminated debt equity exchanges and franchise tax credits)			
Pennsylvania	1, 2, 3, 4	Pennsylvania Chamber of Business & Industry and AFL-CIO	1989	04/05/90	04/90
Ohio	5		1990	1990	
Legislation introduced but not adopted					
Delaware	5		1988		
California	N/A		1989		

Note: Types of statutes are as follows: 1 = control share acquisition; 2 = control share cashout; 3 = fair price; 4 = five-year freeze-out fair price; 5 = business combination statute.
[a] Target of corporate control contest. $ indicates the target is a member of the Business Roundtable; $USX indicates membership through USX at the time of the legislation; $ATL indicates membership at the time of legislation.
[b] Amendments to existing second-generation statutes.

In other areas of the equity market, changes in public policy created additional barriers to capital ownership. Regulations in the area of public equity offerings increased transaction costs for issuers of both initial and secondary equity offerings (Yago and Tanenbaum, 1989). Reversals of certain tax benefits of employee stock ownership plans also helped slow the movement toward employee ownership.

Overview of Restrictive Lending Practices by Financial Institutions on Commercial Bank Lending

At the end of 1991, U.S. businesses had approximately $50 billion less in bank loans to work with than they did a year earlier (Stock, 1992). As part of an effort to tighten bank supervision, the Federal Reserve Board, the FDIC, and the Comptroller of the Currency adopted a broad definition of high leveraged transactions (HLT) in late 1989. The definition covers all buyouts, recapitalizations, and acquisitions that either double a company's liabilities while increasing liabilities to 50% of assets or raise liabilities to 75% of assets. While not prohibiting new loans, the increased scrutiny of HLT loan restrictions resulted in 70% of banks reporting tighter credit standards. Though the U.S. Treasury reported in January 1992 that the 40 regulations on HLT loans were being removed, declines in both merger and small business loans have continued at a level that was much greater than banks would have chosen in the absence of federal intervention. Similarly, other regulations, including higher rates of deposit insurance premiums, higher capital ratios, revised risk-based capital requirements, and increased regulatory oversight pressures, have led to a fundamental departure of banks from their historic role as providers of credit to growth businesses.

FIRREA: Restricting Savings and Loan Lending

In 1989, Congress passed the Financial Institutions Reform, Recovery, and Enforcement Act (FIRREA) to engineer a federal bailout of troubled thrifts. I address the origins and complications of the thrift crisis in another forthcoming study; here, it is important to note the severe effects of these regulations in further weakening both capital markets and other credit channels. The federal government had shaped the mission of the S&L industry through providing both secondary market support for home mortgages and deposit insurance and risk subsidization through federal guarantees. By the late 1970s, as thrifts became long in assets and short in liabilities given their traditional business base, they were subject to interest rate risks and an inability to hedge their portfolios through diversified investment. Rather than reregulate these institutions to accommodate changing financial markets, the government followed wholesale deregulation with reactive regulations that expanded losses furthered by government guarantees.

FIRREA required the nation's thrifts to write down the values of their investments in high-yield securities. Because FIRREA came together with the increase in capital requirements, most S&Ls were effectively forced to liquidate those portfolios within three months of enactment because of accounting rules. The act additionally increased requirements for thrifts to keep their assets in mortgage-related investments (during a period of declining real estate values), limited lending, and created new capital adequacy rules that required further forced liquidation of marketable assets.

Overnight, profitable S&Ls were transformed into government-owned basket cases. The forced sell-off of approximately 7% of the high-yield market caused prices to plummet in what was already a thinly traded market. This initiated a further sell-off in an already depressed high-yield market, thus further aggravating the capital problems of S&Ls and creating a downward regulatory spiral in high-yield bond prices. A steady media attack on the market further undermined values (e.g., Anders and Mitchell, *Wall Street Journal*, November 20, 1990; Winkler, *Wall Street Journal*, April 14, 1989; but also see Winkler, *Wall Street Journal*, September 11, 1989). In the secondary high-yield market, prices of high-yield securities fell sharply and yields soared in the wake of

TABLE 3.4
Survey of Findings: Regulatory and Economic Impacts on Thrift Performance

Regulations	Daly (1972)	Spellman (1978)	Kane (1980)	Brumbaugh and Carron (1987)	Gorton and Haubrich (1987)	Romer (1987)	Aharony, Saunders and Swary (1988)	Fraser and Kolari (1990)	Kane (1990)	Brumbaugh and Litan (1991)
Variable interest rate regulation	policies shortsighted.									
Deposit rate regulations		leads to misallocation of resources.								
DIDMCA			should enhance profitability.	positive			positive			
Regulation of financial system					regulations cause regulations					
Glass-Steagal Act					act is binding limits diversification	unclear				
Prohibition of interstate banking						negative				
Increased monitoring technology					decreases desired loan size, decreases bank capital	no effect				
Garn St. Germain								increased common stock values		
FIRREA									negative	negative
RTC									negative	
FDIC									negative	

regulation-induced sell-offs. Thrifts were unable to realize the full future profitability of their high-yield investments as a result. Thrifts that had high-yield portfolios were instantly saddled with a further market deterioration in their capital positions that hastened their demise.

Table 3.4 summarizes the empirical findings of research on the regulatory and economic impacts of thrifts. It appears that any measures that facilitated diversification of thrift portfolios had positive consequences. Efforts that limited diversification failed to enhance profitability, decreased bank capital, and led to misallocation of financial resources. The distorting effects of federal guarantees and regulations expanded the severity not only of the thrift crisis, but of the funding crisis for U.S. businesses. There appears to be no empirical evidence in all of the currently available research that the thrift crisis was caused by loans to operating businesses. Indeed, business loans provided useful diversification of thrift portfolios. Investments (and effective federal guarantees of those investments) in real estate, agriculture, and energy constituted the greatest source of losses.

Restricting Insurance Company Lending Practices

In both public and private markets, insurance companies developed into a major financial institutional source for long-term financing. In 1990, however, threatened with federal oversight of insurance companies, the National Association of Insurance Commissioners enacted guidelines that effectively made investments in lower-rate credits more costly. This followed state actions in New York, Maryland, and Florida to restrict capital access by businesses to insurance investment funds. Procedures were established to assign risks used by state insurance commissions to determine the size of the securities valuations reserves to be established for each bond. This more stringent rating system forced insurers to increase their reserves held against expected losses on their high-yield portfolios. Additionally, ratings restrictions were applied to private placement investments as well.

Contraction in Money Market and Mutual Funds

Another regulatory salvo came from the Securities and Exchange Commission, which set limits on the type of commercial paper that could be held by the nation's $530 billion money market funds. The rule, which went into effect in May 1992, allowed funds to put no more than 5% of their assets in less than top-grade commercial paper. Previously, funds could have assets of up to 25% in any single issuer. In addition, to qualify for top-grade rating by the SEC, a specific issue must now be considered top grade by two of the five rating agencies.

Indirectly, the thrift regulations affected other major sources of capital to growth businesses, as evidenced by the net flows of capital in high-yield mutual funds, which account for roughly 30% of the total high-yield market. Figure 3.1 shows high-yield mutual funds experienced a net outflow of more than $500 million in the two months following the passage of FIRREA, after averaging net new inflows of $300 million during the first eight months of 1989. The long-term effects of public policies on mutual funds as providers of investment capital for business growth require further assessment.

Discouragement of Investments by Pension Funds

Pension funds have been important institutional investors in both equity and debt markets for corporate securities. In high-yield markets, pension funds hold 15% of all bonds. Pension fund regulators also responded predictably to media and regulatory reactions by the late 1980s, further restricting capital investments in growth firms. In New York, pension rules forbid state pensions to invest in bonds issued to finance leveraged buyouts; California announced its fund would sell its $530 million junk bond portfolio even though that portfolio experienced few defaults and a 13.5% return.

Financial Innovations for Small and Medium-Sized Companies

During the 1980s, new channels of capital were carved that flowed toward firms with the highest prospects for growth. In previous research projects, I have summarized the empirical record to date of the massive innovations of finance and their applications to corporate growth strategies (see, e.g., Yago, 1991). At this point, my objectives in this chapter are to review impacts that have emerged since the onset of the current economic downturn and to suggest a research agenda for assessment of regulatory impacts in the future.

High-Yield Market: Overview of the Fall and Rise of Financial Innovation

The timing of collapses in the new issue high-yield bond market (Figure 3.2), in capital flows in high-yield bond funds (Figure 3.3), and in high-yield bond indices (Figure 3.4) is coincident with the launching of regulatory measures against that market specifically and capital credit access generally. The derivative effects of these capital flow restrictions require further exploration in terms of their macroeconomic impacts. A working hypothesis would be that derivative effects of the collapse of this market in late 1989 and early 1990 severely hampered the capacity of growth firms and firms requiring financial and strategic restructuring to adapt.

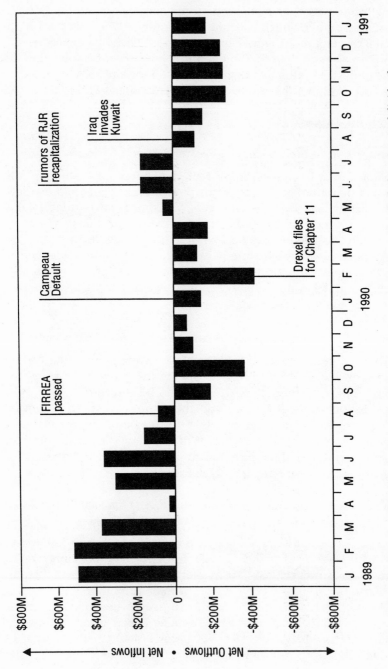

FIGURE 3.1 Flows into High-Yield Bond Funds *Source:* Investment Company Institute. *Note:* Includes reinvested dividends.

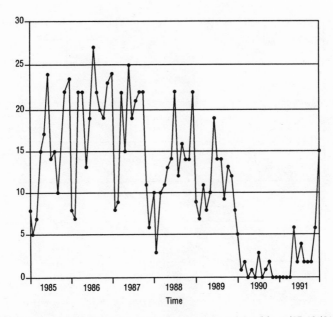

FIGURE 3.2 Number of Non-Investment-Grade New Issues, Monthly, 1/85-12/91
Source: Securities Data Corp.

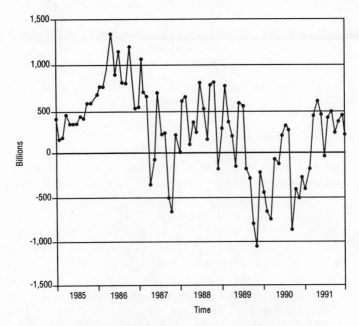

FIGURE 3.3 Capital Flows in High-Yield Bond Funds, Monthly, 1/85-11/91
Source: Investment Company Institute

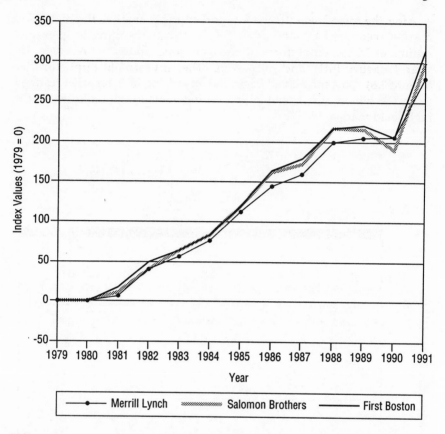

FIGURE 3.4 High-Yield Index Performance, 12/31/79-8/30/91 *Sources:* Knowledge Exchange, Merrill Lynch, Salomon Brothers, First Boston.

The impact of noneconomic regulatory factors upon the collapse of the high-yield market is suggested by further econometric analysis I have done with my colleague Don Siegel at the State University of New York at Stony Brook. Variations in prices, yields, new issues, and capital flows in the high-yield market appear to be explained by variances in default rates, yield spreads with government bonds, equity yields, LBO activity, GNP changes, and other macroeconomic factors. We tested the structural stability of these econometric estimates without requiring prior information concerning the true point of structural change. In each case, instability in the model appears linked to the fourth quarter of 1989, after the introduction of FIRREA and other regulations restricting capital access (Figure 3.5).

After the forced sell-offs were absorbed in the market, the high-yield market recovered by 40% over the past year, resulting in averaged returns of 14.1%, outperforming the Dow Jones Industrial Average, 10-year Treasury bills, and numerous other investment opportunities (Figure 3.6). On a monetized basis, the mispricing of the market resulted in an $80 billion misunderstanding on the valuation of securities in the high-yield market.

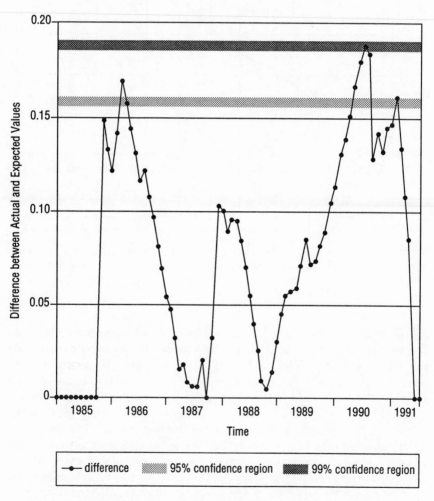

FIGURE 3.5 Dependent Variable: Merrill Lynch High-Yield Index

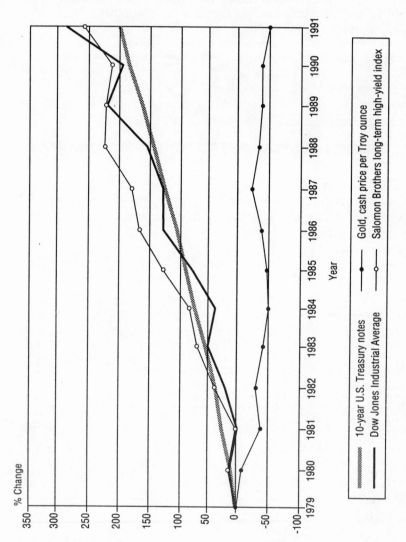

FIGURE 3.6 Cumulative Performance, 12/31/79-8/31/91 *Sources*: Federal Reserve, Knowledge Exchange, Salomon Brothers, Bloomberg.

Long-Term Impacts on Growth, Productivity, and Competitiveness: Restrictions in Capital Market Access by Size

The long-term effects of these policy measures has been to create structural barriers to entrance into the capital markets by small and medium-sized firms. This process was, in part, under way, with changes as the high-yield market matured over the 1980s. With the growth of the high-yield market, the new debt issues were increasingly purchased by larger firms. As Figure 3.7 shows, in 1979, firms with sales below $100 million made up more than 50% of the market. By 1988, the market share of these smaller corporations had dropped to below 10%. Corporations with revenues above $500 million averaged about 11% of the market at the beginning of the 1980s, but had more than 60% of all dollars raised in the high-yield market by the close of the decade. Small and medium-sized firms, which were the backbone of the high-yield market during its growth phase, became underserved in recent years. As in the IPO market mentioned above, the non-investment-grade bond market was not being recharged by new, dynamic firms.

This process was amplified by the regulatory events of 1989 and 1990, which continued in 1992. Even in its recovery during 1991, the high-yield market drifted toward higher credit quality tranches and larger-sized firms that restructured existing debt rather than expanded capital investment (Fridson, 1992).

Other Impacts: Employment and Productivity

In past research, I have demonstrated the linkage between growth firms and access to capital credit and equity markets. My colleagues and I have found consistent rates of job creation performance among firms in the high-yield bond market (Yago, Stevenson, Seifert, and Wu, 1988), among firms undergoing restructuring (Yago et al., 1988), among plants that had been subject to leveraged buyouts or divestiture (Yago, Lichtenberg, and Siegel, 1989), and among IPO firms (Yago and Tanenbaum, 1989). Moreover, we found that rates of job retention were also higher among firms accessing capital markets in declining industries.

These findings are consistent with more aggregate findings about the job creation process:

- Over the 1980s, private sector employment rose by 38%, adding 12.5 million net new jobs; all of these net new jobs were created by non-Fortune 500 firms.
- New firm birth and survival rates and patterns are important because existing large firms in aggregate are net losers of jobs (Brown, Hamilton, and Medoff, 1990). During the 1980s, Fortune

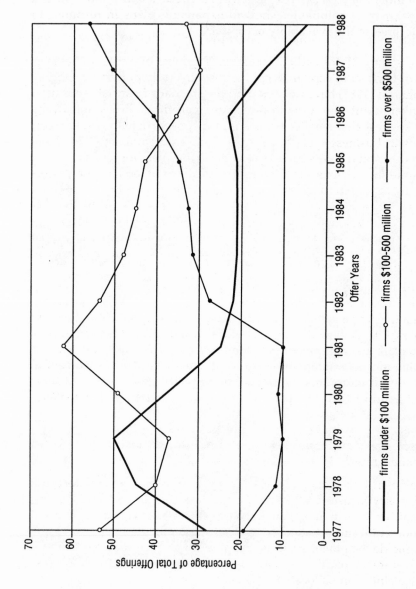

FIGURE 3.7 Distribution of Straight High-Yield Debt Offering by Firm Size, 1977-88 *Source:* Drexel Burnham Lambert.

500 and investment-grade companies experienced net job losses of more than 3.5 million.

- Job growth in the private sector dropped from a peak growth rate of more than 5% per year in 1984 to a virtual standstill in 1990 as a majority of companies shelved expansion plans in response to declines in the availability of capital.

Consistent with the earlier discussion, a number of recent studies suggest that barriers to capital access increase inversely to firm size. Storey and Johnson (1987) have pointed out how standard financial ratios used by bankers limit high-growth-potential small firms. Brock and Evans (1989) suggest that smaller firms suffer disproportionally when credit tightens in business cycle downturns. Bates and Dunham (1991) have shown the capital access barriers to minority business formation.

Despite the obvious social policy implications of job creation performance by capital markets, employment impacts are required for neither disclosure nor assessment by Congress or firms, the Securities Exchange Commission, or any government agency related to financial regulation. The barriers to firm/plant-specific employment analysis of financial change are difficult for researchers to overcome and require further disclosure.

Similarly, substantial evidence has emerged regarding ownership change. Contrary to conventional wisdom, studies of firms undergoing ownership change have found them to have higher rates of productivity increases, less likelihood of plant shutdown, and higher investment rates in new plant and equipment. Measures that have created rigidities in the financial and ownership structure of firms and limited their access to capital inhibit restoration of industrial competitiveness of U.S. business (U.S. Bureau of Labor Statistics, 1990; Yago, 1991; Yago, Lichtenberg, and Siegel, 1989).

Research Agenda to Assess Policy Impacts on Employment and Economic Growth

The absence of economic impact analysis in assessing regulatory and public policy measures affecting financial markets is most telling in this economic downturn. In a regulatory world that has made economic and environmental impact statements legal requirements for physical and economic development projects, the absence of such required analyses for government regulatory measures affecting the investment process and availability and allocation of capital is ironic.

Similarly, the extraordinary availability of financial information about securities and capital markets is deceptive. The current ability to link financial information with economic and employment performance indicators of firms and industrial sectors is undeveloped. In contrast, fiscal, budgetary, and monetary research on economy changes is highly evolved. However, the linkage between broad national aggregates and firm and sectoral performance is less explored. Data limitations obscure policy impacts, limitations that this current economic downturn suggests we cannot afford. Following are brief discussions of several areas that require further exploration if we are to avoid the policy missteps that made it impossible to keep economic growth alive in the early 1990s.

Research on Job Creation, Retention, and Productivity. As mentioned above, there is no required employment disclosure by plant, firm, or location in current SEC financial disclosure rules. Despite what might be crocodile tears shed by regulators on the job creation issue in the 1992 election year's favorite theme, the absence of such required disclosure is glaring. In its absence, we need to be able to build an ongoing data base linking the financial information available in equity and debt securities offering with firm-specific data on employment, investment, and productivity. Such data are available from disparate commercial and government sources and need to be linked and made available to researchers and policymakers for more immediate assessment of policy options, at state, industrial sector, and national levels.

Research on Capital Market Gaps. Institutional changes in banking, thrifts, and capital markets suggest that emerging barriers to capital access by many firms endanger economic growth. Sectoral, racial, regional, and size differences in capital access need to be explored and assessed to inform financial innovations and market developments that could remedy these emerging problems. We need to know more precisely and on a timely basis about the impact of financial regulatory changes on the provision of capital to small and medium-sized growth firms. Again, linking financial data from equity and debt markets with information on size, type, sector, and ownership of firm and financial institutional activities would alert both policymakers and business practitioners to opportunities for capital expansion.

Research on Financial Institutions and Capital Providers. We need to have more systematic information about sources of entrepreneurial finance. Industry information from insurance companies, mutual funds, pension funds, government development finance funds, and the like needs to be compiled and reviewed.

Research on the Application of Financial Innovations. As the search for market solutions to social problems continues, more creative work needs to be done on the transfer of sophisticated financial technologies to recalcitrant social problems in distressed communities, industries undergoing transition, and governments seeking restructuring and privatization.

Conclusion

Today's policymakers are largely out of touch with macroeconomic evolution. The current economic crisis was not induced by macroeconomic or predetermined cyclical events. It was caused by a massive structural and institutional disconnection. Rather than addressing revolutionary trends and dynamics that have emerged over the past two decades, our policymakers are continuing to focus on bygone realities. Sources of capital have shifted, changing the nature and fundamental charters of our traditional providers of capital. At the same time, as is natural in this kind of evolution, new capital sources have developed or have been redirected to make up for resulting gaps and to expand the base. Instead of finding new and productive ways to capitalize on these changes, policymakers are hobbling our mature sources of capital and choking off the more innovative avenues.

We have already seen plenty of evidence in the past few economic cycles, not to mention historical data going back all the way to the late nineteenth century, that restricting capital from growth sectors in the economy during a recession serves only to exacerbate the crisis. Moreover, given the context of an increasingly global economy and the shift in this country and most of the developed world from an industrial base to one that is technology and information driven, we must predicate our economic policy on those metrics that are most relevant to this country. All economic levers should be measured according to their influence on growth, job creation, and capital access. Until there is access to the spectrum of political, financial, and business leadership, we will continue to be doomed to repeat the mistakes of the past and constrained from exploiting the bold new opportunities created by advancing technologies and expanding freedom around the world.

References

Aharony, J., Saunders, A., and Swary, I. (1988). "The Effects of DIDMCA on Bank Stockholders' Returns and Risk." *Journal of Banking and Finance, 12,* 317-331.

Anders, G., and Mitchell, C. (1990, November 20). "Junk King's Legacy." *Wall Street Journal.*

Bates, T. (1989). "Small Business Viability in the Urban Ghetto Milieu." *Journal of Regional Science, 29,* 625-643.

Bates, T., and Dunham, C. (1991, March 7). "Facilitating Upward Mobility through Small Business Ownership." Paper presented at the Urban Opportunity

Program Conference on Urban Labor Markets and Labor Mobility, Arlie House, Virginia.

Bernanke, B. S. (1983). "Nonmonetary Effects of the Financial Crisis in the Propagation of the Great Depression." *American Economic Review, 73*, 257-276.

Birch, D. (1987). *Job Creation in America*. New York: Free Press.

Board of Governors (1992). *Federal Reserve Bulletin*, Vol. 78, No. 9, A39-A42.

Bordo, M. D., Rappoport, P., and Schwartz, A. J. (1992). "Money Versus Credit Rationing: Evidence for the National Banking Era, 1880–1914." National Bureau of Economic Research Reprint 1716.

Brock, W., and Evans, D. (1989). "Small Business Economics." *Small Business Economics, 198*, 7-20.

Brown, C., Hamilton, J., and Medoff, J. (1990). *Employers Large and Small*. Cambridge, MA: Harvard University Press.

Brown, C., and Medoff, J. (1987). *The Impact of Firm Acquisitions on Labor*. Washington, DC: National Bureau of Economic Research.

Brumbaugh, R. D., Jr., and Carron, A. S. (1987). "Thrift Industry Crisis: Causes and Solutions." *Brookings Papers on Economic Activity*, pp. 349-388.

Brumbaugh, R. D., Jr., and Litan, R. E. (1991). "Ignoring Economics in Dealing with the Savings and Loan and Commercial Banking Crisis." *Contemporary Policy Issues, 9*, 36-53.

Chandler, A. D., Jr. (1968). *Strategy and Structure*. Garden City, NY: Doubleday.

Chandler, A. D., Jr., and Daems, H. (1974). "The Rise of Managerial Capitalism and Its Impact on Investment Strategy in the Western World and Japan." In H. Daems and H. van der Wee (Eds.), *Den Haag*. The Hague, Netherlands.

Comment, R., and Jarrell, G. A. (1991). *Corporate Focus and Stock Returns*. Rochester, NY: University of Rochester, Simon Graduate School, Bradley Policy Research Center.

Daly, G. (1972). "The Impact of Monetary Policy and the Maturity of Savings and Loan Association Assets: A Critique of Reform." *Journal of Money, 4*, 441-444.

Dana, J. (1947). *A. P. Giannini: Giant in the West*. New York: Prentice-Hall.

Foner, E. (1976). *Tom Paine and the Revolutionary America*. New York: Oxford University Press.

Fraser, D., and Kolari, J. (1990). "The 1982 Depository Institutions Act and Security Returns in the Savings and Loan Industry." *Journal of Financial Research, 13*, 339-347.

Fridson, M. S. (1992, January/February). "This Year in High Yield." *Extra Credit: The Journal of High Yield Bond Research*.

Fry, M. (1989). *Money, Interest, and Banking in Economic Development*. Baltimore: Johns Hopkins University Press.

Glahe, F. R. (Ed.). (1991). *Keynes's The General Theory of Employment, Interest, and Money: A Concordance*. Savage, MD: Rowman & Littlefield.

Goodwyn, L. (1976). *Democratic Promise: The Populist Movement in America*. New York: Oxford University Press.

Gorton, G., and Haubrich, J. (1987). "Bank Deregulation, Credit Markets, and the Control of Capital." In K. Brunner and A. H. Meltzer (Eds.), *Carnegie-Rochester Conference Series on Public Policy, 26* (pp. 289-319). Amsterdam: Elsevier Science.

Greider, W. J. (1987). *Secrets of the Temple: How the Federal Reserve Runs the Country*. New York: Simon & Schuster.

Investment Company Institute (1991). Washington, DC.

Jensen, M. C. (1989, January). "Capital Markets, Organizational Innovation, and Restructuring." Paper presented to the Board of Governors, Federal Reserve System, Washington, DC.

Kane, E. J. (1980, December 8–9). "Reregulation, Savings and Loan Diversification, and the Flow of Housing Finance." Paper presented at the annual conference of the Federal Home Loan Bank Board of San Francisco, San Francisco.

Kane, E. J. (1990). "Principal Agent Problems in S&L Salvage." *Journal of Finance*, 45, 755-764.

Kelso, L. O., and Kelso, P. H. (1986). *Democracy and Economic Power*. Cambridge, MA: Ballinger.

Lasch, C. (1991). *The True and Only Heaven: Progress and Its Critics*. New York: W. W. Norton.

Lehn, K., and Poulsen, A. (1988). *Free Cash Flow and Stockholder Gains in Going Private Transactions*. Washington, DC: Securities and Exchange Commission and University of Georgia.

Lichtenberg, F., and Siegel, D. (1980). *The Effect of Takeovers on the Employment and Wages of Central-Office and Other Personnel*. New York: Columbia University Graduate School of Business.

Lipset, S. M. (1977). *Union Democracy: The Internal Politics of the International Typographical Union*. New York: Free Press.

McKinnon, R. I. (1973). *Money and Capital in Economic Development*. Washington, DC: Brookings Institution.

Mitchell, M., and Netter, J. (1988, March 30). *Stock Market Evidence from the October 1987 Proposed Takeover Tax Bill*. Washington, DC: U.S. Securities and Exchange Commission, Office of Economic Analysis.

Moore, B., Jr. (1966). *Social Origins of Dictatorship and Democracy*. New York: Harcourt Brace.

National Research Council. (1988). *Manufacturing Studies Board*. Washington, DC: National Academy of Sciences.

Romer, D. (1987). "Comments on Gorton and Haubrich." In K. Brunner and A. H. Meltzer (Eds.), *Carnegie-Rochester Conference Series on Public Policy*, 26 (pp. 336-343). Amsterdam: Elsevier Science.

Schlesinger, A. M., Jr. (1945). *The Age of Jackson*. Boston: Little, Brown.

Securities Data Corp. (1991). New York.

Shaw, E. S. (1973). *Financial Deepening in Economic Development*. New York: Oxford University Press.

Spellman, L. J. (1978). "Entry and Profitability in a Rate-Free Savings and Loan Market." *Quarterly Review of Economics and Business*, 18(2), 87-95.

Stiglitz, J. E. (1985). "Credit Markets and the Control of Capital." *Journal of Money, Credit and Banking*, 17, 133-152.

Stiglitz, J. E., and Weiss, A. (1981). "Credit Rationing in Markets with Imperfect Information." *American Economic Review*, 71, 393-410.

Stock, K. (1992, July 30). "Regulations Drive Lending to Non-Banks." *Wall Street Journal*, p. A13.

Storey, D. J., and Johnson, S. (1987). *Job Generation and Labor Market Change.* New York: Macmillan.

Winkler, M. (1989, April 14). "Harvard Study Notes Defaults." *Wall Street Journal.*

Winkler, M. (1989, September 11). "Wharton Disputes Junk-Bond Study, Fueling Debate." *Wall Street Journal.*

Yago, G. (1991). *Junk Bonds: How High Yield Securities Restructured Corporate America.* New York: Oxford University Press.

Yago, G., Lichtenberg, F., and Siegel, D. (1989). *Leveraged Buyouts and Industrial Competitiveness: The Effects of LBOs on Productivity, Employment, and Research and Development.* Washington, DC: Securities Industry Association.

Yago, G., Stevenson, G., Seifert, C., and Wu, S.-Y. (1988). *The Uses and Effects of High Yield Securities in U.S. Industry.* Stony Brook: State University of New York, Economic Research Bureau.

Yago, G., and Tanenbaum, J. (1989). *The Economic Impact of IPOs on U.S. Industrial Competitiveness.* Washington, DC: National Association of Securities Dealers.

Yago, G., Tanenbaum, J., and Cometta-Berndt, P. (1989). *Leveraged Buyouts in Focus: The Role of Debt in Ownership Change and Industrial Competitiveness in the Eighties.* Stony Brook: State University of New York, Economic Research Bureau.

4

Bank Capitalization Standards, the Credit Crunch, and Resource Allocation under Regulation

Benjamin Zycher

That a "credit crunch" has slowed and continues to afflict the U.S. economy seemingly is the conventional wisdom, the evidence for which is the willingness of senior politicians to allude to it in their quests for votes.[1] Widely observed, for example, but perhaps less understood is the recent shift in the composition of bank portfolios toward a mix in which the value of government securities exceeds that of private sector loans.[2] But the precise nature of the "crunch," other than one implying a vague sense of capital "unavailability," seems not to have been defined carefully in the public discussion; still obscure are the sources of the "crunch," its magnitude, its effects upon various sectors and classes of businesses, and, indeed, its very meaning.

The U.S. money supply and its growth rate are determined by the demand and supply of money, as shaped and constrained by economic conditions, by the supply of reserves from the Fed, and by bank lending behavior as influenced by the system of fractional reserve requirements. Conventional wisdom seems to attribute the "credit crunch" to a newly emerged unwillingness (or reduced willingness) on the part of bankers to lend (for a brief discussion of this conventional wisdom, see Benston, 1992). But total liquidity in the economy depends upon the supply of reserves by the Fed; a credit crunch stemming from gun-shy behavior on the part of banks implies that they are making no use of excess reserves that earn no interest, and thus are allowing excess reserves to grow greatly.[3] That would represent strange behavior indeed, as safe interest-bearing investments always are available. Aggregate reserves of depository institutions grew from $40.6 billion at the end of 1989 to

$49.5 billion in July of 1992, an annual growth rate of 8.3%.[4] But excess reserves grew only from $922 million to $963 million, indicating clearly that the additional reserves were moved through the capital market by banks driven by a profit motive.

Furthermore, a generalized "credit crunch" as seemingly perceived by the conventional wisdom would be equivalent analytically to a backward shift in the supply of capital; the result ought to be an increase in the real rate of interest. Between the beginning of 1989 and July of 1992, yields on three-month Treasury bills fell from 8.29% to 3.28%. Of course, shifts in investment demand affect interest rates; accordingly, part of the decline might have been caused by the effects of the 1990–91 recession. But yields on three-month T-bills during the much sharper recession of 1981–82 fell only from 10.9% in December 1981 to 8.0% a year later. Differences in shifting inflation expectations clearly affect such relative trends, and the choices of starting and ending months are somewhat arbitrary. The central point, however, is that the decline in interest rates during the period of the purportedly generalized credit crunch does not lend support to that conventional view.

This chapter has as its central goals a more precise delineation of the "credit crunch," along with an empirical measurement of its effects in terms of the allocation of capital. Of particular importance are two regulatory capital standards: the Tier 1 leverage ratio, implemented in 1990, and the risk-based (Basle) capital standard, effective for U.S. banks officially at the beginning of 1992, and to be phased in fully by the end of the year.[5] Comparison of bank lending behavior during two recent business cycles—1977 through 1982 and 1985 through 1991—offers insights into the nature of the credit crunch and the effects of the capitalization standards. The central conclusion is that the "credit crunch" is regulatory in origin and sector specific in impact with respect to commercial and industrial firms generally, and small firms in particular. Because the notion of a generalized "credit crunch" is misguided, and because the "crunch" affects specific kinds of borrowers disproportionally, this chapter shall employ the term *sectoral crunch* instead.

The next section summarizes the leverage ratio and risk-based (Basle) regulatory capital standards imposed upon U.S. banks, and outlines the likely implications of the capital standards for bank lending and for the composition of the asset side of bank balance sheets. This is followed by an examination of the reasons for the mutual specialization between banks and bank borrowers, and resulting implications for bank lending in the context of the regulatory capital standards. The final section of the chapter offers a brief discussion of the risk-based standards now in the process of implementation, along with some concluding observations.

The Leverage Ratio and Risk-Based
Bank Capitalization Standards

Suppose that it is the regulatory capital standards—that is, the minimum capital requirements—rather than the fractional reserve requirements that impose the marginally effective constraints on the expansion of credit (money) by banks. That might have important sectoral effects to the extent that banks and given economic sectors are mutually specialized with respect to credit markets, an issue addressed in the next section. Moreover, unlike the case of reserve requirements, in which it is the sum of reserves for the banking system in total that is relevant because a federal funds market can shift reserves among individual banks, there exists no equivalent market within which banks with insufficient capital can obtain overnight transfers from banks enjoying a surplus. Accordingly, it is appropriate to examine the leverage ratio and risk-based capitalization standards and resulting changes in bank lending behavior.

The Leverage Ratio

The Tier 1 leverage ratio standard is a minimum of 3% of Tier 1 capital as a proportion of total assets.[6] Virtually all banks are required to operate with leverage ratios well above that level, as the Fed regulations require leverage ratios "100 to 200 basis points above the stated minimums" for banks with significant credit or interest rate risk, for banks rated less than a composite 1 under the BOPEC and CAMEL rating systems (for bank holding companies and banks, respectively), for banks experiencing or anticipating significant growth, and for banks with "supervisory, financial, or operational weaknesses" (Federal Reserve Regulatory Service, 1991, p. 4–798).[7]

What is of interest in the context of the "credit crunch" is the effect of the regulatory capitalization standards on bank lending behavior. Consider a bank with, say, $300 million in U.S. Treasury securities, $400 million in mortgages, and $800 million in commercial and industrial loans; thus, total assets are $1.5 billion, and the minimum leverage ratio Tier 1 capital requirement would be $75 million if the required leverage ratio for this bank were 5%. Suppose that Tier 1 capital is only $60 million; this bank either must raise an additional $15 million in Tier 1 capital or must reduce its assets by $300 million.

For business firms in general and banks in particular, an increase in Tier 1 capital achieved through acquisition of additional outside equity is quite costly. One implicit reason for this is engendered by the system of federal deposit insurance, which historically has been subsidized heavily.[8] To the extent that a given bank is subsidized by the deposit insurance system, the value of the subsidy declines as equity increases, because future losses will be borne by equity holders first and by the deposit insurance system (i.e., sound banks and the taxpayers) second. Thus, the increase in equity reduces the likelihood that subsidized deposit insurance actually will be used to cover investment losses.

A second reason, more important but perhaps more subtle, for the costliness of additions to outside equity is the asymmetric nature of the information about the firm available to management and to outside investors, respectively.[9] Since, in the context of a new equity offering, management and, implicitly, existing shareholders might misrepresent the true financial condition of the firm, market prices in (equity) capital markets in effect yield a premium for purchasers of new shares; the premium represents market compensation for this risk borne by purchasers of new shares, and must come from dilution of the equity owned by existing shareholders. This dilution takes the form of a reduction in the market value of existing shares.

TABLE 4.1
Total Assets of Domestic Commercial Banks (billions of 1991 dollars)

Year:Quarter	Assets	Year:Quarter	Assets	Year:Quarter	Assets
1992:2	2973.6				
:1	2982.3				
1991:4	3023.4	1986:4	2964.1	1981:4	2326.9
:3	2993.1	:3	2862.7	:3	2319.9
:2	2999.9	:2	2848.0	:2	2326.8
:1	3011.8	:1	2797.8	:1	2297.6
1990:4	3072.8	1985:4	2780.9	1980:4	2352.2
:3	3053.4	:3	2718.6	:3	2290.8
:2	3062.5	:2	2671.3	:2	2319.7
:1	3068.6	:1	2636.4	:1	2307.1
1989:4	3074.5	1984:4	2636.0	1979:4	2337.0
:3	3016.6	:3	2569.9	:3	2302.7
:2	3022.3	:2	2575.7	:2	2295.1
:1	3004.1	:1	2573.2	:1	2277.9
1988:4	3038.5	1983:4	2582.3	1978:4	2313.2
:3	2995.3	:3	2526.6	:3	2316.7
:2	2982.8	:2	2501.3	:2	2353.6
:1	2955.6	:1	2483.7	:1	2287.6
1987:4	2982.5	1982:4	2458.0	1977:4	2305.7
:3	2936.5	:3	2390.5	:3	2240.1
:2	2957.9	:2	2363.8	:2	2227.6
:1	2938.9	:1	2341.5	:1	2192.6

Source: Board of Governors of the Federal Reserve System, Federal Reserve Bulletin, various issues. Note: Quarterly data are averages.

That is consistent with the traditional literature on the relationships among retained earnings, new equity, and debt in the capital structure of the firm (see, e.g., Modigliani and Miller, 1963; see also Masulis, 1980; Myers and Majluf, 1984; Sametz, 1964). It is consistent also with a number of empirical findings; for example, Asquith and Mullins (1986) find that for nonfinancial corporations, new equity offerings on average reduce the existing value of the firm by 31% of the size of the new offering.[10] Wall and Peterson (1991) find for bank holding companies that "announcements of plans to issue common stock have a significant absolute effect on firm wealth" (p. 82) that is negative.[11]

The costliness of new equity for banks suggests that asset reduction will be a major means by which banks will adapt to the constraints imposed by the leverage ratio capital standard. This is consistent with the growth of real commercial bank assets, shown in Table 4.1, upon implementation of the leverage ratio standard in 1990.

Between the fourth quarter of 1987 and that of 1988, total commercial bank assets increased by $56 billion, or 1.9%; between 1988:4 and 1989:4,

TABLE 4.2
Annual Change of Total Commercial Bank Assets

Year	Change from Year Earlier (billions of 1991 dollars)	Growth Rate from Year Earlier (%)
1991	−49.4	−1.6
1990	−1.7	−0.1
1989	36.0	1.2
1988	56.0	1.9
1987	18.4	0.6
1986	183.2	6.6
1985	144.9	5.5
1984	53.7	2.1
1983	124.3	5.1
1982	131.1	5.6
1981	−26.3	−1.1
1980	15.2	0.7
1979	23.8	1.0
1978	7.5	0.3
1977	—	—

Source: Computed from data in Table 4.1. *Note:* Computed as fourth quarter over fourth quarter.

bank assets increased by $36 billion, or 1.2%. But between the fourth quarter of 1989 and the fourth quarter of 1990, total bank assets fell slightly, by $1.7 billion; and by the second quarter of 1992, bank assets fell by an additional $99.2 billion, or 3.2% of 1990:4 bank assets. Table 4.2 presents annual changes and growth rates (fourth quarter over fourth quarter) for total commercial bank assets.

TABLE 4.3
Real GDP and Real GDP Growth, Two Business Cycles

Year:Quarter	Real GDP (billions of 1991 dollars)	Real GDP Growth (%)
1992:2	5763.2	1.5
:1	5741.2	2.9
1991:4	5699.8	0.6
:3	5691.9	1.2
:2	5674.5	1.7
:1	5650.5	−3.0
1990:4	5694.2	−3.9
:3	5751.7	−1.6
:2	5775.4	1.0
:1	5761.4	2.8
1989:4	5721.2	1.5
:3	5700.3	0
:2	5700.3	1.8
:1	5675.1	3.2
1983:4	4726.3	7.0
:3	4646.5	6.1
:2	4578.3	11.3
:1	4457.0	2.6
1982:4	4428.8	0.6
:3	4422.7	−1.8
:2	4442.4	1.6
:1	4424.7	−4.9
1981:4	4480.1	−6.2
:3	4552.4	2.1
:2	4528.7	−1.7
:1	4547.7	5.6
1980:4	4486.4	8.3
:3	4398.1	0.1
:2	4397.0	−9.9
:1	4512.7	1.7

Source: Council of Economic Advisers, Economic Indicators, various issues. Note: Quarterly data at seasonally adjusted annual rates.

Part of this recent reduction in bank assets may have been caused by the effects of the 1990–91 recession, the trough of which occurred in the first quarter of 1991. Table 4.3 presents quarterly data for real GDP and real GDP growth for the 1980–83 and 1989–91 business cycles. In the six quarters (1989:1–1990:2) preceding the beginning of the 1990–91 recession (1990:3), total bank assets grew by $58.4 billion, or 1.9%. As noted above, bank assets were roughly constant between the fourth quarters of 1989 and 1990, and then began a nearly steady decline of 3.2% over the ensuing six quarters.[12]

In the six quarters (1980:2–1981:3) preceding the beginning of the much sharper recession of 1981–82 (1981:4), total bank assets essentially were unchanged,[13] but in sharp contrast with the current recovery period, total bank assets over the six quarters (1982:4–1984:1) after the recession trough (1982:3) grew by $115.2 billion, or 4.7%. This anomalous behavior of commercial bank assets after the trough of the 1990–91 recession is consistent with the findings of several other researchers;[14] it is not only weak demand in credit markets but also the leverage ratio regulatory constraints that explain the decline of bank lending during the current business cycle.

The Risk-Based Standards

Under the risk-based (Basle) capital standards, to be phased in fully for U.S. banks by the end of 1992, banks must adhere to two risk-based capital ratio requirements: Tier 1 capital must be at least 4% of risk-weighted assets, and total capital must be at least 8% of risk-weighted assets.[15] A weight of zero—implying a regulatory assumption of zero risk—is assigned to U.S. Treasury securities, government-backed mortgages, and mortgage-backed securities guaranteed by the Government National Mortgage Association. A weight of 20% is assigned to most other mortgage-backed securities and securities issued by federal agencies. Most conventional mortgages and general-obligation revenue bonds are assigned a weight of 50%, and a weight of 100% is assigned to commercial/industrial, consumer, and commercial real estate loans.

For our hypothetical bank with $300 million in U.S. Treasury securities, $400 million in mortgages, and $800 million in commercial and industrial loans, total assets are $1.5 billion but risk-weighted assets are only $1.0 billion.[16] Thus, required Tier 1 capital would be only $40 million, whereas required total capital would be $80 million. Banks can achieve the mandated capital/asset ratios under the risk-based standards not only by reducing total assets or acquiring (expensive) new equity, but also by changing the composition of their balance sheets in favor of assets carrying lower weights; thus, for example, a reduction of commercial/industrial loans of, say, $100 million combined with an equal increase in government securities would reduce risk-weighted assets by the full $100 million, required Tier 1 capital by $4 million, and required total capital by $8 million.

This suggests that the risk-based capital standards may enhance the downward effect upon commercial/industrial lending engendered by the leverage ratio standards,[17] and may strengthen a trend already manifest toward the acquisition of government securities as commercial bank assets. Consider Tables 4.4 and 4.5, which present quarterly data since 1977 on commercial/industrial loans and on U.S. government securities held by domestic commercial banks. Commercial/industrial loans held by commercial banks began a steady decline in 1990; between 1990:1 and 1992:2, such loans fell by more than $113 billion, or more than 20%. Similarly, government securities held as assets by commercial banks increased by $28.4 billion (7.9%) over 1988–89, but then increased by $108 billion (27.8%) over 1990–91, and an additional $33.9 billion

TABLE 4.4
Total Commercial/Industrial Loans of Domestic Commercial Banks (billions of 1991 dollars)

Year:Quarter	C/I Loans	Year:Quarter	C/I Loans	Year:Quarter	C/I Loans
1992:2	439.8				
:1	448.2				
1991:4	464.1	1986:4	558.1	1981:4	454.1
:3	475.5	:3	543.9	:3	447.4
:2	496.5	:2	552.1	:2	440.4
:1	511.2	:1	546.8	:1	428.9
1990:4	526.3	1985:4	545.3	1980:4	436.1
:3	532.4	:3	547.0	:3	422.8
:2	545.9	:2	546.9	:2	428.8
:1	547.4	:1	544.6	:1	435.3
1989:4	552.9	1984:4	543.8	1979:4	436.3
:3	554.1	:3	534.6	:3	435.7
:2	558.8	:2	528.9	:2	430.1
:1	554.1	:1	512.6	:1	417.4
1988:4	555.3	1983:4	498.0	1978:4	413.6
:3	553.8	:3	488.3	:3	430.4
:2	560.5	:2	487.3	:2	n.a.
:1	549.8	:1	488.0	:1	n.a.
1987:4	551.8	1982:4	493.4	1977:4	n.a.
:3	548.0	:3	487.7	:3	n.a.
:2	560.3	:2	483.6	:2	n.a.
:1	566.0	:1	467.0	:1	n.a.

Source: See Table 4.1. *Note:* n.a. = not available.

TABLE 4.5
Total U.S. Government Securities of Domestic Commercial Banks (billions of 1991 dollars)

Year:Quarter	Government Securities	Year:Quarter	Government Securities	Year:Quarter	Government Securities
1992:2	529.9				
:1	511.4				
1991:4	496.0	1986:4	334.8	1981:4	157.5
:3	469.8	:3	321.3	:3	164.5
:2	450.6	:2	305.5	:2	170.7
:1	436.4	:1	304.8	:1	171.2
1990:4	431.4	1985:4	306.9	1980:4	170.4
:3	426.9	:3	316.2	:3	164.3
:2	422.1	:2	312.7	:2	158.2
:1	406.5	:1	307.4	:1	158.7
1989:4	388.0	1984:4	302.0	1979:4	160.3
:3	380.9	:3	307.9	:3	162.6
:2	378.0	:2	317.0	:2	169.1
:1	372.9	:1	278.0	:1	172.3
1988:4	366.9	1983:4	239.2	1978:4	177.1
:3	363.9	:3	226.0	:3	185.1
:2	363.1	:2	218.7	:2	194.4
:1	362.3	:1	195.5	:1	200.0
1987:4	359.6	1982:4	171.2	1977:4	203.2
:3	354.6	:3	159.3	:3	207.8
:2	350.2	:2	159.0	:2	218.0
:1	343.9	:1	161.5	:1	223.2

Source: See Table 4.1.

(6.8%) in the first two quarters of 1992. Tables 4.6 through 4.8 present quarterly ratios of commercial/industrial loans to total bank assets, government securities to total assets, and commercial/industrial loans to government securities, respectively.

Again, it is difficult to ascribe these patterns to the effects of the business cycle. In the five quarters following the 1990–91 recession trough, commercial/industrial loans held by commercial banks declined by $71.4 billion, or almost 14%. In the six quarters following the 1981–82 recession trough, commercial/industrial loans grew by $24.9 billion, or 5.1%. Indeed, the decline in commercial/industrial loans began in the third quarter of 1989, well before the 1990–91 recession, and continued throughout the following 11 quarters for which data are available. By contrast, during the 1980–83 cycle, commercial/industrial loans fell only in mid-1980, early 1981, and early 1983, corresponding roughly to periods of negative or slow growth.

TABLE 4.6
Domestic Commercial Banks, C/I Loans/Total Assets

Year:Quarter	C/I Loans/Assets	Year:Quarter	C/I Loans/Assets	Year:Quarter	C/I Loans/Assets
1992:2	.148				
:1	.150				
1991:4	.154	1986:4	.188	1981:4	.195
:3	.159	:3	.190	:3	.193
:2	.166	:2	.194	:2	.189
:1	.170	:1	.195	:1	.187
1990:4	.171	1985:4	.196	1980:4	.185
:3	.174	:3	.201	:3	.185
:2	.178	:2	.205	:2	.185
:1	.178	:1	.207	:1	.189
1989:4	.180	1984:4	.206	1979:4	.187
:3	.184	:3	.208	:3	.189
:2	.185	:2	.205	:2	.187
:1	.184	:1	.199	:1	.183
1988:4	.183	1983:4	.193	1978:4	.179
:3	.185	:3	.193	:3	.186
:2	.188	:2	.195	:2	n.a.
:1	.186	:1	.196	:1	n.a.
1987:4	.185	1982:4	.201	1977:4	n.a.
:3	.187	:3	.204	:3	n.a.
:2	.189	:2	.205	:2	n.a.
:1	.193	:1	.199	:1	n.a.

Source: See Tables 4.1 and 4.4. *Note:* n.a. = not available.

TABLE 4.7
Domestic Commercial Banks, Government Securities/Total Assets

Year:Quarter	Securities/ Assets	Year:Quarter	Securities/ Assets	Year:Quarter	Securities/ Assets
1992:2	.178				
:1	.171				
1991:4	.164	1986:4	.113	1981:4	.068
:3	.157	:3	.112	:3	.071
:2	.150	:2	.107	:2	.073
:1	.145	:1	.109	:1	.075
1990:4	.140	1985:4	.110	1980:4	.072
:3	.140	:3	.116	:3	.072
:2	.138	:2	.117	:2	.068
:1	.132	:1	.117	:1	.069

(continues)

TABLE 4.7 (*continued*)

Year:Quarter	Securities/ Assets	Year:Quarter	Securities/ Assets	Year:Quarter	Securities/ Assets
1989:4	.126	1984:4	.115	1979:4	.069
:3	.126	:3	.120	:3	.071
:2	.125	:2	.123	:2	.074
:1	.124	:1	.108	:1	.076
1988:4	.121	1983:4	.093	1978:4	.077
:3	.121	:3	.089	:3	.080
:2	.122	:2	.087	:2	.083
:1	.123	:1	.079	:1	.087
1987:4	.121	1982:4	.070	1977:4	.088
:3	.121	:3	.067	:3	.093
:2	.118	:2	.067	:2	.098
:1	.117	:1	.069	:1	.102

Source: See Tables 4.1 and 4.5.

TABLE 4.8
Domestic Commercial Banks, C/I Loans/Government Securities

Year:Quarter	Loans/ Securities	Year:Quarter	Loans/ Securities	Year:Quarter	Loans/ Securities
1992:2	.83				
:1	.88				
1991:4	.94	1986:4	1.67	1981:4	2.88
:3	1.01	:3	1.69	:3	2.72
:2	1.10	:2	1.81	:2	2.58
:1	1.17	:1	1.79	:1	2.51
1990:4	1.22	1985:4	1.78	1980:4	2.56
:3	1.25	:3	1.73	:3	2.57
:2	1.29	:2	1.75	:2	2.71
:1	1.35	:1	1.77	:1	2.74
1989:4	1.43	1984:4	1.80	1979:4	2.72
:3	1.45	:3	1.74	:3	2.68
:2	1.48	:2	1.69	:2	2.54
:1	1.49	:1	1.84	:1	2.42
1988:4	1.51	1983:4	2.08	1978:4	2.34
:3	1.52	:3	2.16	:3	2.33
:2	1.54	:2	2.23	:2	n.a.
:1	1.55	:1	2.50	:1	n.a.
1987:4	1.53	1982:4	2.88	1977:4	n.a.
:3	1.55	:3	3.06	:3	n.a.
:2	1.60	:2	3.04	:2	n.a.
:1	1.65	:1	2.89	:1	n.a.

Source: See Tables 4.4 and 4.5. *Note:* n.a.: = Not available.

Similarly, the business cycle cannot explain the shift toward government securities among bank assets. Government securities held as bank assets increased every quarter during 1989 through 1992 regardless of real GDP growth, but that pattern was not observed in the 1980–83 period. Government securities held as bank assets grew 6.3% in 1980, when real GDP fell 0.5%; fell 7.6% in 1981, when real GDP growth was 1.8%; increased 8.7% in 1982, when real GDP growth was –2.2%; and increased 39.7% in 1983, when real GDP growth was 3.9%.

The next section discusses some ensuing implications of the capital standards for bank lending to the commercial/industrial sector.

Sectoral Effects of the Bank Capitalization Standards

To the extent that the capitalization standards are likely to constrain bank lending, it is important to ask whether the tighter credit market conditions will affect all firms and sectors proportionally, or whether some sectors are disproportionally dependent upon banks for credit. The general answer in the literature is that banks tend to specialize in making loans that are "nonstandard," that is, that require some customizing in order to meet the needs of particular borrowers. Furthermore, banks seem to specialize in meeting the credit demands of borrowers for whom commercial paper and other forms of debt instruments, for a variety of reasons, are not cost-effective; among suppliers of credit to such borrowers, banks seem to have a comparative advantage in processing information about and screening potential borrowers, and in monitoring their performance in terms of repayment (see, e.g., Bernanke and Gertler, 1987; Gertler, 1988).

Another way to approach this issue is to recognize that banks finance the acquisition of assets with certificates of deposit, which ought to be close substitutes from the viewpoint of lenders for commercial paper and other kinds of debt instruments (for a fuller discussion of bank lending specialization, see Fama, 1985). Thus, CDs must yield the same returns as other securities of comparable risk; but, unlike other kinds of debt instruments, CDs until recently were subject to a reserve requirement, and such reserves do not bear interest. That condition is analogous analytically to a tax on CDs; but because holders of CDs must earn competitive returns, the incidence (burden) of the implicit reserve tax cannot be borne by lenders. Instead, the tax must be borne by borrowers.

That this tax is viable—that is, that borrowers are willing to pay the higher interest rates incorporating it rather than shift to other kinds of securities—suggests that bank loans provide services to borrowers not available (as cheaply) with other kinds of debt. Bank loans are an example of "inside debt," that is, debt that allows the lender access to information about the borrower not publicly available.[18] Because bank loans are short-term and usually low in priority among business firm contracts promising fixed payments, the renewal process provides the market with a signal that (in the view of the bank) the higher-priority payment promises made by the borrower can be believed; other creditors, then, need not undertake their own costly evaluations of the borrower, thus reducing credit costs for the borrower overall.[19] This bank signal is credible because the bank offers or refuses real financial resources on the basis of its evaluation.

Historically, the use of both outside equity and outside debt imposes high information and contracting costs; thus, both traditionally have been uneconomic for small firms (see Fama and Jensen, 1983a, 1983b). As bank loans have been used by firms of all sizes and types, it is reasonable to conclude that contracting costs for bank loans historically have been lower for small firms than those attendant upon the use of outside debt. Even with the rise of high-yield debt available to smaller firms, it still is likely to be the case that bank debt will be used disproportionally by smaller firms. This suggests that the capital standards will yield a sectoral crunch weighing disproportionally upon small business.[20] This is consistent with the observation that among all manufacturing firms with assets greater than $25 million, the ratio of bank debt to nonbank debt was 0.42 in the first quarter of 1992; for manufacturing firms with assets not greater than $25 million, the ratio was more than 1.8.

The discussion above suggests that a reduction in the supply of C&I credit induced by regulation ought to result in a decline in bank lending to small firms proportionally greater than any decline in bank lending to larger firms, or relative to the decline in total C&I lending; that outcome ought to obtain because smaller firms presumably have less (or no) access to commercial paper or national credit markets served by other types of intermediaries. The data in Table 4.9 are roughly consistent with that expectation. Between the first quarter of 1990 and the first quarter of 1992, total bank debt for manufacturing firms with assets greater than $25 million fell by 6.6%. For the three categories of smaller manufacturers, the comparable figures are 17.6%, 2.3%, and 21.1%.

Another implication of a sectoral crunch yielded by regulation is an increase in the differences ("spreads") between C&I lending rates and other short- and long-term interest rates.[21] Table 4.10 shows three short-term spreads and one long-term one. No pattern of increasing spreads is discernible in the 1990–91 period, a finding that does not support the central hypothesis of this chapter. However, it is likely that banks faced with increased regulatory constraints on C&I credit would reduce lending to

TABLE 4.9
Total Bank Debt, Manufacturing Corporations (billions of 1991 dollars)

	Corporation Asset Size			
Year:Quarter	Less Than $5 Million	$5-$10 Million	$10-$25 Million	More Than $25 Million
1992:1	15.5	8.4	13.1	202.3
1991:4	15.5	8.6	12.8	197.0
:3	16.0	8.4	13.1	205.6
:2	15.9	9.5	14.5	206.8
:1	16.6	9.0	14.8	212.4
1990:4	16.3	9.6	14.6	216.5
:3	16.8	9.2	15.3	218.8
:2	18.1	9.5	15.6	213.3
:1	18.8	8.6	16.6	216.6
1989:4	18.0	9.0	15.9	206.6
:3	18.9	9.3	17.3	202.6
:2	18.4	11.4	17.5	199.0
:1	20.6	11.4	17.6	188.8

Source: U.S. Department of Commerce, *Quarterly Financial Report,* various issues. *Note:* Asset sizes are nominal dollars.

the worst risks first; the remaining loans would be better risks, thus possibly reducing interest rates observed for C&I lending. In other words, the spreads shown in Table 4.10 are not for an identical (or similar) group of loans, this may explain the absence of an increasing interest rate spread.[22]

Concluding Observations

The risk-based standards provide incentives to shift assets toward categories carrying lower weights; for example, a shift from commercial loans to residential loans would reduce commercial loans and also risk-weighted assets, but might actually increase risks borne by banks or by the deposit insurance system, because mortgage loans tend to be long-term fixed-rate obligations financed with shorter-term deposits. This is only one problem among many engendered by the risk-based standards, but it is highly revealing in terms of the mischief that can result when government attempts to substitute bureaucratic fiat for outcomes yielded by market forces.

The weights specified in the risk-based standards obviously are arbitrary, and they are crude in that risk variation within categories is ignored. Is the worst municipal bond really less risky than the best mortgage? And how is it that the international bureaucrats have come to

TABLE 4.10
Interest Rate Spreads (percent)

Week Ending	Spread 1	Spread 2	Spread 3	Spread 4
11/08/91	2.26	1.92	1.99	0.60
08/09/91	2.37	0.99	2.01	1.15
05/10/91	2.15	1.85	1.71	1.16
02/08/91	2.48	2.11	2.07	1.52
11/09/90	3.42	2.53	2.78	2.83
08/10/90	2.42	1.65	2.08	2.00
05/11/90	2.20	1.77	1.72	2.27
02/09/90	0.61	0.21	0.39	0.86
11/10/89	2.79	1.81	2.43	3.44
08/11/89	2.85	1.80	2.58	3.60
05/05/89	3.30	2.01	2.30	3.68
02/10/89	2.42	1.87	1.69	2.58
11/11/88	2.56	1.80	1.77	1.88
08/05/88	2.86	1.91	1.67	1.40
05/06/88	2.34	1.67	1.36	0.12
02/05/88	2.66	1.60	1.76	1.21
11/06/87	2.76	2.04	1.27	0.25
08/07/87	2.28	1.45	1.38	0.03
05/08/87	2.53	0.94	1.33	0.43
02/06/87	1.86	1.24	1.59	1.28
11/07/86	2.03	1.22	1.66	0.93
08/08/86	2.03	1.37	1.60	1.44
05/09/86	2.07	1.26	1.71	1.63
02/07/86	2.30	1.36	1.78	1.28
11/08/85	2.45	1.38	1.97	0.39
08/09/85	2.02	1.36	1.46	-0.09
05/10/85	2.10	1.67	1.75	-0.14
02/08/85	1.94	1.51	1.62	-0.27
11/09/84	2.55	1.42	2.09	0.98
08/10/84	2.77	1.70	2.13	1.14
05/11/84	2.47	1.99	1.59	-0.11
02/10/84	1.99	1.48	1.83	0.18
11/11/83	2.15	1.59	1.80	1.14
08/05/83	1.70	1.50	1.30	-0.12
05/06/83	2.28	1.51	2.17	1.22
02/11/83	1.96	1.70	1.66	0.89

Source: Board of Governors of the Federal Reserve System, *Annual Statistical Digest,* various issues. *Note:* Spreads 1–4: short-term commercial bank C&I rate minus three-month T-bill rate; short-term commercial bank C&I rate minus federal funds rate; short-term commercial bank C&I rate minus six-month commercial paper rate; long-term commercial bank C&I rate minus 10-year T-bond rate.

130   *Benjamin Zycher*

know that 4% of risk-weighted Tier 1 capital and 8% of risk-weighted total capital are the efficient standards? Moreover, the riskiness of a portfolio of assets is very different from the riskiness of the individual assets themselves; the risk-based standards ignore the covariance among assets—and resulting riskiness of the portfolio—that is far more relevant for purposes of both analysis and policy formulation.

The international nature of the agreement is consistent with the cartel view of government, in which bureaucrats and politicians seeking greater budgets and power for themselves reduce the scope of competition among governments. The exercise of such monopoly power by governments acting in concert increases the speed with which market forces will find routes around the arbitrary constraints imposed by decision makers. The rise of nonbanks, securitization, and money market funds is the wave of the future.

Politics is the art of wealth redistribution, and economic regulation is the continuation of politics by other means. As regulation is used as a vehicle for the redistribution of wealth, and for the protection of existing concentrated interests against new competition, market forces attempt to find routes around the artificial constraints imposed by regulators. (For an early discussion of the tax/transfer view of economic regulation, see Posner, 1971; see also Becker, 1983; Peltzman, 1976; Posner, 1974; Stigler, 1970, 1971.) Government responds by attempting to constrain this unregulated market behavior or by including it under the regulatory umbrella. But government cannot regulate more and more endlessly, or attempt to do so, without creating sizable economic losses. As the problem of bank capital stems from the perverse incentives engendered by the system of deposit insurance, it is difficult to believe that real reform will be able to preserve that system over time.

Notes

1. President Bush, for example, called on banks in his last State of the Union Address to "make more sound loans." Then-Commerce Secretary Robert A. Mosbacher argued in mid-1990 that the economic slowdown was due in substantial part to a "credit crunch" (see Murray, 1990).

2. This point will be discussed in greater detail below, but it is interesting to note that in 1990 and 1991 commercial and industrial lending by all insured banks fell by 0.3% and 7.8%, respectively, while holdings of U.S. government securities grew by 16.% and 23.4%, respectively.

3. Excess reserves are simply the difference between total reserves and required reserves held by commercial banks. Some implications of the implicit tax imposed upon banks by the fact that reserves do not earn interest are discussed below.

4. See Board of Governors of the Federal Reserve System, *Federal Reserve Bulletin*, various issues. Data are in nominal dollars, seasonally adjusted, and adjusted for changes in reserve requirements.

5. The Basle agreement was negotiated under the auspices of the Bank for International Settlements (BIS). Approved in 1988 by an international committee of central bankers, the agreement received no formal congressional approval or (apparently) administration review, and appears to have no statutory basis whatever. Such agreement among otherwise competing governments on tax and regulatory policies implicitly is a way to reduce such competition, and thus is analogous to a cartel arrangement. See for example, McKenzie and Staff (1978).

6. Tier 1 capital is predominantly common stockholder equity and perpetual preferred stock. Tier 2 capital includes loan-loss reserves up to 1.25% of risk-weighted credit exposure, other types of preferred stock, mandatory convertible debt, and subordinated debt.

7. Former FDIC Chairman William Seidman has estimated that 99% of all U.S. banks have to maintain Tier 1 equity ratios above 4.5%. See Garsson (1990).

8. The value of the subsidy for a given bank is determined by the degree to which the deposit insurance premiums for which the given bank is responsible fail to cover expected losses and administrative costs.

9. This information problem inherent in the market for equity capital is the capital market analogue of the "lemons" problem discussed by Akerlof (1970) in the context of the market for used automobiles.

10. Asquith and Mullins find the median dilution effect to be 28% (see also Marsh, 1979; Taggart, 1977).

11. Wall and Peterson do not estimate directly the wealth effect on existing shares. (see also Myers and Majluf, 1984).

12. Bank assets grew fairly steadily in 1987 and 1988, fell in the first quarter of 1989, and then began a monotonic decline in the first quarter of 1990, interrupted only in 1990:4. Interestingly, that quarter was distinguished by the weakest economic performance of the current business cycle.

13. Real GDP growth was negative in the second quarter of 1981; if that is counted as the beginning of the 1981–82 recession, total bank assets in the six preceding quarters (1979:4–1981:1) fell by $39.4 billion, or 1.7%.

14. Bernanke and Lown (1991) compare lending growth for domestically chartered commercial banks over six business cycles by year of cyclical peak as follows:

Year	Lending Growth (%)
1990	1.7
1981	9.3
1980	3.1
1973	14.6
1969	4.1
1960	4.4

See also Furlong (1988), Wall and Peterson (1987), Baer and McElravey (1992), and Keeley (1988).

15. Total capital is the sum of Tier 1 and Tier 2 capital. See footnote 6.

16. The U.S. Treasury securities carry a weight of zero, and the mortgages and loans carry respective weights of 50% and 100%.

17. Bernanke and Lown (1991, p. 217) conclude from data on securitization of commercial/industrial loans that the securitization phenomenon does not explain the decline of commercial/industrial loans held as commercial bank assets.

18. "Outside debt" is publicly traded debt with respect to which debt holders must rely upon information available publicly, such as information provided by the borrower or purchased from auditors or rating agencies.

19. Higher-priority debts include, for example, payments owed to suppliers of inputs. The value of this signal about the creditworthiness of an organization is illustrated by the fact that many firms pay periodic fees for lines of credit from banks that are used little if at all. Fama (1985) notes that "large corporations often purchase lines of credit from banks for the sole purpose of providing a signal about outside debt (commercial paper) to be issued publicly rather than held by the bank" (p. 37).

20. Moreover, the liabilities of such other financial intermediaries as insurance companies and finance companies are not subject to a reserve requirement; that such alternative lenders have not competed away bank borrowers suggests that there is something special about banks themselves. Fama (1985, pp. 37–38) argues that monitoring costs are lower for banks than for other financial intermediaries because the deposit history of a borrower provides inside information.

21. The reduction in the supply of credit in the C&I market would drive interest rates up there, and a market shift toward government securities and other instruments might drive the prices of the latter up, thus reducing their yields.

22. Although the spreads did not increase, they do not seem to have decreased, either.

References

Akerlof, G. (1970). "The Market for Lemons: Quality Uncertainty and the Market Mechanism." *Quarterly Journal of Economics, 84,* 488–500.

Asquith, P., and Mullins, D. W. (1986). "Equity Issues and Offering Dilution." *Journal of Financial Economics, 15,* 61–89.

Baer, H., and McElravey, J. (1992). "Capital Adequacy and the Growth of U.S. Banks." Federal Reserve Bank of Chicago Working Paper WP–92–11.

Becker, G. S. (1983). "A Theory of Competition among Interest Groups for Political Influence." *Quarterly Journal of Economics, 98,* 371–400.

Benston, G. J. (1992). "Is There a Credit Crunch? And What Should We do About It?" *Journal of Applied Corporate Finance, 4,* 86–91.

Bernanke, B. S., and Gertler, M. (1987). "Banking and Macroeconomic Equilibrium." In W. A. Barnett and K. J. Singleton (Eds.), *New Approaches to Monetary Economics.* New York: Cambridge University Press.

Bernanke, B. S., and Lown, C. S. (1991). "The Credit Crunch." *Brookings Papers on Economic Activity, 2,* 205–247.

Fama, E. F. (1985). "What's Different about Banks?" *Journal of Monetary Economics, 15,* 29–39.

Fama, E. F., and Jensen, M. C. (1983a). "Agency Problems and Residual Claims." *Journal of Law and Economics, 26*, 327–349.

Fama, E. F., and Jensen, M. C. (1983b). "Separation of Ownership and Control." *Journal of Law and Economics, 26*, 301–325.

Federal Reserve Regulatory Service. (1991). *Capital Adequacy Guidelines for Bank Holding Companies: Tier 1 Leverage Measure* (Regulation Y; 12 CFR 225). Washington, DC: Government Printing Office.

Furlong, F. T. (1988, Spring). "Changes in Bank Risk-Taking." *Economic Review* (Federal Reserve Bank of San Francisco), pp. 45–56.

Garsson, R. M. (1990, September 11). "Seidman Decides to Back the Fed's Capital Proposal." *American Banker*, p. 1.

Gertler, M. (1988). "Financial Structure and Aggregate Economic Activity: An Overview." *Journal of Money, Credit, and Banking, 20*, 559–588.

Keeley, M.C. (1988, Winter). "Bank Capital Regulation in the 1980s: Effective or Ineffective?" *Economic Review* (Federal Reserve Bank of San Francisco), pp. 3–20.

Marsh, P. R. (1979). "Equity Rights Issues and the Efficiency of the U.K. Stock Market." *Journal of Finance, 34*, 839–862.

Masulis, R. W. (1980). "The Effects of Capital Structure Change on Security Prices: A Study of Exchange Offers." *Journal of Financial Economics, 8*, 139–178.

McKenzie, R., and Staff, R. (1978). "Revenue Sharing and Monopoly Government." *Public Choice, 33*, 93–97.

Modigliani, F., and Miller, M. H. (1963). "Corporate Income Taxes and the Cost of Capital: A Correction." *American Economic Review, 53*, 433–443.

Murray, A. (1990, June 15). "Mosbacher Says 'Serious' Credit Crunch Grips U.S., Isn't Limited to Real Estate." *Wall Street Journal*, p. A3.

Myers, S. C., and Majluf, N. S. (1984). "Corporate Financing and Investment Decisions When Firms Have Information That Investors Do Not Have." *Journal of Financial Economics, 13*, 187–221.

Peltzman, S. (1976)."Toward a More General Theory of Regulation." *Journal of Law and Economics, 19*, 211–240.

Posner, R. A. (1971). "Taxation by Regulation," *Bell Journal of Economics and Management Science*, Spring.

Posner, R. A. (1974). "Theories of Economic Regulation." *Bell Journal of Economics and Management Science, 5*, 335–358.

Sametz, A. W. (1964). "Trends in the Volume and Composition of Equity Financing." *Journal of Finance, 19*, 450–469.

Stigler, G. J. (1970). "Director's Law of Public Income Redistribution." *Journal of Law and Economics, 13*, 1–10.

Stigler, G. J. (1971). "The Theory of Economic Regulation." *Bell Journal of Economics and Management Science, 2*, 3–21.

Taggart, R. A., Jr. (1977). "A Model of Corporate Financing Decisions." *Journal of Finance, 32*, 1467–1484.

Wall, L. D., and Peterson, D. R. (1987). "The Effect of Capital Adequacy Guidelines on Large Bank Holding Companies." *Journal of Banking and Finance, 11*, 581–600.

Wall, L. D., and Peterson, P. P. (1991). "Valuation Effects of New Capital Issues by Large Bank Holding Companies." *Journal of Financial Services Research, 5*(1), 77–87.

Comment

George J. Benston

Both Glenn Yago and Benjamin Zycher consider the effect of constraints on financial institutions, particularly commercial banks, on economic growth. Yago examines a broad spectrum of constraints on capital markets before concentrating on the current presumed bank "credit crunch." Zycher limits his analysis to that event, examining the hypothesis that it was caused by regulatorily imposed higher capital standards. In this comment, I discuss each chapter in some detail before presenting a framework for analysis of my own and a proposal for bank regulation that would reduce "credit crunches" to being the consequence of government policies that attempt to allocate or otherwise control bank credit.

Glenn Yago's Chapter

Yago's thesis is that "this recession [and credit crunch are] not cyclical and macroeconomic, but structural and institutional—the result of rigidities that artificially inhibit business and financial innovation through restrictive government regulation and financial institutional behavior" (p. 82). He begins with "historical background," describing capital ownership as "a long-standing tradition and aspiration in our political culture of seeking economic independence" (p. 83). "Capital ownership," he says, "requires capital access" (p. 84). He then asserts that "the current capital crunch that torpedoed economic growth has historical precedents during earlier periods of American history" (p. 84). He gives three examples. The first occurred in 1914 as a result of a run to gold. The second, the 1930–33 depression, was characterized by a reduction in the money supply and bank failures (neither of which he mentions). Rather, he emphasizes declines in the demand for credit and in creditworthiness and "bank bashing" by Washington.

The third and only example from more recent times is the "credit crunch of 1974" when a "sharp increase in oil prices sent inflation and interest rates soaring" (a causal relationship that monetarists, at least, would dispute), and "deteriorating bank capital positions and declining real estate and stock market values led banks to curtail lending to all but the largest and highest-rated companies" (p. 87). Perhaps the most important special feature of this period, President Nixon's wage and price controls, is not mentioned. These controls included a Federal Reserve-imposed ceiling on prime interest rates. Yago does not mention the widely cited 1966 credit crunch, which was characterized by Federal Reserve and Johnson administration calls for credit rationing as a means of restraining (or giving the appearance of restraining) inflation and disintermediation caused by deposit interest rate ceilings below market rates of interest (see Burger, 1969). Nor does he include the 1969–70 episode in which the Fed and the Nixon administration called on banks to reduce credit extensions through nonprice allocations of credit. Or the 1980 situation, when the Federal Reserve and the Carter administration imposed consumer credit controls and restrictions on bank growth (see Schreft, 1990).

Yago turns next to "financial repression: redlining American business" (p. 87). He delineates two forms of repression. One takes the form of "low interest rate ceilings and selective credit policies that inhibit saving" (p. 88). Both logic and evidence support this conclusion that these policies restrict access to capital. However, neither constraint has been present in the current recession. The second is "regulatory restrictions on both financial institutions and capital markets that constrict capital flow channels and thereby inhibit growth" (p. 88). At this point he is not more specific.

He then analyzes the 1989-92 period. He first presents figures showing a sharp decline in bank loans to nonfinancial corporations and in funds raised from high-yield bond floatations and initial public offerings of equity. His Table 3.1, however, does not fully support his statement that "trends in financing of nonfinancial corporations reflect the larger role of capital markets played relative to banks as a source of capital growth" over the years 1985 through 1990 (p. 90). The proportions of total debt capital raised from corporate bonds were 55% in 1985 and 63% in 1990, with a low of 46% in 1989. Commercial paper was 7% of the total in 1985 and 15% in 1990, with a low of –5% in 1989. Bank loans did decline substantially, from 24% in 1985 to 2% in 1990, but this source of debt was only 3% of the total in 1987 and at 21% in 1989 almost equaled the 1985 percentage. It is difficult to draw much of anything from these figures for the six-year period included in the table.

In the next section of his chapter, Yago "examines patterns of regulation that have inhibited change and growth in the economy" (p. 90). His Table 3.2 presents a chronology of "measures inducing rigidity in capital structures and markets" from 1985 through 1990. In the table, 29 events are listed and described briefly. Almost all of these are measures that were proposed to or introduced in the Congress or statements of concern about takeovers and junk bonds. Very few laws are listed as having been passed, and most of the regulations adopted appear to affect capital markets rather trivially. The only measures of some significant importance appear to be the Tax Reform Act of 1986, which reduced marginal tax rates, thereby reducing the tax benefits of debt; the Financial Institutions Reform, Recovery, and Enforcement Act (FIRREA) of 1989, which limited thrifts' permissible holdings of junk bonds; and some state restrictions on junk bond investments by insurance companies. Table 3.3 lists 39 laws restricting corporate takeovers enacted by 27 states between November 1982 and April 1990. These laws, Yago says, were "designed to protect existing managers of public companies" (p. 94). He does not show the actual effect of these laws on economic activity during the late 1980s compared with other periods.

Restrictions on bank and thrift lending are considered next. The bank restrictions Yago mentions are "increased scrutiny of HLT" (highly leveraged transactions) in late 1989, "higher rates of deposit insurance premiums, higher capital ratios, revised risk-based capital requirements, and increased regulatory oversight pressures" (p. 98). The restriction on thrifts discussed is the requirement imposed by FIRREA in 1989 that savings and loans mark junk bonds to market and limit their holdings of these investments. Insurance companies were affected by higher reserves required against lower-rated credits, and money market and mutual funds were affected by restrictions on holdings of lower-rated commercial paper and assets of a single issuer. Yago does not consider the extent to which these changes were necessary to protect the deposit insurance fund, insurees and their beneficiaries, and investors in presumably safe investment funds.

Yago next goes on to present some graphs depicting the high-yield bond market. His Figure 3.2 does indicate that the number of non-investment-grade new issues declined after 1989, which is consistent with his view that FIRREA had a negative impact on this market. His Figure 3.3 shows that capital flows in high-yield bonds (presumably the same as non-investment-grade new issues) declined after 1989. However, the flows recovered almost to 1988–89 levels in 1991, which is somewhat inconsistent with the FIRREA hypothesis. Yago then refers to a multivariate analysis he conducted, in which the variation in high-yield bond prices, yields, new issues, and capital flows are explained by a number of economic variables. His Figure 3.5 shows the residuals (actual less expected) from this model, where the dependent variable is the Merrill Lynch High-Yield Index. I see the figure as showing two things. First, there appears to be a considerable amount of autocorrelation among the residuals, which indicates a specification error. Assuming that this error is not serious, as best I can tell the residuals are negative from 1986 through sometime in 1991, except for a few months in 1990. Thus, whatever explains the negativity, it predates FIRREA by about three years. Furthermore, the residuals decline rather similarly in 1986, 1988, and 1991. This pattern is not explained.

Yago then gives a very brief description of findings from his previous research, from which he says "My colleagues and I have found consistent rates of job creation performance among firms in the high-yield bond market . . . , among firms undergoing restructuring . . . , among plants that have been subject to leveraged buyouts or divestiture . . . , and among IPO firms" (p. 107; references omitted). (I presume he means consistently higher rates of job creation than among other firms.) From his description, I cannot tell whether other factors that might be related to job creation but are not necessarily related to the source of financing were accounted for.

Finally, Yago suggests four areas for future research. For research on "job creation, retention, and productivity," he calls for additional required disclosure by firms subject to the SEC's rules of employment data by plant, firm, or location. Although such data might be interesting to researchers (Yago does not specify how these data would speak to specific hypotheses), this call would seem to be inconsistent with his previous remarks about the burden of regulation on enterprises. He says that "research on capital market gaps" is needed because "institutional changes in banking, thrifts, and capital markets suggest that emerging barriers to capital access by many firms endanger economic growth" (p. 110). He does not specify which *emerging* barriers he has in mind (as contrasted with barriers that have been in place since the early 1930s). Indeed, recent institutional and technological changes have tended to reduce distinctions among firms providing financial services. The third research topic Yago recommends concerns "systematic information about sources of entrepreneurial finance" (p. 110). Assuming that such information does not now exist, it would seem to be useful if well-structured hypotheses about this financing were specified before data were gathered. Finally, Yago suggests research is needed on "the transfer of sophisticated financial technologies to recalcitrant social problems" (p. 111). This research might be useful if it is well specified. It should include tests of the null hypothesis—that financing is not part of the problem.

To summarize, Yago's chapter really does not offer much in the way of analysis of the effect of political and regulatory barriers to economic growth. Many of his conclusions are not supported by the data he presents. Perhaps most important for present purposes, he does not provide support for his introductory statement that the current "recession is not cyclical and macroeconomic, but structural and institutional—the result of rigidities that artificially inhibit business and financial innovation through restrictive government regulation and financial institutional behavior" (p. 82).

Benjamin Zycher's Chapter

Zycher is much less ambitious than Yago. He restricts his analysis to the present "credit crunch" and to the role of commercial banks. He points out in the beginning of his chapter that, according to conventional economic wisdom, given the supply of reserves by the Federal Reserve, banks' unwillingness to lend implies that they are holding excess reserves, which is inconsistent with the data. Furthermore, he says, real interest rates should have increased, and they have declined. Nevertheless, bank loans have decreased, a situation he concludes "is regulatory in origin and sector specific in impact with respect to commercial and industrial firms generally, and small firms in particular" (p. 116). The regulation that is responsible, he finds, is increased bank capital requirements, particularly the risk-based (Basle) requirement effective at the beginning of and phased in during 1992.

Zycher maintains that capital is costly to banks for two reasons. First, "to the extent that a given bank is subsidized by the deposit insurance system, the value of the subsidy declines as equity increases, because future losses will be borne by equity holders first and by the deposit insurance system (i.e., sound banks and the taxpayers) second" (p. 117–118). Second, new equity offerings generally result in declines in the market value of existing shares because information is asymmetrically available to management but not to outside investors. Consequently, Zycher concludes, "asset reduction will be a major means by which banks will adapt to the constraints imposed by the leverage ratio capital standard" (p. 119).

He supports this conclusion with data presented in his Table 4.1, which shows bank total assets in 1991 dollars declining in 1991, following implementation of the leverage ratio standard in 1990. He also compares the 1980–83 recession with the 1990–91 recession with quarterly gross domestic product (GDP) data (presented in his Table 4.3). These data, he concludes, support the hypothesis that "it is not only weak demand in credit markets but also the leverage ratio regulatory constraints that explain the decline in bank lending during the current business cycle" (p. 121).

The relationship can be seen a bit more clearly in the figures I have prepared from Zycher's data. In Figure 1, bank total assets and gross domestic product (both in 1991 dollars) are plotted, with each series

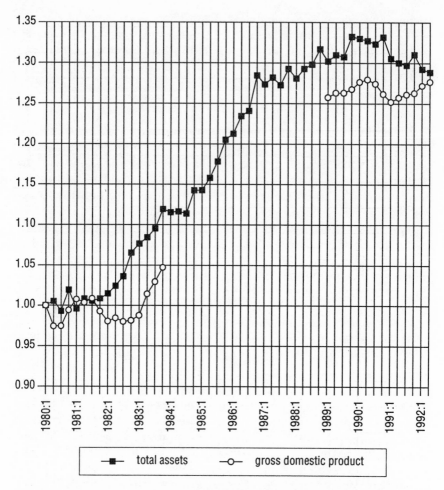

FIGURE 1 Bank Total Assets and Gross Domestic Product, 1980:1–1992:2 (constant 1991 dollars; 1980 = 1.00) *Source:* Zycher (Chapter 4, this volume, Table 4.2).

equal to 1.00 in 1980. After 1981 bank total assets increased, despite a decrease in GDP. In the current recession, bank total assets decreased at a similar point in time, and continued to decrease even after GDP increased. However, the decrease in bank total assets started in 1990, before the capital standards were imposed.

My Figures 2 and 3 compare the ratios of banks' securities to assets and C&I loans to assets, and GDP, with the values for 1980:1 equal to 1.00, over the 1980–83 and 1990–91 recessions. In both recessions the securities-to-assets ratio increased considerably and similarly. The loans-

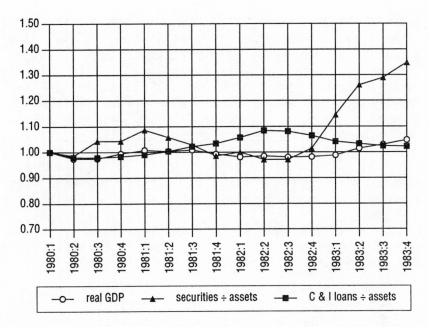

FIGURE 2 Changes over 1980:1–1983:4 Recession (1980:1 = 1.00) *Source:* Zycher (Chapter 4, this volume, Tables 4.1, 4.3, 4.4, 4.5).

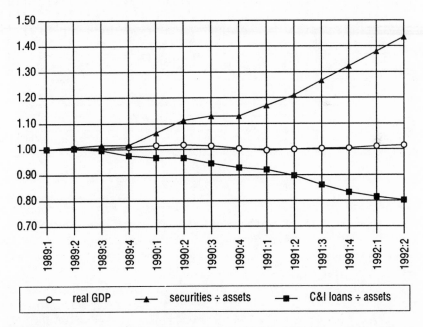

FIGURE 3 Changes over 1989:1–1992:2 Recession (1989:1 = 1.00) *Source:* Zycher (Chapter 4, this volume, Table 4.1, 4.3, 4.4, 4.5).

to-assets ratio decreased in both recessions, but much more so in the 1990–91 recession. However, as noted above, the decrease started a year before the more stringent capital requirements were imposed.

Finally, Zycher examines the presumed effects of the higher bank capitalization standard on corporations classified into four size groupings. From the data presented in his Table 4.9, he concludes that "the capital standards will yield a credit crunch weighing disproportionally upon small business" (p. 127). My Figure 4 presents the data graphically for the three smaller groups of corporations. This figure shows that all three groups borrowed proportionally less than did corporations with more than $25 million in assets. However, their relative decline began at least as early as 1989; indeed, the decline was greater before 1990 than after the higher capital standards were imposed. Hence, while these data are consistent with the hypothesis that the recession reduced bank lending to smaller corporations more than to larger ones, they are not consistent with Zycher's more-stringent-capital-standard explanation.

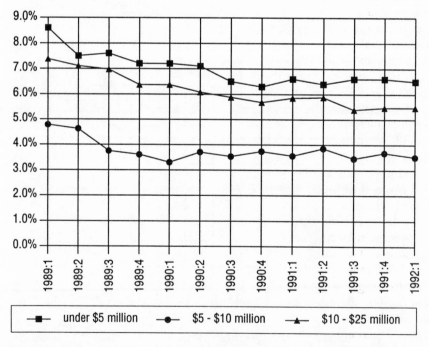

FIGURE 4 Manufacturing Corporations' Bank Debt: Three Total Asset Size Groups' Debt as Percentages of All Manufacturing Corporations *Source:* Zycher (Chapter 4, this volume, Table 4.9)

To summarize, Zycher shows that bank loans declined during the present recession, and he does make a strong theoretical argument for banks, downsizing and reducing lending as a result of their having to hold more capital. However, his data do not appear to support this explanation for the credit crunch, if there is a crunch.

Conclusions with Respect to Yago's and Zycher's Findings on the Credit Crunch

Neither Yago nor Zycher demonstrates that a credit crunch characterized or exacerbated the 1990–91 recession. Neither author accounts for changes in the demand for bank credit or isolates other reasons for the reduction in bank lending that occurred during this period. Nor does either of them analyze whether the decline in bank lending worsened the recession or was desirable, from a societal point of view, given the reduced demand by entrepreneurs for loans and the higher risk to creditors of making loans. The chapters of both authors suffer from an absence of theory from which testable hypotheses could be drawn.

Because it is insufficient simply to criticize others, I now put forth a theory that I believe is useful for analyzing the situation, with an eye toward delineating supportable policy conclusions. For this purpose, I assume that society is best served when individuals are free to make decisions about the disposition of their human and nonhuman capital, with two caveats. One is that these decisions do not result in externalities that impose costs on others, unless the cost of dealing with the externalities (including preventing individuals from acting) exceeds the costs from the externalities. The second caveat is that the distribution of wealth among persons is considered to be fair, or that wealth redistributions are considered to be made most efficiently through means other than by constraining individuals' private decisions.

I proceed as follows. First, I assume that entrepreneurs can self-fund their projects. This permits me to concentrate on their investment decisions independent of financing. Next, I delineate the benefits and costs of outside investment and then the role of commercial banks. In the latter section, I examine the caveats of externalities and fairness. This analysis leads to the conclusion that the only reason beneficial to society that justifies regulating banks' activities is to prevent costs from being imposed on the deposit insurance fund, although banks are more pervasively regulated to reduce competition among suppliers of financial services. I then apply the concepts developed to a bank credit crunch and the appropriate public policy actions that might be taken. Finally, I outline a regulatory scheme, based on higher capital requirements and structured early intervention and resolution, that would allow banks to serve the public efficiently and would obviate the possibility of a bank-caused "credit crunch."

Entrepreneurs' Investment Decisions
When They Are Self-Funding

Let us assume, first, that entrepreneurs (who, I assume, organize their activities through limited liability corporations) are self-funding. That is, they have sufficient resources to invest in any projects that they believe will be beneficial to them and are not concerned with diversifying their investments among outside and inside projects. Thus, they will undertake all projects that offer them positive present values. In the absence of externalities and concerns about the initial distribution of wealth and fairness to people afflicted with poor skill and bad luck, such decisions will tend toward optimizing societal welfare.

In making their investment decisions, entrepreneurs estimate the amounts and timing of cash flows (or their equivalent in other resources) expected from projects and the opportunity cost of investing in these projects. The cash flows almost never are certain. Hence, the entrepreneur must estimate the distribution of possible outcomes and the probabilities of their occurrence, which can be expressed as certainty equivalent amounts.[1] The rate at which these amounts are discounted reflects the entrepreneurs' opportunity cost of not investing in other projects or of personally consuming resources. The discount rate includes four elements that are particularly important for this analysis. One is the cost of forbearance, of delaying consumption—the opportunity cost of time. The second is the expected purchasing power of the monetary unit (cash)—the expected rate of inflation. Third is the cost of uncertainty if the entrepreneur is risk averse. Fourth is the entrepreneur's transactions cost of making and monitoring the decisions.

The Benefits and Costs of Outside Investment

Benefits

Because the initial assumptions—that entrepreneurs are self-funding and are not interested in outside diversification—are not generally correct, people can benefit from markets for funds (capital markets). Entrepreneurs with potentially valuable projects need not have the resources to invest, and people with the resources may not be able to generate positive-present-value projects or may not have the skills or desire to manage projects effectively. Thus, capital markets can increase societal welfare considerably. Furthermore, entrepreneurs who are risk averse are faced with "putting all their eggs in one basket." Even if these entrepreneurs had sufficient resources to fund their projects, they could benefit from diversification made possible by capital markets.

Costs

However, capital markets are subject to several important information costs not faced by self-funding entrepreneurs. One is the cost of search, as entrepreneurs and investors have to learn about each others' existence and evaluate each others' claims. A second is probity cost, as entrepreneurs and investors must determine and evaluate each others' reputations and incentives to misrepresent and cheat on contractual performance. For example, entrepreneurs must determine whether investors actually have the funds they say they want to invest and will not displace the entrepreneurs and take over their enterprises if they are successful. A third information cost is agency cost, which results from people tending to act (albeit honestly) so as to enhance their own interests, even when this imposes costs on others. For example, investors have reason to believe that entrepreneurs will overstate the cash flows expected from projects and understate the risk that these cash flows might not be forthcoming as stated. Entrepreneurs will bear these agency costs to the extent that they are unable to assure investors that the funds will be used as promised.

Additional important transactions costs arise from monitoring, administration, and bankruptcy collection. Monitoring usually is desirable because investors face the possibility that entrepreneurs will put the funds invested at higher risk than was originally promised or will mismanage the projects. Therefore, it generally is cost-effective for investors to monitor the use of their funds rather than wait to see what happens or to charge entrepreneurs a sufficiently high premium to offset losses. Administration costs are incurred by investors in keeping track of their investments and in documenting transactions against the event that legal proceedings are undertaken. Bankruptcy collection costs result from investors having to enforce their contracts when events turn out badly. These "deadweight" costs include the operations cost of attempting to collect amounts due, legal fees, and court costs, as well as the loss of investments should entrepreneurs misappropriate or misuse resources when they expect their equity in the enterprise is gone and they have little more to lose.

It should be noted that self-funded enterprises are subject to many of these same costs once entrepreneurs must hire people to manage their projects. These enterprises are also subject to agency costs, as employees tend to manage projects in their own interests rather than solely in the entrepreneurs' interests. The entrepreneurs thus must incur monitoring and administration costs. The costs delineated above for capital markets are in addition to the costs that are generated internally.

The Role of Commercial Banks

Commercial banks are institutions that profit from reducing the costs of information (including search, probity evaluation, and agency hazards) and of transactions (including monitoring, administration, and bankruptcy collection), and by offering risk-averse entrepreneurs and investors the advantage of diversification. Although many institutions offer these services, commercial banks are special in several regards. First, they also offer funds transfer services, primarily to and from deposit accounts. Consequently, they often have conveniently located and well-recognized offices that reduce the cost of search. Banks' joint production of deposit and lending services also reduces their and their customers' information costs with respect to probity. Their offering deposit services makes their maintenance of a reputation for probity and security particularly important, as (absent creditable deposit insurance) depositors have reason to fear putting their funds with dishonestly and incompetently run and insufficiently capitalized banks. Depositors realize that banks operate with fractional reserves and that there would be insufficient funds to repay all depositors should a bank incur losses that use up its capital. Indeed, some researchers have explained banks offering deposits repayable at par on demand as a means by which banks inform the public that they do not expect to be subjected to runs.

Commercial banks have comparative advantages over specialized lenders in that banks can achieve economies of scope from commonly producing deposit, lending, and collateral services (such as collections, investments, safekeeping, foreign exchange, letters of credit, and acceptances). Customers can benefit from "one-stop shopping" and from dealing with a banking officer who knows their total requirements and can offer a full range of services to meet those requirements. Banks, in turn, benefit from internal sharing of facilities among deposit, lending, and other services and of information about customers. Banks can achieve economies of scale by hiring and training specialists and using specialized equipment and information services. These economies reduce the costs of monitoring, administration, collections, and bankruptcy resolution.

Banks also can reduce their and their customers' costs of uncertainty and the transactions costs of reducing uncertainty by offsetting cash flows from deposits and loans, which lowers the amount of funds they must invest or lend in outside capital markets. Specialization in working with these markets (such as assessing interest rate and prepayment risk, hedging currency and interest rate risk, and purchasing, selling, evaluating, and creating financial instruments) gives banks a comparative advantage over entrepreneurs and many other institutions. This advantage reduces banks' costs of operations and provides them with products that they can sell directly for fees.

Constraints on Commercial Banks' Operations

Constraints on commercial banks are likely to reduce their considerable contribution toward increasing societal wealth, unless two assumptions do not hold. The most important is the absence of negative externalities that would be cost-effectively reduced by constraints. The other is the assumption that, if wealth were not distributed "fairly" or if banks were operated "unfairly," constraints could be effective in improving the situation.

Unlike manufacturing enterprises, banks do not impose the possible externality of air and water pollution. Indeed, bank buildings tend to be architecturally pleasing, offering positive externalities. The two possible important externalities of banks' operations are financial collapse and deposit insurance costs. Both may be quite costly, but, as the following analysis shows, only the latter should be of concern.

Financial Collapse

Three types of financial collapse should be distinguished: the collapse of an individual insolvent institution, the related collapse of a similar solvent institution that is mistakenly believed to be insolvent, and the collapse of the banking system. The collapse of an individual bank can result in deposits (investments) being lost, loans and other banking services being disrupted, and employees losing their jobs. Although this can cause distress to some people, it is a relatively small problem, particularly when entry into banking markets is not constrained. Furthermore, the collapse of an individual bank should not be identified as an externality. Depositors, similar to other investors, can bargain *ex ante* for compensation for the risk that they might lose their investments. Banks have incentives to inform depositors of the risks involved, and depositors have incentives to determine whether this information is credible. The fact that bank deposits (other than time-dated certificates of deposit) can be removed on demand gives banks considerable incentive to allay depositors' concerns.

Furthermore, unlike the situation when the manufacturer of a specialized product fails, bank customers can shift their business at relatively little cost to other banks that offer the same kinds of services and products. Bank employees tend to have transferable skills and usually can find employment in other banks and financial service firms. However, if entry into banking markets is restricted, such that only a few banks serve an area, the failure of even one bank could cause considerable economic distress, as the remaining banks (if there are any) might not be capable of serving the failed bank's customers except after some time for adjustment. Nevertheless, the failed bank's customers and employees should have considered the possibility of its failure when they established relationships with the bank, and adjusted accordingly the interest rates, fees, and wages they paid and received. Hence, although an individual bank failure may be distressing, it should not be considered as an externality.

The second type of financial collapse is the failure of solvent institutions that are misperceived to be insolvent because they are seen as similar to a failed bank. This may be labeled the *asymmetric information problem*; it results from depositors' not being able to determine the value of bank assets and liabilities. Although this lack of ability also affects other enterprises, banks are said to be special because, unlike other enterprises, creditors (depositors) can withdraw their funds at par on demand. Should such a run occur, the affected bank must sell assets at reduced "fire sale" prices or borrow at high rates, both of which can cause it to go from solvency to insolvency.

I believe contagious collapse is unlikely to occur. *Ex ante*, banks have incentives to avoid being misperceived as insolvent, by holding higher levels of capital, by being audited by reputable public accountants, and by being supervised by government authorities. Indeed, there is considerable evidence that depositors recognize differences among banks, as shown by several studies of contagion when Continental Illinois and other major banks failed (see Swary and Aharony, 1983; Wall and Peterson, 1990). Other large banks did not experience runs, and their stock prices did not decline. In any event, several institutional arrangements exist to reduce the cost of this type of financial collapse. The central bank as lender of last resort is the principal modern arrangement. Correspondent relationships among banks before (and coincident with) the establishment of the central bank have been effective in preventing the failure of solvent banks. Thus, I conclude that this second type of financial collapse should not be of much concern.

The third type is a systemic financial collapse. This collapse results from a run to currency (or, in earlier days, to gold) as people take their money out of banks and do not redeposit it. Banks suffer a loss in reserves that is not replenished, which causes them to reduce their deposits and assets. This multiple contraction of the money supply and bank credit almost always causes great economic distress, as prices and wages do not instantly readjust and as debt contracts unexpectedly become more onerous. However, the central bank can prevent such a systemic collapse from occurring. Through open market operations it can provide banks with the reserves that customers withdraw and provide consumers with the currency they demand. Indeed, a systemic collapse can be caused only by actions taken or not taken by the central bank.

Furthermore, credible deposit insurance now makes a run to currency extremely unlikely. Depositors whose accounts are fully insured have no reason to remove their funds, even from insolvent banks. Depositors with large, partially insured accounts would not run to currency, because this would saddle them with considerable costs. They would risk being robbed of cash and would lose the benefits from paying bills by check. Rather, if they believed that their banks might fail, they would transfer their deposits to other, safe banks and the funds would stay within the banking system.

Deposit Insurance Costs

Deposit insurance removes the cost to depositors of evaluating and monitoring their banks, with the exception of those depositors whose account balances exceed the insurance limit. These depositors, however, need only monitor their banks so that when the banks get close to insolvency they can transfer their funds to other institutions before their banks are closed. This absent and limited monitoring represents a saving in resources, but two additional costs are incurred. One is the moral hazard that results from banks' not having to be concerned about most depositors' welfare. The second cost follows from the first: the deposit insurance agency must evaluate and monitor banks' solvency. Hence, in the absence of constraints imposed by the deposit insurance agency or other regulators, bank owners have incentives to take greater risks than they would have taken in the absence of deposit insurance. If the risks turn out well, the bank owners benefit fully; if they turn out so badly that the bank's capital is exhausted, the owners lose only their capital investments. This situation is present for any firm with debt. Consequently, private debt holders' risks are reduced by contractual arrangements (such as collateral and covenants restricting the distribution of dividends and specified investments) and by firms' having sufficiently high levels of equity to absorb most losses. The deposit insurance agencies similarly must impose constraints on banks with insured deposits. The essential issue is, What constraints would do the least damage to the societal advantages of fund intermediation and transfer and the related services that banks can offer the public?

Ostensibly because of concerns about bank solvency, banks now are restricted in the assets in which they may invest and the services they may offer. In particular, their investments in presumably high-risk loans, such as equity participations, junk bonds, and merger and acquisition financing, have been restricted. They generally are not permitted to invest in equities and real estate (other than for banking operations). They also are restricted from offering several banking-related products, particularly securities brokerage and underwriting and insurance sales and underwriting, although these restrictions are more the result of demands by competitors (discussed below) than of realistic expectations of risk reduction.

"Unfair" Wealth Distribution and Bank Operations

In an unconstrained market, consumers can purchase what they please and producers can make and distribute what they believe consumers will purchase. This situation usually is seen as optimal from the viewpoint of social welfare, given the distribution of wealth (human and nonhuman). However, some might consider this situation to be unfair because people are differently endowed and thus might not be able to afford to purchase what they "need." (Although *need* and *fairness* may not be readily defined in concept, or even definable operationally, these concerns should not be ignored.) For example, some basic level of medical treatment and education might be provided to all citizens regardless of their economic wealth. Whether or not this concern is accepted politically, it has little application to capital markets. If anything, the value of capital markets and access to banking services should be proportional to people's economic wealth. Hence, whether or not wealth is "unfairly" distributed, there is little reason for government to interfere in capital markets on this account.

Bankers might treat individuals unfairly if they allow invidious discrimination (bigotry) to interfere with their decisions to make loans and provide other services to consumers and businesses. Such acts might be (and have been) declared illegal for all enterprises, particularly for decisions involving individuals, race, gender, religion, and national origin. There is no reason for such laws to apply especially to financial institutions. Indeed, invidious discrimination is less likely to occur in the provision of financial services, as these rarely involve interpersonally close relationships. In any event, unconstrained competition among providers of financial services should provide the most effective means to reduce, if not entirely eliminate, invidious discrimination.

Anticompetitive Reasons for Constraints on Banks

Perhaps the most important reason (in terms of political effectiveness) for constraining banks' operations is to restrict competition for the benefit of particular people and industries. For example, securities brokers and insurance agents and companies do not want banks to compete for their customers. Real estate agents similarly do not want banks to enter their markets. Small banks tend to favor restrictions on branching to reduce competition from large banks. Domestic banks might want to reduce competition from foreign banks (although this desire tends to be blunted by their concern that the foreign banks might get their governments to reciprocate).

Bankers often complain about regulation, but they value laws that limit their competitors and competition among banks, and that provide subsidies. Hence, many bankers favor restrictions on entry, including prohibitions against other institutions' providing deposit services. They also favor the prohibition of interest on demand deposits and in the past have favored ceilings on time-deposit interest (until market forces made these limits untenable). Some bankers prefer to be regulated and restricted if, in return, they get underpriced deposit insurance. Some bankers also do not protest when all banks are prevented from offering some products (such as securities underwriting and junk bond holdings) if they believe they are not well suited for these activities and, particularly, if they have established profitable networking relationships with other organizations that offer these products.

As a consequence of demands to limit competition, banks are restricted in the following important ways:

- Interstate branching (and, in some states, intrastate branching) is prohibited.
- Banks may not directly offer full-service securities brokerage services and corporate securities underwriting.
- Banks may not own equity securities.
- Banks may not sell or underwrite insurance.
- Banks may not offer real estate brokerage or invest in real estate.

Application of the Concepts to a Bank Credit Crunch

A "bank credit crunch" may be defined operationally as the failure of banks to provide loans to borrowers who, in the absence of the "crunch," would be granted loans. The decline in bank loans made and outstanding, as such, is insufficient to demonstrate the existence of a credit crunch. As described above, entrepreneurs may have lesser demands for loans because the cash flows expected from projects have declined, perhaps because of lower demands by consumers. Or shifts by the public toward present rather than future consumption, or to government rather than private spending, might reduce the demand for business loans.

Increases in banks' production costs would result in a lower supply of bank loans, as banks lose comparative advantage to other suppliers. Other suppliers might use newer technology more effectively than banks. Higher-priced deposit insurance increases the marginal cost to banks of the funds they lend. Higher bank capital requirements also might increase banks' costs.

Banks might shift to other earning assets if these offered higher returns. In particular, government securities might become more profitable as yields increase because of the greater amount the government must float to fund deficits. Alternatively, business loans would offer lower expected net yields if bankers expected default losses and collection costs to be higher.

Finally, extensions of business credit might be reduced as a result of demands by government that banks refrain from lending to businesses and shift their investments to government securities. Similarly, bank supervisors may instruct examiners to criticize business loans more harshly than do bankers.

Thus, bank credit might decline for several reasons that differ public policy implications. I suggest that the following policies would be consistent with the alternative explanations for declines in bank credit discussed above.

1. If bank loans decline because of lesser demands from entrepreneurs or individuals, *no government action should be taken.* Individuals are the best judges of whether projects should be undertaken and how they should be funded or whether present consumption is preferred to future consumption.

2. If banks shift to other earning assets because loans offer lower returns, net of expected losses, *no government action should be taken.* Bankers are the best judges of whether the returns on loans are sufficient compared with alternative available investments. If there is reason to stimulate the economy, such action should be undertaken with open market operations to increase bank reserves. If there are externalities or fairness considerations that justify subsidies, these should be granted directly.

3. If bank loans have declined because alternative suppliers have lower production or distribution costs, *no government action should be taken, except as noted next.*

4. However, banks' costs may be higher because they must pay deposit insurance assessments that exceed the value of the insurance, perhaps because they are charged for past losses that politicians do not want to pass directly to taxpayers. Or banks may have

to pay supervisory and examination costs that exceed the benefits they gain from being viewed by consumers as safely and honestly run institutions, compared with nonregulated firms with which they compete. If these events obtain, *unless the politicians are willing to have banks be displaced by their competitors, the costs should be lowered to a level approximately equal to the user benefit obtained by banks.*

5. If bank loans are restrained by authorities' demands or by overly harsh examinations, the credit crunch should be recognized as the result of government policy, which presumably was undertaken for benefits that government officials believe are sufficient to offset the inefficiency introduced into the economy. *In this event, the government might be changed.*

6. If bank loans have decreased because of higher bank capital requirements, *this policy should not be changed, but* (as is discussed next), *it can be improved.*

Bank Regulatory Policies That Would Avoid Bank Credit Crunches and Other Dysfunctional Situations

As noted above, the major reasons for regulating banks are to protect the deposit insurance fund and to restrict competition by and among banks. Unfortunately, restrictive regulations and laws also constrain banks from serving their customers. These constraints become particularly important when banks have been weakened by losses or fail in markets where there are few alternative suppliers of credit to the banks' usual customers.

All of these problems (assuming that restrictions on competition are not desired) can be solved with "early structured intervention and resolution." George Kaufman and I proposed this system in 1988 (Benston and Kaufman, 1988; see also Benston and Kaufman, 1989). Since then, it has been endorsed and improved by a group of economists (following many days of discussions) (Benston et al., 1989) and by the Shadow Financial Regulatory Committee (1992). A modified version is included in the Federal Deposit Insurance Corporation Improvement Act of 1991 (FDICIA). It is based on the belief that banks can and should be permitted to provide any product or service as long as the banks' owners have sufficient capital investments to absorb almost all of the losses that result.

The Benston-Kaufman Proposal[2]

Bank capital should include equity and all debt that is explicitly not guaranteed by the deposit insurance agency or government and that cannot be redeemed by the bank before the supervisory agencies can act. Subordinated debentures with present maturities of at least one year fit this requirement. If these debentures are publicly traded, the market rates of interest on these obligations can provide bank supervisors with early warning signs of banks' financial difficulties. Alternatively, closely held banks probably would find placing subordinated debentures with investors (such an pension funds, insurance companies, and other banks) preferable to selling stock that might dilute the control of present owners or that could not be sold to investors who would be minority stockholders. Most important, allowing banks to hold subordinated debentures as capital puts them in the same situation as other corporations with respect to their cost of capital. Hence, requiring banks to hold higher levels of capital (defined as being explicitly uninsured) up to the amount that the market would demand in the absence of deposit insurance does not impose higher costs on them, with the exception of reducing or removing a subsidy because of underpriced deposit insurance. In effect, banks would only be required to hold explicitly uninsured debentures in place of insured certificates of deposits. In addition, capital should be measured in terms of economic market values. However, the proposed scheme also can be effective when capital is measured according to traditional accounting values.

Four explicit, predetermined ranges or tranches of capital-to-asset ratios are specified.[3] Assets include off-balance sheet accounts, but assets are not classified according to risk because of the difficulties in measuring *ex ante* risk accurately.

1. Banks are considered to have *adequate capital* if it is, say, 10% or more of their total assets, preferably measured in terms of market or current values. Those falling into this first tranche would be subject to minimum regulation and supervision.
2. Banks with capital-to-asset ratios of, say, 6% to 9.9% are at the *first level of supervisory concern*. A bank in this second tranche is subject to increased regulatory supervision and more frequent monitoring of its activities. It is required to submit a business plan to raise more capital. At its discretion, the supervisory authority could require the bank to suspend dividend payments and obtain approval before transferring funds within a holding company system and could restrict the bank's asset growth.
3. The third tranche is the *second level of supervisory concern*; it is reached when a bank's capital ratio falls below 6% and is at least 3%. Banks in this range are subject to intense regulatory supervision and monitoring. The supervisory authority is required to suspend

dividends, interest payments on subordinated debt, and outflows of funds to the bank's parent or affiliates. The institution must submit an emergency plan for its immediate recapitalization to the tranche one level.

4. Finally, when a bank's capital falls below 3% of its assets, it is in tranche four—*mandatory recapitalization and reorganization.* The supervisory authority must place the bank in a conservatorship, which is charged with recapitalizing the bank or liquidating it in an orderly fashion within a short period by merger or sale of individual assets. The present owners and subordinated debt holders have the option of implementing quickly the plan submitted when the institution moved into tranche three or of electing not to inject additional funds into the bank. If the owners and debt holders elect not to recapitalize the bank, any residual value from its sale or liquidation of its assets is returned to them, after allowing for costs incurred.

The proposed scheme offers several advantages. In particular, market forces are likely to correct a deteriorating situation before the supervisory authority intervenes. The authority can exercise discretion until a bank falls into the third tranche, when it must act. To avoid these actions (particularly mandatory resolution), bankers can and probably would recapitalize, merge, or voluntarily dissolve their banks. Thus, except in abnormal cases of very rapid failure or massive fraud, losses would accrue only to shareholders, not to depositors, other creditors, or the FDIC. Deposit insurance costs would be very small and banks' activities need not be restricted.

In particular, banks would not be prohibited from opening branches at whatever locations (inter- and intrastate) they believe will be profitable. Banks could offer any product or service the public might desire. Should a bank suffer losses, its stockholders and subordinated debenture holders would bear the costs, and the bank would be recapitalized or sold to another, well-capitalized, institution. Denials of credit, then, would be the result entirely of decisions made by bank managers who are restrained only by the relative expected profitability of the loan. A potential borrower who believes that a banker's decision is misplaced can turn to alternative suppliers, whose entry into the bank's market would not have been constrained. Any future "credit crunch," then, would be the consequence of advertent or inadvertent government actions to control bank credit.

Notes

1. The *certainty equivalent* is the sum of the products of possible payoffs times the probability that they will be forthcoming.
2. This description is essentially the same as that given in Benston and Kaufman (1992).
3. The material that follows is taken largely and often verbatim from the Shadow Financial Regulatory Committee (1992).

References

Benston, G. J., Brumbaugh, R. D., Jr., Guttentag, J. M., Herring, R. J., Kaufman, G. G., Litan, R. E., and Scott, K. E. (1989). *Blueprint for Restructuring America's Financial Institutions*. Washington, DC: Brookings Institution.

Benston, G. J., and Kaufman, G. G. (1988). *Risk and Solvency Regulation of Depository Institutions: Past Policies and Current Options*. New York: New York University, Salomon Brothers Center.

Benston, G. J., and Kaufman, G. G. (1989). "Regulating Bank Safety and Performance." In W. S. Haraf and R. M. Kushmeider (Eds.), *Restructuring Banking and Financial Services in America* (pp. 63–99). Washington, DC: American Enterprise Institute for Public Policy Research.

Benston, G. J., and Kaufman, G. G. (1992). "Comment on Deposit Insurance Reform: A Functional Approach." *Carnegie-Rochester Conference Series on Public Policy, 38*.

Burger, A. E. (1969). "A Historical Analysis of the Credit Crunch of 1966." *Federal Reserve Bank of St. Louis Review, 51*, 13–20.

Schreft, S. L. (1990). "Credit Controls: 1980. *Economic Review* (Federal Reserve Bank of Richmond), *76*, 25–55.

Shadow Financial Regulatory Committee. (1992). "An Outline of a Program for Deposit Insurance and Regulatory Reform" (Statement 41; February 13, 1989). *Journal of Financial Services Research, 6* (supplement), S78–S82.

Swary, I., and Aharony, J. (1983). "Contagion Effects of Bank Failures: Evidence from Capital Markets." *Journal of Business, 56*, 305–322.

Wall, L. D., and Peterson, D. R. (1990). "The Effect of Continental Illinois on the Financial Performance of Other Banks." *Journal of Monetary Economics, 26*, 77–99.

Comment

Paul H. Rubin

Glenn Yago's chapter is one of the more depressing pieces I have read in some time. As a student of health and safety regulation and of antitrust, I realized that regulation in these areas was increasing. However, while I was aware that there was some increase in financial regulation as well, I did not understand the magnitude of this increase. In order merely to *list* the increases in financial regulation since 1985, Professor Yago needs a lengthy table; he identifies 29 "measures inducing rigidity in capital structures and markets."

Moreover, as depressing as this list is, it is not complete. Professor Yago lists explicit regulatory changes, but regulation can increase even if the laws on the books do not become any more restrictive as long as people who want to regulate are put in place in regulatory agencies. While President Reagan did deregulate the economy, he did so largely by appointing less enthusiastic regulators, not by changing laws. President Bush appointed more zealous regulators to the antitrust agencies (the FTC and the Antitrust Division of the Department of Justice), and they have increased regulation. One effect of this sort of regulation is to make mergers more difficult, again reducing the flexibility of capital markets. Bittlingmayer (in press) has shown that increased antitrust activity is associated with reduced economic activity; thus the tendencies addressed by Professor Yago have been exacerbated by Bush appointees. The SEC also became more regulatory in the Bush years, as did many other agencies.

Although I have no deep quarrel with Yago's arguments, there are one or two issues I would like to address. First, Yago indicates that the goal of Americans to own their own businesses is culturally determined. This may be, but it is more likely (and more satisfying, particularly now that Gary Becker has won his Nobel) that this goal can be explained in terms of economic criteria. There are well-known benefits to ownership, including reductions in agency costs of all sorts, that can explain this behavior without introducing cultural factors (for discussion, see Rubin, 1990).

My only other criticism is that some of Yago's analysis may be interpreted as advocating more regulation. He argues in his section on policy that there are "glaring" omissions in SEC-mandated data regarding employment. I hope that he is not advocating that the SEC begin to mandate these additional data. Although it would be nice to have them, I do not believe that economists should impose costs on businesses in order to obtain desired data. After all, as Hayek long ago told us, an economy can function quite well when there is little public information available. Indeed, I sometimes think that the economy (but not economists) would be better off with less information.

Ben Zycher identifies yet another capital restriction. In his chapter, he argues that the recent requirements of increased capital holding and risk-based capital standards for banks have caused the existing "credit crunch" and have had a disproportionally detrimental effect on small business. However, it is possible that almost everything claimed by Zycher is true and that nonetheless there is no major inefficiency caused by the regulations. This is not to defend regulation; numerous problems in banking and in the economy are caused by regulation. But the problems in banking may be caused by different regulations, as discussed by Yago: deposit insurance, excessive regulation of bank behavior, and excessive regulation of the market for high-yield bonds.

The first issue to address is whether or not a credit crunch exists at all. Zycher cites as primary evidence statements made by various politicians, including President Bush and Commerce Secretary Mosbacher. However, the statements of politicians provide weak evidence of anything, including even politicians' own intentions. In particular, politicians are always happy to blame adverse economic conditions on others (banks, the Federal Reserve) rather than on their own misguided policies.

Others (including Yago) have also found evidence of some sort of credit crunch (see, e.g., Benston, 1992; Bernanke and Lown, 1991). But Bernanke and Lown (1991) assert that, although there may be a credit crunch, it is not a major factor in our current economy. They find, for example, that in New England (where the credit crunch may be most significant because of real estate failures), reductions in bank capital explain only 2–3% of the decline in lending. Indeed, Bernanke and Lown conclude that "the credit crunch has not been a major cause of the recession." Thus, it appears that the credit crunch exists, but is of relatively small magnitude. Yago argues that the regulations he has identified have reduced credit, but provides no formal definition of a credit crunch.

The capital standards and leverage ratio requirements criticized by Zycher are an attempt to require that stockholders of banks have some capital at risk. Given the moral hazard problems associated with deposit insurance, which Zycher recognizes, banks have an incentive to acquire excessively risky portfolios. That this theoretical possibility can become real is demonstrated by the savings and loan fiasco.

It is in this context that we must view the requirements discussed by Zycher. Indeed, he demonstrates the effects of this requirement in his discussion of the acquisition of new capital by banks. Zycher argues that banks do not want to acquire new capital because capital is not subsidized through the deposit insurance system. That is, existing equity is subsidized because banks can make excess (relative to expected values, properly discounted for risk) loans and the deposit insurance system bears the risk. Therefore, he argues, banks will not acquire additional equity capital, but rather will reduce their loan portfolios in order to reduce capital requirements. However, this is exactly the purpose of capital requirements; they are designed to provide incentives for banks to eliminate loans acquired only because of the moral hazard engendered through limited liability. It is therefore inappropriate to argue that this policy of necessity creates an inefficiency in the system.

The policy may create an inefficiency. As Zycher correctly argues, the risk weights for differing types of capital are arbitrary and may be incorrect for any one bank (or even for all banks). Moreover, the requirements may induce some banks to cancel or refuse desirable loans; a regulatory system will not respond optimally. Nonetheless, some regulation may be a second-best response to the problems created by the deposit insurance system. We all know the difficulty of performing proper second-best analysis, but without such analysis we cannot be sure that the regulations are inefficient.

As Benston argues in his comment on Yago's and Zycher's chapters, however, the risk-based capital standards are only a small part of the problem with bank regulation. He suggests that more efficient reforms would include limiting the FDIC guarantee to only a fraction of a bank's demand deposits; elimination of restrictions on intrastate and interstate branching, which have exacerbated the credit crunch by not allowing banks from one region to make efficient numbers of loans in other regions that may be more subject to the credit crunch; and modification or elimination of the Glass-Steagall and Bank Holding Company Acts, which limit the ability of banks to offer the optimal mix of services (including provision of equity) to their customers.

In addition, problems of small business are exacerbated by excess regulation in the high-yield bond market. Although this source of capital may not be available to the smallest businesses, some middle-sized firms that suffer from the credit crunch in banks might have benefited from this market if it were allowed to function without excess control.

I am in agreement with the major point of both Yago's and Zycher's chapters. The current economic downturn has been exacerbated, if not caused, by excessive regulation from Washington. This regulation has taken the form of the appointment of administrators with excessive regulatory zeal to existing agencies, such as the Justice Department, FTC, FDA, SEC, and EPA, and also the passage of additional regulatory statutes. Moreover, I have not even mentioned the problems associated with the U.S. legal system, the "torts crisis."

I propose a hypothesis for testing: the U.S. economy cannot now function at a high level with the existing regulatory structure if these laws are vigorously enforced.

As to enforcement: under Bush, antitrust agencies were much more active than under Reagan. Increased regulatory activity by other major agencies such as the EPA and the regulations discussed by Yago also imposed huge costs on the economy.

There have also been new regulatory initiatives, in addition to the financial regulations discussed by Yago. I believe that the Disabilities Act will have a major negative impact on the economy, and may already have begun to do so. After all, the other civil rights acts may induce firms to hire employees with low marginal products, but under the Disabilities Act any given employee may have a large *negative* marginal product, and the firm cannot know this until after the hiring decision has been made. Because firms are limited in their ability to determine before hiring the qualifications of any employee, they may be forced to spend large sums on such things as special equipment after hiring to enable some employees to function.

People who worry about competitiveness and industrial policy have discussed the government's picking "winners" and subsidizing them. But consider three industries in which it is generally agreed that the United States is world class: pharmaceuticals, software, and entertainment. What have we done with those industries? David Kessler, the commissioner of the FDA, has viciously attacked the pharmaceutical industry. The FTC is investigating Microsoft, the world's leading software firm, for purported antitrust violations. Congress has just passed a law regulating the cable television industry. I suggest that the way to determine which industries are "winners" is to look at those industries in which the rate of increase of regulation is greatest. In such a world, is it surprising that the current recovery is weak and delayed, whether or not there is a "credit crunch"?

References

Benston, G. J. (1992). "Is There a Credit Crunch? And What Should We Do About It?" *Journal of Applied Corporate Finance, 4,* 86–91.

Bernanke, B. S., and Lown, C. S. (1991). "The Credit Crunch." *Brookings Papers on Economic Activity, 2,* 205–247.

Bittlingmayer, G. (in press). "Antitrust and the Economy: The First 25 Years," in C. England (Ed.), *A Century of Antitrust.* Atlanta, GA: Cato Institute.

Rubin, P. H. (1990). *Managing Business Transactions.* New York: Free Press.

PART THREE

Monetary and Fiscal Policy

Introduction

The literature on monetary policy is vast and expanding rapidly, a growth pattern influenced heavily by modern realizations that the growth in nominal income is influenced heavily by the rate of monetary growth, that this nominal income growth is the prime influence determining the inflation rate, and that shifts in the monetary growth rate can have important implications for short-run changes in the growth of real income. For an economy in which the power of money creation is held in substantial part by government, those variables therefore clearly are subject to the factors and incentives driving government behavior, in this case, the growth rate of the money supply.

Given that government can within broad limits influence those important economic variables, what are the considerations that should drive sound monetary policy? Or, alternatively, ought such considerations even be addressed? That is, should monetary policy be changed in light of shifting economic conditions or should monetary policy be fixed, and thus predictable from the viewpoint of the private sector?

Discretion versus fixed rules—that is the question. Allan H. Meltzer summarizes the literature on optimal monetary growth, and then points out that changes in monetary policy always have engendered shifts in economic activity only after a time lag. That means that discretionary policy necessarily must be based upon economic forecasting, an activity undertaken by economists that always has been afflicted with very great difficulty. This difficulty inherent in economic forecasting means necessarily that discretionary monetary policy must be based upon forecasts that invariably turn out to be wrong, often by substantial margins. Meltzer argues that economic forecasts on average prove so inaccurate that discretionary policy based upon forecasts is unlikely to minimize variability in economic outcomes. Or, as Meltzer puts it, "Policymakers who adjust policy based on the forecast for the following year have little reason to be confident that they have changed policy in the right direction" (p. 172). Meltzer goes on to endorse a fixed monetary growth rule defined in terms of the monetary base.

Robert H. Rasche examines the recent divergence in the measured growth rates of different monetary aggregates; in particular, the difference between the growth rates of M1 and M2 seems to be unprecedented in the postwar period. Several economists and policymakers have interpreted this pattern as a reflection of the need for a discretionary monetary policy, not only in terms of the target growth rates, but also in terms of the choice among the monetary aggregates and/or various interest rates to be used for targeting. Thus can policy adapt as the behavior of the monetary aggregates shifts in unexpected ways.

Rasche argues that appearances are deceiving: the recent behavior of both M1 and M2 is consistent with historical patterns, and can be explained in the context of shifts in other economic variables. In particular, he shows that the growth patterns of M1 and M2 (that is, of M1 and M2 velocity) are consistent with historical shifts attendant upon changes in the level and term structure of interest rates. This suggests that discretionary monetary policy could under similar conditions prove mischievous, in that shifts in economic variables, subtle but wholly consistent with historical experience, might induce policymakers to assume substantial change in the economic environment when in reality none has taken place.

The general discussion during the session in which Meltzer's and Rasche's papers were presented began with a consideration of whether discretionary shifts in monetary policy can or ought to be used to offset the effects of such economic shocks as sudden increases in the price of oil. As economic shocks affect such real variables as relative prices and aggregate wealth, whereas monetary policy can affect only the nominal quantity of money, something of a consensus emerged that discretionary shifts in monetary policy cannot offset economic shocks and therefore ought not be used under such conditions.

Another point made in the general discussion concerned the "instability" in prices and employment attendant upon monetary instability—that is, discretion—along with ensuing political responses harmful to economic growth. Although this view shunts aside the issue of "rational expectations" of Fed behavior on the part of the market, there was some agreement about the adverse effects of such political responses as price controls, financial market regulations, and the like. On the whole, little support for discretionary monetary policy was voiced.

5

Monetary Policy:
Some Theory and Evidence

Allan H. Meltzer

Few topics have a larger or more rapidly growing literature than monetary policy. The literature has wide diversity, ranging from highly abstract analyses of optimal money growth to the commentary ground out daily or weekly by central bank watchers in many countries.[1] In between are such issues as the choice of rules over discretion, the strategies and tactics of monetary action, the advantages of activism, and, recently, the positive analysis of policymakers' decisions.

It is daunting to attempt a full summary and assessment of even the most actively researched topics of the recent past. The assessment is made more difficult by the many conflicts found in this literature and by the absence of empirical work that resolves the conflicts. This absence reflects several problems, of which the most important is the sensitivity of empirical results to the choice of sample period or specification.

From the menu of choices, I have selected two topics. The sponsors of the conference are concerned with growth, so I discuss, first, what has been learned about the relation of money to economic growth. Then I consider and attempt to evaluate the costs or benefits of relying on forecasts when choosing monetary (or other) aggregate policy actions.

Money and Economic Growth

From the earliest systematic writings on monetary theory, writers have observed a relation between money and the price level. Two features of this early literature are (1) the relation was observed and noted independently in many different places and times, and (2) a common observation was of an inverse relation between the stock called money and the value of a unit of that stock. Often, these or later observers asserted the relation that later was known as[2] neutrality: an increase in money has no effect on the real value of the stock of money or other real values.

Neutrality remains a central proposition for all monetary theory. Differences remain about the importance of departures from neutrality and the speed of return, but departures from neutrality are attributed to misperception, costs of acquiring information, costs of changing prices or responding to such changes, and other impediments to immediate response. The neutrality of money is accepted as an implication of rational behavior.

When one turns from the static theory of money and output to the steady-state relation between inflation and production or output, issues about temporary nonneutrality drop away. At issue is whether a fully anticipated rate of inflation can affect real economic activity. If individuals choose to hold money to satisfy desires for liquidity or safety, their higher demand for money raises the real rate of interest. To the individual, the higher interest rate is the return he or she forgoes to get more safety or liquidity. But society can provide the additional liquidity at zero (low) cost by producing money at a rate that satiates the demand for money. This rate of money growth is optimal for society.

In principle, government can increase economic welfare by providing the optimal rate of monetary expansion and inflation. My 1969 survey of the literature establishing this proposition showed that the size and even direction of the effect of inflation on economic activity were not robust to the assumptions made (Meltzer, 1969). Of particular importance to the conclusion is the nature of the production function, the types of services provided by money, the extent to which the services of money substitute for other forms of consumption (and therefore alter the saving rate), or, if money is treated as a productive asset, the relative size of the effect of money growth on the ratio of money to capital and of capital to labor.

Recent surveys by McCallum (1990), Orphanides and Solow (1990), and Woodford (1990) discuss different parts of this literature. A common conclusion is that the direction of any effect of inflation or money growth on output is ambiguous. McCallum (1990, p. 973) suggests that any effect may be quantitatively unimportant, but Orphanides and Solow (1990) argue that it is difficult to move directly from this literature to actual economies until there is better understanding of the reasons people hold and use money.

If the services of money include saving of transaction and information costs, "money" serves as a substitute for time used to gather information and transact. The "money" that provides these services is not just pieces of colored paper or claims at financial institutions. The meaning of *money* here should include the set of institutions that permit the public to develop optimal payment schedules—schedules that minimize the costs of carrying out current and intertemporal transactions. The choice of a wealth-maximizing rate of inflation requires analysis of how this institutional structure evolves under different known and fully anticipated rates of inflation.

Missing also from the literature is the distinction between a world economy with one source of paper money and a number of independent countries with independent monetary authorities in several countries. If the optimal rate of inflation is positive, as might occur with distortionary taxation, individuals can avoid the tax on cash balances by using less inflationary foreign money.[3]

In principle, empirical work relating inflation to growth could capture relevant features missing from the models of optimal inflation. Unfortunately, there has been little effort to resolve the ambiguity about sign and magnitude of the optimal rate of inflation and money growth. Friedman (1969) assumes values for the relevant parameters and conjectures that the rate may be between –5% and –17% per annum, but he does not use his estimates when he makes his policy recommendation for money growth.

In earlier work, I estimated the relation between average growth rates and average inflation rates for the years 1965–88 (Meltzer, 1992). The sample consists of data for 100 countries from the *World Bank Development Report* and for three subsets of countries at different levels of income. These are shown in Table 5.1.

TABLE 5.1
Dependent Variable: Per Capita Real GDP Growth, 1965-88

	Constant	Average Rate of Inflation	Adjusted R^2
100 countries	2.00 (7.38)	–0.02 (1.94)	0.03
30 low income	1.69 (2.84)	–0.08 (2.32)	0.13
32 middle income	2.34 (5.36)	–0.02 (1.63)	0.05
38 upper-middle and high income	2.63 (6.07)	–0.02 (1.08)	0.004

Note: t statistics are shown in parentheses.

For the group as a whole, and for each of the subsets, the simple relation between growth and inflation is negative. Inflation lowers growth and deflation raises it, as Friedman's (1969) analysis implies. The effect is not negligible; a 10% rate of deflation would raise the average growth rate by 0.2 percentage points or 10% of the mean growth rate shown if we interpret the intercept as showing the average growth of per capita income resulting from factors other than inflation.

These estimates have both strengths and weaknesses. Judged by goodness of fit, the inflation rate explains little. This is not surprising; differences in the quantity and quality of human and physical capital are far more important sources of differences in growth. Perhaps a more relevant problem is the treatment of the average rate as the relevant rate for inflation and growth. This ignores the variability of inflation rates. Variability may be related to the average rate, so the coefficient may be biased. An advantage of rates of growth and inflation averaged over more than 20 years, however, is that one-time changes from oil shocks, controls and decontrol, changes in sales or value-added taxes, and so on have less influence.

A disadvantage is that, strictly speaking, the relation we want to observe is between the long-run level of output and the rate of inflation, since optimal monetary policy would lower the real rate of interest once and for all. For this interpretation, the growth rates of output in the regressions should be interpreted as the rates computed over an interval rather than as steady-state rates that would be maintained forever. This does not tell us the optimal rate of inflation, however. The reason is that the linear relations in Table 5.1 imply that there are large (possibly infinite) gains if only the deflation rate is sufficiently high. To correct for this problem, I estimated the relations among average per capita economic growth, average inflation, and the squared value of average inflation for the same sample of 100 countries and the three subgroups. In three of the four cases, including the full sample, the coefficient of the linear term is negative and the coefficient of the quadratic term is positive. This implies, as in the linear relation, that growth is maximized at an extreme point. Low rates of inflation minimize economic growth. This result is surely wrong.

Results from theory and data analyses about the optimal rate of inflation or rate of money growth are inconclusive. It is not clear whether there is a unique, optimal monetary policy in the sense used in this literature. Given the many strong assumptions used to develop the theory— such as a representative consumer, a single world money (or common optimal inflation rate in all countries), a government that seeks to maximize individual welfare, a constant returns to scale production function with neutral technological change, to name only a few—the choice of monetary policy must continue to rest on considerations other than those stressed in the literature on optimal policy.

Rules or Discretion: Some Evidence from Forecasts

In practice, countries neither seek nor choose an optimal or even constant rate of money growth. Brunner and Meltzer (1964), Lombra and Moran (1983), and Hetzel (1986) describe central aspects of policymaking in the United States at different times. They report no evidence of a fixed set of objectives. Objectives shift about. Greatest weight may be given to disinflation at one time, unemployment at another, and financial markets or exchange rates at other times. Cukierman and Meltzer (1986) analyze the shifting weights on objectives as changing randomly in response to changing concerns about the business cycle and inflation. These random shifts represent the nonsystematic (or discretionary) behavior of the authorities.

In practice, the Federal Reserve's decisions to shift the weights on different objectives are based on forecasts of future values of unemployment, inflation, and the pace of economic activity. Forecasts are made by different methods, including both judgment and more systematic procedures. A central tenet of those who favor reliance on discretion is that the use of current information and forecasts when making decisions to change interest rates and money growth improves welfare.

If policy actions affect the economy with a lag, as much evidence suggests, discretionary actions must be based on forecasts. The case for replacing discretionary action with feedback rules that do not depend on forecasts is based on evidence that forecasts are so inaccurate relative to the average rate of change that they provide a poor foundation for discretionary policy decisions and actions or for rules based on forecast values.[4]

The thesis I present is that forecasts of main economic aggregates are so inaccurate on average that discretionary policies based on forecasts are unlikely to minimize variability. The thesis does not depend on any particular method of forecasting. It applies to all methods of forecasting that have been studied, including some based on judgment and some that are entirely mechanical. Nor does it depend on the choice of a particular time period. It appears to be true of all the recent time periods for which forecasts have been compared. Nor is it intended as a criticism of economists' forecasts. Their forecasts, though wide of the target, may be the best available.

The record of more than 20 years of economic forecasting in the United States is summarized by the finding that, on average, the most accurate forecasters cannot predict reliably at the beginning of the quarter whether the economy will be in a boom or a recession during that quarter. Although forecasting improves as the quarter passes and additional information becomes available, the statement remains true; after more than half of the current quarter has passed, forecasters cannot distinguish reliably between an above-average expansion and a recession.

For several major countries, forecasts of annual values are available, in many cases for nearly 20 years. These data support a similar conclusion.[5] Policymakers who adjust policy based on the forecast for the following year have little reason to be confident that they have changed policy in the right direction. Forecast errors are so large relative to the mean rate of change that forecasts cannot distinguish slow growth or recession from a boom. Similar conclusions hold for forecasts of inflation; forecast errors are so large relative to changes in the rate of inflation that reliance on forecasts will often mislead policymakers about the rate of inflation.

The size of average forecast errors poses a major problem for those who base discretionary policy on forecasts or propose rules that rely on forecasts. A study of forecast errors using different, and possibly changing, techniques suggests that the problem is likely to remain. No single method or model seems to be superior to others. Indeed, we should not expect one method to dominate the others completely or significant differences in forecast accuracy to persist. Economists would have difficulty explaining the survival of inferior models or methods in a competitive market for valuable information about the future.

One plausible explanation of the size of forecast errors is that, for the best forecasts, the average errors reflect mainly unpredictable, random shocks that hit the economy. The shocks may result from real events—changes in productivity, weather, and the like—or from unanticipated or misperceived policy actions. Each model or method may weight the responses to a particular surprise or change in a particular time period differently, but the resulting differences—while important for explaining differences in forecasts for a particular quarter—appear to have little effect on measures of forecast accuracy.

A main objective of economic stabilization policy should be to reduce the uncertainty faced by consumers and producers to the minimum inherent in nature and trading arrangements. As always, there are two types of errors. Policy can be so active that uncertainty is increased. This can occur if policy actions are so unpredictable that observation of past behavior misleads the public or provides little information to guide current decisions. As Friedman (1951) has noted, activist policies can increase uncertainty and variability also, if policymakers act on misjudgments—for example, if they mistake transitory for permanent changes, misinterpret nominal shocks as real shocks, or base decisions on unreliable forecasts. On the other hand, policymakers can be too passive, as they were in the U.S. monetary collapse of the 1930s or in Europe and Japan when they maintained the Bretton Woods arrangement long after it had become clear that fixed exchange rates transmitted U.S. inflation to the rest of the world.

A standard conclusion in the literature on decision making is that actions should be based on all available information. Applications of this proposition to economic policy use the argument to show that a policymaker who maximizes social welfare will follow a contingent rule. The rule replicates the actions that would be chosen by a policymaker with complete discretion who acts to maximize social welfare. Assume that the policymaker seeks to stabilize the economy and reduce uncertainty. To say that the policymaker should not neglect current information is not the same as saying that he or she should rely on predictions or forecasts. Inaccurate forecasts can cause well-intentioned policymakers to increase variability and uncertainty, to destabilize rather than stabilize.

The United States

For the United States, there are a large number of public and private forecasts of quarterly and annual data. I have chosen data mainly on forecasts of real GNP and inflation, because comparative data are available for many countries, and these measures are prominent among the measures of social welfare.[6] Table 5.2 shows the size of quarterly forecast errors for various periods. Sources do not measure the error in the same way, so I have used root mean square error (RMSE) or mean absolute error (MAE) when RMSE is not available. RMSE magnifies the effect of large errors, such as those made in many countries at the time of the first oil shock. My impression is that the two measures rarely give conflicting interpretations, although numerical values differ.

To judge the forecast errors, it is useful to compare average growth rates for the period. The mean growth rate of real GNP is 2.7% for 1970–85 and 2.4% for 1980–85. The rate of inflation (deflator) is 6.7% for 1970–85 and 5.4% for 1980–85. Nominal GNP growth is 9.5% for 1967–82, 9.8% for 1973–82, and 9.9% for 1970–83.

Root mean square errors are a large fraction of the reported growth rates of nominal and real GNP. Using twice the median value of the RMSE, the range within which real growth can fall during the current quarter, covers the range from deep recession to a strong boom. For example, the median error for the four forecasters considered by Zarnowitz (1986), 3%, exceeds the average growth rate of real GNP, 2.4%, for the period. On average, forecasters have not been able to distinguish between booms and recessions beginning in the same quarter.

One standard error covers the range –0.6% to 5.4% and two standard errors cover the range of real growth rates –3.6% to 8.4%. For nominal GNP growth, errors reported by Zarnowitz are smaller relative to nominal GNP growth for the period (9.8%). Still, the errors are large relative to the information required for stabilizing policy; two times the standard deviation covers the range 2.2% to 17.4%.

These data give no support for the idea that discretionary policy based on forecasts is likely to increase stability. The data make clear that the same conclusion follows for all quarterly forecasts considered, even if the lowest available value of the RMSE is used in place of the median, and for each of the periods considered. Large errors associated with the oil shocks may have increased forecast errors at the time, but cannot explain the persistent pattern. The note to Table 5.2 reports the RMSE for forecasts made late in the quarter—for the current quarter—after one or two official estimates of monthly data on prices, industrial production, money, sales, jobless claims, employment, and other data have been released. Forecast accuracy improves, but it remains true that the RMSE is a large fraction of the average growth rate of the period.

The errors for quarterly forecasts come from different models and methods that cover the range of techniques in common use. McNees (1986) compares judgmental forecasts compiled by the American Statistical Association and the National Bureau of Economic Research, large-scale econometric model forecasts sold commercially, forecasts

TABLE 5.2
Quarterly Root Mean Square Forecast Errors, United States (annual percent)

Variable	Time Period	Range	Median or Actual	Source
Real GNP growth	1980:2–1985:1	3.1–4.4	3.8	McNees (1986)[a]
	1970–73		2.1	Lombra and Moran (1983)
	1970:4–1983:4	2.8–3.6	3.0	Zarnowitz (1986)
	1970:1–1984:4	4.4–5.4	4.7	Webb (1985)
Inflation	1980:2–1985:1	1.4–2.2	1.6	McNees (1986)[a]
	1970:4–1983:4	2.0–2.6	2.2	Zarnowitz (1986)
	1970:1–1984:4	1.8–2.1	1.9	Webb (1985)
Nominal GNP growth	1967–82		5.5	Federal Reserve[b]
	1973–82		6.2	
	1970:4			
	1983:4	3.5–4.3	3.8	Zarnowitz (1986)

[a] Twelve forecasts early in the quarter. Median values for three late quarter forecasts: real GNP, 2.4; inflation, 1.4.
[b] From Federal Reserve "green" books, various issues.

issued by banks, the federal government's Bureau of Economic Analysis, economic consulting firms, university research groups, and the Bayesian vector autoregression model developed by Robert Litterman. Webb (1985) compares seven mechanical forecasting procedures that use the autoregressive properties of economic time series to forecast interest rates, real GNP growth, and inflation.

At times, policymakers and their staffs have access to information that is not available to others. They have earlier access to some data of particular importance. For example, they know more about current policy than the public. Can they use this advantage to forecast more accurately than outsiders?

Lombra and Moran (1983), using mean absolute error of forecast, compare quarterly forecasts by the staff of the Board of Governors for 1970–73 with an earlier study of forecast accuracy by McNees covering six private forecasts. They note a small advantage in favor of the Board, 0.1% for real growth and 0.2% for inflation in quarterly forecasts for the current quarter. The advantage disappears for forecasts made four quarters ahead. Lombra and Moran also report root mean square errors for the Federal Reserve staff forecasts for the same period. The RMSE is shown in Table 5.2. For real growth, the reported error is the lowest value in the table. However, superior performance is not repeated in the nominal GNP growth forecasts available for a longer period. These are shown in the lower part of Table 5.2, where Federal Reserve forecast errors are substantially larger than errors by other forecasters for a comparable period.

The Federal Reserve staff forecasts of nominal GNP growth for 1973–82 appear to be biased. The mean absolute error for the current quarter is 5.4%, very similar to the mean error.[7] A plausible reason is that the Federal Reserve staff consistently underestimated inflation during the 1970s. This systematic error may have been the result of unwillingness to recognize internally the inflationary consequences of past policies, or the use of adaptive models that adjust slowly to the new information, or evidence of a Keynesian model structure that minimizes or denies the effect of money growth on inflation. Whatever the reason for the bias, the presence of persistent bias over a relatively long period, combined with lower accuracy than private forecasters, gives little support to arguments for discretionary policy actions intended to stabilize growth of output and the price level.

Recently, several economists have proposed using targets for expected nominal GNP growth to guide monetary policy, (e.g., Gordon, 1983; Tobin, 1983). The claimed benefit of a rule for expected nominal GNP growth is that policy offsets changes in velocity growth; money should grow faster in periods when expected velocity growth is low and vice versa. In this way, monetary policy stabilizes the growth of aggregate demand.

The nominal GNP growth forecasts in Table 5.2 cast doubt on the stabilizing properties of expected nominal GNP growth targets if the targets are forecast values. The Federal Reserve's forecast error for nominal GNP growth in the current quarter is as much as 60% of the average rate of change. The smallest RMSE for private forecasts is 3.5%, more than one-third of the average growth rate for 1970–83. These data give little reason for confidence in the stabilizing properties of this type of rule.

Quarterly data may reflect seasonal changes or transitory variations that distort the accuracy of current forecasting techniques. Also, quarterly data are not readily available for many countries, but annual data are. Table 5.3 shows annual data for the United States. Several of the annual forecasts are from the same source as the quarterly forecasts, so we can observe whether the size of errors differs for quarterly and annual forecasts. No uniform pattern emerges from the comparisons available.

One notable feature of the inflation forecasts is the comparatively large errors made by the Federal Reserve for 1970–73 and by the OECD for 1973–85. I noted earlier that the Federal Reserve persistently underestimated inflation during the period of rising inflation. Artis (1987, p. 46) shows that the OECD forecasts also underestimated inflation when the inflation rate rose in the 1970s and overestimated inflation when the inflation rate fell in the 1980s.

TABLE 5.3
Annual[a] Root Mean Square Forecast Errors, United States (annual percent)

Variable	Time Period	Range	Median or Actual	Source
Real GNP growth	1980:2–1985:1	2.2–3.4	2.7	McNees (1986)[b]
	1970–73		3.5	Lombra and Moran (1983)
	1970:1–1984:4	2.0–3.2	3.0	Webb (1985)
	1973–1985		2.0	IMF, Artis (1987)
	1973–1985		1.7	OECD, Artis (1987)
Inflation	1980:2–1985:1	2.2–3.4	2.7	McNees (1986)[b]
	1970–1973		3.5	Lombra and Moran (1983)
	1970:1–1984:4	1.9–3.1	1.9	Webb (1985)
	1973–1985		1.7	IMF, Artis (1987)
	1973–1985		4.6	OECD, Artis (1987)

[a] Four-quarter-ahead forecasts are included with annual forecasts.
[b] Twelve forecasts early in the quarter.

The RMSE in both cases is a relatively large fraction of the average rate of inflation. For 1970–73, the deflator rose at a compound annual rate of 5.7%, so the Federal Reserve RMSE is more than 60% of the average. For 1973–85, the average rate of inflation is 7.0%, and the RMSE is 66% of average inflation. Using two standard deviations as a measure of accuracy, the data suggest that neither the Federal Reserve nor the OECD could distinguish accurately between stable prices and double-digit inflation a year in advance.[8]

Wolf (1987) compares the forecasting records of 15 private and public forecasters of the U.S. economy for the years 1983–86. The average forecast error for real GNP growth for the 15 forecasts in each of the four years has a mean of 28%. Mean errors range from 19% (1984) to 44% (1983). For inflation, as measured by the CPI, the overall mean is higher and the range is wider. The mean error for the four years is 44% of the rate of inflation, and the mean errors range from 13% (1985) to 99% (1986). The year 1986 includes a large one-time change in the price level that temporarily reduced the measured rate of change, so the 99% error may be extreme. One-time shocks occur frequently, however. Discretionary policy or rules that depend on forecasts are subject to errors of this kind. Moreover, Wolf's data, like Artis's, show large errors in predicting the rate of inflation when the rate changes. For 1983, Wolf reports an average error of 50%.

Wolf computed a measure of overall forecast accuracy for each forecaster in each year and ranked forecasters by the accuracy of their forecasts of four variables. His measure assumes that users (and society) weight errors in each variable equally, so his results may change if forecast accuracy for unemployment and real growth are given different weights than inflation or Treasury bill rates. Using his rankings, he cannot reject the hypothesis that the ranking for each forecaster in each year is independent.

The low correlation that Wolf finds between ranks suggest that differences in the quality of forecasts may arise by chance. This inference receives support from the data in Tables 5.2 and 5.3. These show that there is some suggestion of a lower bound, in the neighborhood of 1.5%, for the RMSEs shown for inflation and real growth in the United States. Further, several different forecast methods produce similar results. Similarity would arise if forecasters were to remove most of the systematic information in past data.

Remaining errors may not be entirely random. The managers of the various models often adjust their forecasts to reflect available information or perceptions. These adjustments do not appear to have much value on average; they do not reduce measured mean square errors for real GNP relative to the autoregressive models included in the data presented in

Tables 5.2 and 5.3. Possibly the adjustments affect errors in particular periods without changing the root mean square error or other measures of forecast accuracy.

Evidence showing negative correlation between the forecast errors obtained using different procedures would suggest that forecast errors can be reduced by combining either procedures or forecasts. Evidence of positive correlation is consistent with the hypothesis that the errors remaining in the most accurate forecasts are mainly random deviations that are missed by different models. Although I have not found a systematic study, some work suggests that forecast errors for IMF, OECD, and private forecasters are positively correlated. For real GNP growth and inflation forecasts in six countries, Artis (1987, pp. 51–52) finds most correlations between errors above 0.8 and many above 0.9.

Litterman (1985) has published an analysis of the source of his forecast error and some evidence on the relation of errors to policy actions. He computes the effect of unanticipated policy changes in 1985 on his forecast for 1986 by comparing the model forecasts for 1986 made late in 1984 with the forecasts made approximately one year later. Since Litterman's autoregressive forecasting model adjusts only to past errors, changes in forecast values occur only when there are unanticipated changes— changes that were unanticipated from the history of the series and related series at the time of the previous forecast. If there were no unanticipated changes in 1985, the forecast for 1986 would remain the same.

After adjusting for the relatively small changes in forecast values arising from the major revision of published historical time series, Litterman (1985, Table 5) shows that most of the new information in 1985 was information about unanticipated monetary policy actions. Specifically, he reports that 80% of the change in his forecast of real growth and 50% of the change in the forecast of inflation were the consequences of differences between expected and actual monetary actions in 1985. These estimates suggest that monetary policy actions account for a large part of the uncertainty and variability experienced during the sample period. Holding monetary policy constant, or otherwise making policy more predictable, would reduce this source of variability.[9]

Europe and Japan

As differences in policy rules and in the extent of discretionary action can affect the size of forecast errors, I now consider annual forecast errors for other developed countries. The results are broadly comparable to the findings for the United States, so I limit the comparison to forecasts of real output growth.[10] Comparisons are facilitated by the availability of data on OECD and IMF forecasts for several countries and for the same time periods. These are shown in Table 5.4.

TABLE 5.4
Annual Forecast Errors, Europe and Japan
(RMSE annual percent) Real Output Growth

Country	Time Period	Actual Growth [a]	Mean Absolute Actual	RMSE	Source
Germany	1969–86	2.4		1.9	Council of Economic Experts
	1978–86	1.8		0.7	Council of Economic Experts
	1973–85	1.8	2.7	2.2	IMF, Artis (1987)
	1973–85	1.8		1.1	OECD, Artis (1987)
The Netherlands	1953–85	3.6		3.2	Central Economic Plan
	1975–85	1.6		2.0	Central Economic Plan
Japan	1973–85	4.3	4.7	3.2	IMF, Artis (1987)
	1973–85	4.3		2.8	OECD, Artis (1987)
France	1973–85	2.1	2.5	1.1	IMF
	1973–85	2.1		1.5	OECD
Italy	1973–85	2.0	3.0	2.5	IMF
	1973–85	2.0		2.5	OECD
United Kingdom	1973–85	1.3	2.4	1.8	IMF
	1973–85	1.3		1.6	OECD

[a] From Federal Reserve Bank of St. Louis (1987).

The IMF and OECD forecasts have very similar RMSEs for four of the six countries, and substantial differences between countries. Forecast errors by the IMF and OECD are lowest for France, both absolutely and relative to the reported growth rate.[11] Forecast errors are highest for Japan, but the growth rate is highest also, so the relative forecast error for Japan is among the lowest.

The mean ratio of RMSE to actual growth is approximately 1.0 for the set of forecasts in Table 5.4. As in the United States, forecasts on average cannot distinguish booms from recessions, so they are not a useful guide for setting policies in advance of events to smooth growth. Reliance on these forecasts to direct policy would mislead policymakers at critical times. Forecast errors tend to be largest at turning points. Artis (1987) investigated the source of errors by studying the relation of forecast errors to policy changes and OPEC shocks. He found that the effects of the first OPEC shocks were largely unforeseen. This is not surprising. Like Litterman (1985), Artis also found that the effects of monetary restraint were often underestimated. Unanticipated fiscal policy changes proved relatively unimportant and often had the "wrong" sign (Artis 1987, pp. 74, 78). Most of the errors appear to be random.

Forecast errors may depend on the choice of monetary regime. Melt-zer (1985) found that forecast errors for Japan declined following the shift to fluctuating exchange rates and preannounced targets for mone-tary growth. The variability of annual forecast errors for Germany and the Netherlands, based on forecasts of output by the Council of Experts and the Central Planning Bureau, also declined under the system of pre-announced monetary growth, adjustable pegged rates within the EMS, and fluctuating rates against other major currencies.[12] For Germany, forecasts are relatively accurate. The root mean square error is less than one-half the average growth rate for the period 1978–86. It remains true, however, that policymakers who rely on forecasts to determine the time for discretionary changes would mistake booms and recessions.

Smythe (1983) studied the accuracy of OECD forecasts for seven countries—the United States, Japan, Germany, France, the United Kingdom, Italy, and Canada—for the years 1968–79. He found no corre-lation between the errors and the year of the forecast, suggesting that forecast accuracy has not improved significantly but did not worsen after major currencies adopted the fluctuating rate system. Zarnowitz (1986) reports a similar result.

Smythe reports the results of several tests. He used Theil's decomposi-tion to show that most of the errors for output growth and inflation are random. He also compared the accuracy of forecasts to a naive model, the latter a random walk using preliminary data for the preceding year to forecast real output. He found that the OECD forecast for each country is more accurate than the random walk but, as Smythe notes, all of the improvement is in 1974–76, following the first round of oil price increas-es. Information about the oil shock was available to private individuals as well as to public bodies, so the mechanical procedure probably overstates the error that people would have made. The results for other years sug-gest that any private information available to the OECD could not be translated into greater forecast accuracy.

Table 5.5 permits one additional set of comparisons. The table com-pares the mean absolute error for year-ahead forecasts by government, private, and international agency groups. Mean absolute errors give less weight to large errors than do RMSEs, so the reported errors are lower than in previous tables. The errors by the IMF staff are typically higher than domestic sources, with France an exception. None of the errors is less than 1.0; the best forecasters have been able to do on average is to make errors equal to 28% of the average rate of growth (Japan). For coun-tries other than the United States and Japan, the mean absolute errors are 50% or more of the average rates of growth shown in Table 5.4.

TABLE 5.5
Mean Absolute Errors, Year-Ahead Forecasts:
Real Output Growth, 1973–85 (in percent)

Country	Official [a]	Private [a]	IMF [b]
United States	1.4	1.0	1.4
Japan	1.2		1.8
France	1.2		1.1
Germany	1.2	1.5	1.6
Italy		1.9	2.2
United Kingdom		1.1	1.4

Source: Artis (1987) based on Llewellyn and Arai (1984), updated.
[a] For details, see Artis (1987).
[b] Artis (1987), World Economic Outlook.

Private forecasters do not make larger errors in general than do official agencies. Any advantage of classified information as a guide to discretionary management either does not affect the forecast or is offset by other errors. Timing cannot fully explain these data, since similar results were found using the quarterly data in Table 5.2.

Table 5.5 also compares the United States with Japan and the European countries. The differences appear to be relatively small in most cases. The results for the United States, and the implications for policy, apply as much to Europe and Japan as to the United States. Discretionary policies that rely on forecasts are likely to increase variability and uncertainty.

The comparisons are suggestive, not conclusive. We have no direct evidence on the variability that would have resulted if a rule had been used instead of discretion or, in the case of countries that followed a rule, the variability that would have resulted under an alternative rule. Lucas's (1976) critique warns us that it is difficult to compare alternative policies. Further, forecast errors often reflect more than differences in models, methods of forecasting, and policies. Many forecasters use current information or intuition to adjust their forecasts. These well-known problems probably do not alter the main conclusions drawn from these comparisons.

Neither policy making agencies nor private forecasters, using the techniques currently available, have been able to forecast, on average, whether the economy will be in a boom or recession one to four quarters ahead. Given that econometric research has been relatively unsuccessful at determining whether the lag between policy action and its effect is short or long, it is not clear whether more accurate forecasts could be used to reduce variability and uncertainty even if economists were capable of producing them. While one cannot dismiss the possibility that new research may change forecast accuracy, reliance on forecasts to make discretionary changes in policy action does not seem useful in the current state of knowledge. Even well-intentioned efforts, based on forecasts, to dampen fluctuations can have the opposite effect of increasing fluctuations and the uncertainty borne by consumers and producers.

What Rule Should Be Followed?

As yet, research has not provided a basis, formal or empirical, for an optimal monetary policy. A choice of policy cannot be avoided. In the United States, for many years, monetary policy has been discretionary; the objective given greatest weight shifts about without a predictable pattern. This practice is common but not universal. Some countries fix their exchange rates. A few have chosen rulelike behavior to achieve domestic price stability or relatively low inflation.

Typically, the case for rules or rulelike policies is entirely analytic. Here, and elsewhere, I have taken an empirical approach by presenting evidence that one of the necessary conditions for discretionary policy changes is not satisfied. The evidence shows that forecast accuracy is sufficiently imprecise that it cannot rule out the possibility that destabilizing actions will be avoided. Brunner and Meltzer (1983) show that in the 1970s, inappropriate policy actions increased variance relative to a rule. McCallum (1987) compares variability under some alternative rules to actual variability and shows that rulelike policies would reduce variability.

Since Keynes (1923/1971), economists who favored the goal of internal price stability have proposed rules for monetary policy under fluctuating (or adjustable) exchange rates. Friedman (1959) argues that this goal is more readily achieved if the central bank specifies the rule in terms of the money stock or its growth rate. I have long argued that the path for monetary policy should be stated as a growth rate for the monetary base. The base is available daily and is much less affected by institutional changes than are other measures of money.

A rule to achieve price stability[13] must specify whether the policymaker accommodates or reverses one-time changes in the price level resulting from permanent changes in productivity or other one-time changes in output. A rule that reverses permanent price changes requires the policymaker to identify all such changes. A rule that does not reverse price level changes allows the price level to adjust as part of the process by which the economy adjusts real values to unanticipated supply shocks. Once adjustment is complete, real values are the same under either rule. Differences arise during the adjustment, however. To reverse the price level change, the policymaker must know the proper amount by which to change money and other nominal values, and so must know structural parameters, including the size of the real wealth effect, the magnitude of the productivity shock, and the price elasticity of aggregate supply. The public must have confidence that the policymaker knows these magnitudes. Such confidence would be misplaced. We simply do not know and, after several decades of empirical work in macroeconomics, we should not expect to learn these values with enough precision to improve on market adjustment of the price level to one-time shocks.

Further, there is no reason current owners of nominally denominated assets should not share in the gains and losses resulting from changes in productivity or supply shocks. One of the main benefits of price stability is that stability of anticipated prices reduces uncertainty faced by transactors, thereby lowering the risk of long-term investment. This is, of course, the argument stressed by proponents of the classical gold standard. Another main benefit is that individuals who save for retirement (or for the distant future) and those who borrow at long term to finance housing and other durables have less reason for concern about the form in which assets are held and less reason to fear that the real value of accumulated saving will be altered by unanticipated price changes. Stability of the price level reduces these risks.

Accommodating unanticipated price level changes does not forsake these benefits. Although the price level changes, and the anticipated price level adjusts to the changes, the rational anticipation at any point is that prices remain at their current level. There is no risk of price level drift. Under the proposed rule, the oil shocks of the 1970s would have raised the price level. The negative oil shocks of the 1980s would have reversed the direction of change, without eliminating all of the prior increases, so the actual and anticipated price levels would have increased. Productivity shocks are mainly positive shocks to the level of output that lower the price level. A bunching of positive (or negative) productivity shocks to firms, if sufficiently strong, would change the measured rate of change of output and, under the proposed rule, induce a change in money. The increased money stock would reverse the effects of supply shocks to the price level. For these reasons, and others, the price level would fluctuate, but there is no reason the rule would produce a trend of the price level in either direction.[14]

The rule I have proposed in several places has two parts: one domestic, one international. To achieve domestic price stability, the rule requires that the monetary base grow at a rate equal to the difference between the moving average growth of output and the moving average rate of growth of velocity computed to the most recent quarter for which data are available. This rule requires no assumption about trends in output or velocity. If velocity and output are approximately random walks with drift and subject to unforeseen changes in the drift, this rule remains applicable. If velocity and output growth are constant, the rule converges to Friedman's rule for constant growth of money. If the drift is constant or if mean reversal is rapid, the Friedman rule yields a smaller variance of the price level. If mean reversal is relatively slow or does not occur, the adaptive rule is superior.

The international part of the rule reduces exchange rate variability. This benefit can be achieved if the major countries in international trade and finance—the United States, Japan, Germany, and perhaps the United Kingdom—adopt compatible rules for stability of the anticipated domestic price level. The rate of growth of the monetary base would differ with the experience of each country and would change over time. Anticipated and actual exchange rates would be subject to change with changes in relative productivity growth; rates of growth of intermediation; differences in saving rates, in expected returns, and in labor-leisure choice; or other real changes. Prices would continue to fluctuate, but anticipated price levels would be constant in all countries that follow the rule, so the rule eliminates this source of short-term instability in real and nominal exchange rates. The remaining changes in real exchange rates would work to facilitate the efficient allocation of resources in response to changes in tastes and technology at home and abroad.

An international rule for compatible monetary policies creates a public good. Smaller countries could choose to import enhanced price and exchange rate stability by fixing their exchange rate to a basket of the currencies of major countries or to one of those currencies. There would be no international agreement and no reason to impose the costs of a coordinating organization. Each country would choose its own course. If all countries choose independent policies, or make frequent discretionary changes, uncertainty would not be at a minimum.

There are opportunities for cheating, as with any agreement. A country may choose to expand money growth to gain some temporary increase in output and employment. Cheating cannot be wholly avoided. Monitoring is improved, however, if the monetary base is chosen as the policy variable and prompt publication of data for the base is provided. The base can be controlled with precision by any central bank that chooses to do so. Prompt publication of the base provides the public with information to protect their wealth against loss from inflation.

Protection of individual wealth does not avoid the social cost of variability. As discussion of the gold standard has long recognized, rules can be abandoned in periods of crisis. There are opportunities for cheating in many ways, such as shaving gold coins in one case or raising the growth rate of the base in the other. A public choice perspective requires some concern for incentives that raise the cost of departing from the rule.

On several occasions I have proposed a system of incentives to enforce a monetary rule. My specific proposal treats the problems of responsibility and accountability. An independent central bank has responsibility for monetary policy and inflation but it is not accountable directly to the public. If monetary growth produces inflation, recessions, and uncertainty, the public holds elected officials accountable, not central bank governors.

The solution is to make the monetary authority accountable for its actions without making it subservient to elected officials. An independent central bank has some merit. Because it is not directly under the control of political authorities it can, but does not always, protect the public from inflation. The value of independence is increased if the central bank is accountable.

My proposal allows the central bank to choose the growth rate of money consistent with the announced monetary rule. If the central bank fails to keep the growth of the base at (or near) the announced rate, the governor (or governors) must resign. The president can accept responsibility for the deviation by reappointing the governor if the president is satisfied that the deviation is appropriate.

Resignation was, at one time, a standard response for a minister of finance whose policies had led to devaluation of the currency. My proposal would produce a similar result. Excessive money growth would devalue the currency relative to other countries following compatible rules or pursuing less inflationary policy. Failure to follow the rule would require resignation. The rule would be symmetric; too little money growth would require resignation also. Recently, New Zealand adopted a process of this kind; one can hope that their action will succeed and spread.

Notes

1. I mention the latter because their commentary reveals the current state of average informed opinion, which, to some unknown degree, may affect asset managers' decisions about portfolio allocation.

2. Hegeland (1951) provides an excellent summary that traces these observations to Confucius, Xenophon, and Copernicus, among others.

3. Woodford (1990) gives a detailed discussion of the optimal tax rate.

4. The rest of this section and most of the following section is taken, with minor changes, from Brunner and Meltzer (1992, Lecture 4) and, is based in part, on Meltzer (1987).

5. Artis (1987) has some evidence on forecasts by IMF staff for less developed countries. Generally, these forecasts are less accurate than the forecasts discussed.

6. Forecasts for other data that I have reviewed include interest rates, money growth, investment, trade balance, and balance of payments. Forecast errors are usually larger for these variables relative to mean values.

7. The mean absolute error four quarters ahead is 5.2% and is also very similar to the mean error. Lombra and Karamouzis (1989) provide a more detailed discussion of Federal Reserve forecasts in the 1970s.

8. The errors reported in Artis (1987) are taken from the World Economic Outlook prepared by the IMF staff. Artis computes the errors for year-ahead forecasts by comparing the forecasts to the first reported results. The data for annual growth rates used in the comparisons are based on revised data published by the Federal Reserve Bank of St. Louis. The difference between the first report and the revised data affects the magnitudes but does not appear to affect the qualitative conclusions based on Tables 5.3 and 5.4. Note also that the year-ahead forecasts for 1973–79 were usually made in December. For 1980–85, forecasts were made in August or September.

9. Litterman's quantitative estimates overstate the effect of unanticipated monetary policy action. The reason is that Litterman includes common stock prices, the value of the dollar, and bond yields as well as monetary aggregates and short-term interest rates in his measure of monetary policy action. Several of these variables are affected by real shocks and by foreign nominal shocks.

10. One difference that is neglected is the difference between OECD and IMF forecasts. OECD has lower errors for growth but larger errors for inflation.

11. Artis (1987) measures errors from the absolute value of the first reported data. These differ from the actual growth rates reported in Table 5.4. The difference is shown by a comparison of absolute growth and mean absolute actual shown for each of the five countries.

12. Data for seven additional German forecasters are available, but I have not computed the root mean square errors for each forecaster.

13. If there is an optimal rate of inflation and the optimal rate is nonzero, the rule should be stated as an optimal rate of inflation.

14. George Von Furstenberg pointed out that the variance of the price level in period t + n would increase with n.

References

Artis, M. J. (1987). "How Accurate Is the World Economic Outlook? A Post Mortem of IMF Forecasting." Working paper, Manchester University.

Brunner, K., and Meltzer, A. H. (1964). *The Federal Reserve's Attachment to the Free Reserve Concept.* Washington, DC: U.S. House of Representatives, Committee on Banking and Currency.

Brunner, K., and Meltzer, A. H. (1983). "Money Supply." In B. Friedman and F. Hahn (Eds.), *Survey of Monetary Economics.* Amsterdam: North-Holland.

Brunner, K., and Meltzer, A. H. (1992). *Money and Economic Activity: Issues in Monetary Analysis* (The 1987 Raffaeli Mattioli Lectures). Cambridge: Cambridge University Press.

Cukierman, A., and Meltzer, A. H. (1986). "A Theory of Ambiguity, Credibility and Inflation under Discretion and Asymmetric Information." *Econometrica, 54,* 1099–1128.

Federal Reserve Bank of St. Louis. (1987). *International Economic Conditions.* St. Louis, MO: Author.

Friedman, M. (1951). "The Effects of a Full-Employment Policy on Economic Stability: A Formal Analysis." *Economie Appliquee, 4,* 441–456.

Friedman, M. (1959). *A Program for Monetary Stability.* New York: Fordham University Press.

Friedman, M. (1969). *The Optimum Quantity of Money.* Chicago: Aldine.

Gordon, R. J. (1983). "Using Monetary Policy to Dampen the Business Cycle: A New Set of First Principles." National Bureau of Economic Research Working Paper 1210.

Hegeland, H. (1951). *The Quantity Theory of Money.* Göteborg, Sweden: Elanders.

Hetzel, R. L. (1986). "A Congressional Mandate for Monetary Policy." *Cato Journal, 5,* 797–820.

Keynes, J. M. (1971). *A Tract on Monetary Reform.* In *The Collected Writings of John Maynard Keynes* (Vol. 4). London: Macmillan. (Original work published 1923)

Litterman, R. B. (1985). "How Monetary Policy in 1985 Affects the Outlook." *Quarterly Review* (Federal Reserve Bank of Minneapolis), *9,* 2–13.

Llewellyn, J., and Arai, H. (1984). "International Aspects of Forecasting Accuracy." *OECD Economic Studies,* 73–117.

Lombra, R., and Karamouzis, N. (1989). "Federal Reserve Policymaking: An Overview and Analysis of the Policy Process." *Carnegie-Rochester Conference Series on Public Policy, 30,* 7–62.

Lombra, R., and Moran, M. (1983). "Policy Advice and Policymaking at the Federal Reserve." *Carnegie-Rochester Conference Series on Public Policy, 13,* 9–68.

Lucas, R. E., Jr. (1976). "Econometric Policy Evaluation: A Critique." In "The Phillips Curve and Labor Markets." *Carnegie-Rochester Conference Series on Public Policy, 1,* 19–46.

McCallum, B. T. (1987). "Optimal Monetary Policy in the Light of Recent Experience: The Case for Rules." Working Paper, Carnegie-Mellon University.

McCallum, B. T. (1990). "Inflation: Theory and Evidence." In B. M. Friedman and F. H. Hahn (Eds.), *Handbook of Monetary Economics* (Vol. 2, pp. 963–1012). Amsterdam: North-Holland.

McNees, S. K. (1986, March/April). "The Accuracy of Forecasting Techniques." *New England Economic Review* (Federal Reserve Bank of Boston), 20–31.

Meltzer, A. H. (1969). "Money, Intermediation, and Growth." *Journal of Economic Literature, 7,* 27–56.

Meltzer, A. H. (1985). "Variability of Prices, Output and Money under Fixed and Fluctuating Exchange Rates: An Empirical Study of Monetary Regimes in Japan and the United States." *Bank of Japan Monetary and Economic Studies, 3,* 1–46.

Meltzer, A. H. (1987). "Limits of Short-Run Stabilization Policy." *Economic Inquiry, 25,* 1–14.

Meltzer, A. H. (1992). "Some Lessons from the Great Inflations." *Bank of Japan Monetary and Economic Studies, 1,* 1–19.

Orphanides, A., and Solow, R. M. (1990). "Money, Inflation and Growth." In B. M. Friedman and F. H. Hahn (Eds.), *Handbook of Monetary Economics,* (Vol. 1, pp. 223–261). Amsterdam: North-Holland.

Smythe, D. (1983, January-March). "Short-Run Macroeconomic Forecasting: The OECD Performance." *Journal of Forecasting, 2,* 37–49.

Tobin, J. (1983). "Monetary Policy Rules, Targets and Shocks." *Journal of Money, Credit and Banking, 15,* 506–518.

Webb, R. H. (1985). "Toward More Accurate Macroeconomic Forecasts from Vector Autoregressions." *Economic Review* (Federal Reserve Bank of Richmond), 7, 3–11.

Wolf, C., Jr. (1987, Summer) "Scoring the Economic Forecasters." *The Public Interest, 88,* 48–55.

Woodford, M. (1990). "The Optimum Quantity of Money." In B. M. Friedman and F. H. Hahn (Eds.), *Handbook of Monetary Economics* (Vol. 2, pp. 1067–1152). Amsterdam: North-Holland.

Zarnowitz, V. (1986). "The Record and Improvability of Economic Forecasting." *Economic Forecasts, 3,* 22–30.

6

Monetary Aggregates and Monetary Policy

Robert H. Rasche

At a first glance, the behavior of various monetary aggregates in the recent past is quite bewildering. From the beginning of 1991 through June 1992, M1 grew at an annual rate of 10.5%, the adjusted monetary base at an annual rate of 7.8%, and adjusted reserves at an annual rate of 11.1%, but M2 grew at an annual rate of only 2.4%. From January 1992 to June 1992, M1 grew at an annual rate of 11.3%, but M2 at an annual rate of only .8%. In the summer of 1991 M2 effectively stayed constant, whereas from February 1992 to June 1992 it actually fell slightly.

This disparate behavior of the various monetary aggregates has provoked recent discussions of monetary policy that are reminiscent of and appear to parallel closely the debate over the behavior of the narrowly defined monetary aggregates approximately a decade ago. In his most recent Humphrey-Hawkins testimony, Chairman Greenspan stated:

> The relationship between money and spending also has been profoundly affected by the process of balance sheet restructuring . . . . My previous testimony to the Congress noted that aberrant monetary behavior emerged in 1990 and has since intensified . . . . reduced depository intermediation stemmed from emerging problems of asset quality, which in turn prompted both the pulling back of depositories from lending and responses by regulators that reinforce those tendencies . . . . Looking ahead, the recent increases in M2 velocity may well continue, although the uncertainties in this regard are considerable.

Ten years ago, in February 1983, Chairman Volcker stated in his Humphrey-Hawkins presentation:

> In setting our monetary and credit objectives for 1983, the Federal Reserve has had no choice but to take into account the fact that "normal" past

relationships between money and the economy did not hold in 1982, and may be in the process of continuing change. Part of the problem lies in the ongoing process of deregulation and financial innovation that has resulted in a new array of deposit and financial instruments, some of which lie at the very border of "transactions" and "savings" accounts, defying clear statistical categories.

The common thread in both of these presentations is that there is something historically unprecedented and perhaps unique in the behavior of the aggregate under consideration. The experience of 1982 led to the removal of M1 from the pantheon of aggregates that the Fed monitored and the reestablishment of a borrowed reserves operating procedure, which over time has evolved back to the federal funds rate operating procedure that existed throughout the 1970s. The singular distinction between the present funds rate operating procedure and that of the 1970s is that the current FOMC appears to be much more aggressive about implementing changes in the funds rate target, and hence the operating procedure is not characterized by the inertia of the 1970s. It seems possible that the current allegations that M2 behavior is not consistent with past patterns could lead to a downgrading of this aggregate in discussions of appropriate monetary policy.

For example, in a recent San Francisco Federal Reserve Bank *Weekly Letter* it is noted:

> M2 was selected for an important role because over the past three decades its relationship with total spending on goods and services has been relatively stable and predictable. However, over the past three years, this relationship has deteriorated, casting doubts upon M2's usefulness as a policy indicator. In this letter we argue that these difficulties are the result of continuing financial innovation, in which M2 has been strongly affected by changes in the way that credit is channeled through the economy. (Judd and Trehan, 1992).

If M2 loses status as a monetary indicator, then the monetary policy operating procedure of the late 1960s in which short-term interest rates were the exclusive focus of policy discussions may be reinstated in the near future. Such a turn of events would be unfortunate. No one, to my knowledge, has evidence of a well-defined relationship between short-run movements in short-term interest rates and nominal income. Absent such information it will be difficult or impossible for the Fed to establish credibility for its stated long-run objective of stable inflation at sufficiently low rates that it is not a factor in the economic decisions of private agents.

The Behavior of Monetary Aggregates:
A Great Mystery?

Are we really in a situation in which the behavior of monetary aggregates is inexplicable, and where there are no discernible relationships between monetary aggregates and economic activity? Some analysts clearly are convinced that this is the case, and argue that the behavior of monetary aggregates should be minimized in policy discussions (see, e.g., Friedman, 1988; Friedman and Kuttner, 1992). Other analyses of the U.S. data suggest that systematic historical relationships are responsible for the behavior of M1 over the past decade (see Hoffman and Rasche, 1991; Lucas, 1988; Poole, 1988). Similarly, recent behavior of M2 can be shown to be consistent with previous episodes.

M1 Behavior since 1980

The velocity of M1 on a quarterly basis from 1959–92:1, relative to gross domestic product (GDP), is plotted in Figure 6.1. Clearly this series has behaved much differently since about 1980. Gone is the upward trend that had persisted since the 1950s. If anything, there is a slight negative trend over the most recent 11 years. In addition, fluctuations in this velocity measure over the recent period have huge amplitude compared with the fluctuations of the previous 25 years. At first glance it is tempting to dismiss any claim to systematic velocity behavior before and after 1980 as lunacy.

Figure 6.2 presents M1 velocity data in a somewhat different light. The data plotted here are annual averages of the Treasury bill rate and the reciprocal of M1 velocity—a textbook representation of a money demand specification. The solid line is a long-run (or equilibrium) velocity relationship estimated from the quarterly data in Figure 6.1 over a sample period of 1956–90, using the model that Dennis Hoffman and I have published (Hoffman and Rasche, 1991).[1] That model allows for a substantial long-run interest elasticity (approximately .55) of velocity with respect to the Treasury bill rate. The boxes are a scatter plot of the actual annual observations of the Treasury bill rate and the reciprocal of M1 velocity. The solid box is the 1991 observation (which is not included in the sample period of the estimation). A plot of the quarterly observations would exhibit more variation around the estimated long-run money-demand relationship, but the story is the same: with a simple constant elasticity relationship the movements of interest rates describe the fundamental behavior of M1 velocity over the three and a half decades.

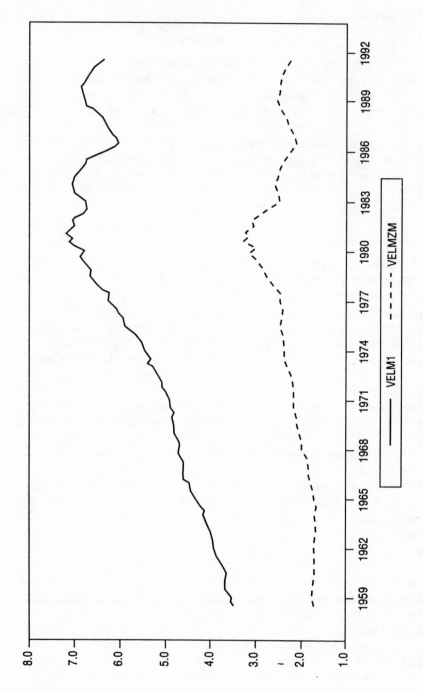

FIGURE 6.1 M1 and Zero-Maturity Money Velocities, 1959–92 *Source:* Citibase and Federal Reserve System.

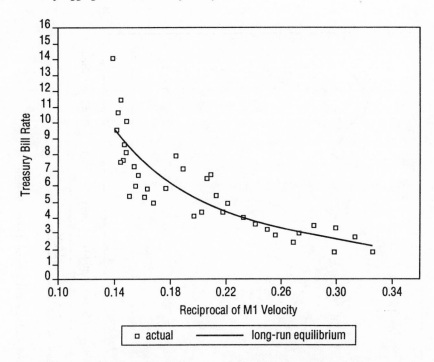

FIGURE 6.2 Annual M1 Velocity, 1955–91 *Source:* Citibase and Federal Reserve System.

A somewhat different picture, using the quarterly data, is presented in Figure 6.3. Here the actual quarterly M1 velocity is plotted as the solid line, while the predicted long-run M1 velocity, *based on the current quarterly value* of the Treasury bill rate, is plotted as the broken line. There are large deviations between the two lines, but these deviations are not permanent: the two lines cross repeatedly.[2]

There are two conclusions to be drawn from this analysis of Figures 6.2 and 6.3. The first is that the recent rapid growth of M1 relative to nominal income growth (the decline in M1 velocity) is a predictable consequence of the decline in the Treasury bill rate from its peak of 7.90% in March 1990 to the recent level of approximately 3%. The second is that the full impact on M1 velocity of the 92% decline in the Treasury bill rate (measured as log differences) over the past two and a half years has not been fully realized yet. Note in Figure 6.3 that the dotted line is considerably below the actual velocity line. The implication of this is that if the Fed maintains the Treasury bill rate at current levels for some period of time (say, over the next year), we should expect to see M1 velocity continue to fall. While the dynamics of the adjustment process to the reduction in nominal interest rates is not identified in the model used here, the adjustments of velocity to various shocks appear to be largely completed

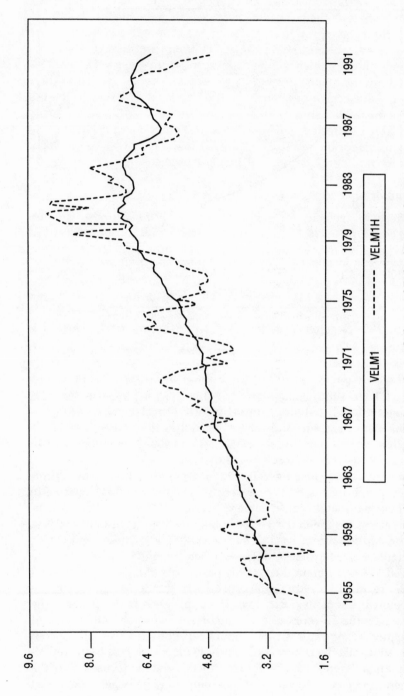

FIGURE 6.3 M1 Velocity and Predicted Long-Run Velocity *Source:* Citibase and Federal Reserve System.

in about two years. Hence, prolonged growth in M1 relative to GDP will be inconsistent with the Fed's stated objective of reducing inflation.

The same type of relationship held for base velocity for the two decades through the end of the 80s (see Hoffman and Rasche, 1991), but probably with a somewhat lower long-run interest elasticity than M1 velocity. With the major currency exports of a couple of years ago, there appears to have been a permanent shift in the level of base velocity, but otherwise the relationship driving the long-run behavior of base velocity was probably unaffected. Therefore, it is likely that the same factors that are responsible for the rapid growth of M1 in the recent past are responsible for the rapid growth of the monetary base measures.

M2 Behavior since 1990

Quarterly M2 velocity for 1955–92:1 is plotted in Figure 6.4. The broken line is the mean of M2 velocity for that period. Again, velocity is measured relative to the recently revised GDP numbers. The mean here is changed very little from that reported by Hallman, Porter, and Small (1991) for quarterly M2 velocity relative to GNP over the period 1955–88:1. As in the case of M1 velocity deviations from the estimated long-run M1 demand equation, the deviations of M2 velocity from the mean M2 velocity are strictly transitory.[3] However, it is important to note that the variance of M2 velocity around its mean is very large.

The shaded areas in Figure 6.4 represent the NBER recession phases. I have arbitrarily dated the end of the 1990–91 recession with the second quarter of 1991, though it should be noted that the NBER has yet to establish an official trough for this recession. The characteristic postwar historical behavior of M2 velocity is a sharp decline during recessions or shortly thereafter. The traditional explanation of this is that market rates of interest fall quickly during these periods, but that the rates of interest paid on various components of M2 are considerably more sluggish, so that the opportunity cost of holding M2 balances (measured by the spread between market rates and own rates) falls and M2 velocity falls. This spread between the Treasury bill rate and the "own rate" on M2 as measured by the staff of the Board of Governors is plotted in Figure 6.5. Note that this spread dropped substantially in 1985–86, so the large decline in M2 velocity at this time is consistent with the conventional wisdom. The last two years do not fit the conventional wisdom. The rate spread plotted in Figure 6.5 dropped throughout the most recent recession as it did in past recessions and remains close to the postwar minimum value. However, it can be seen from Figure 6.4 that M2 velocity did not behave in the characteristic manner. There was a very small decline in M2 velocity in the year following the cyclical peak, but since

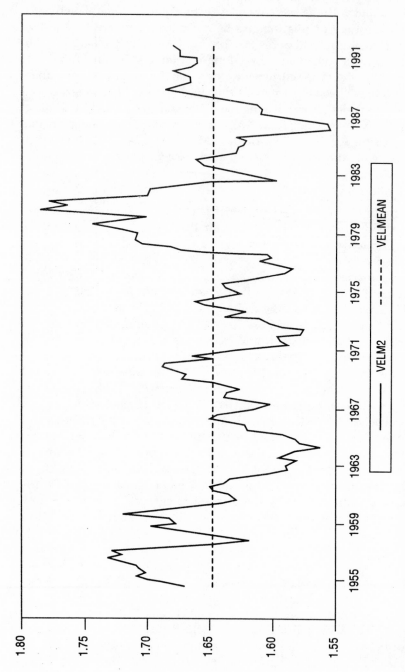

FIGURE 6.4 M2 Velocity, 1955–92 *Source:* Citibase and Federal Reserve System.

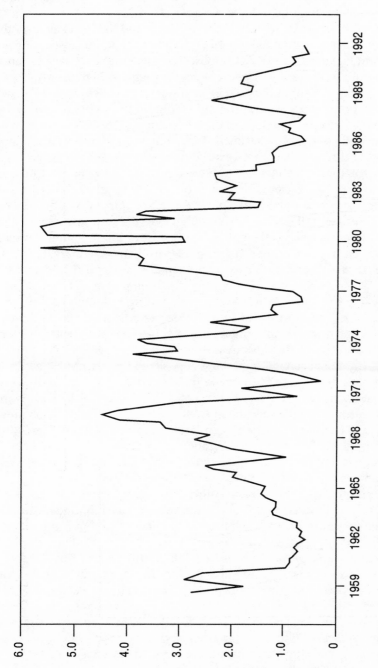

FIGURE 6.5 Treasury Bill Rate-M2 Rate Spread *Source:* Citibase and Federal Reserve System.

then it has increased so that at the latest observation (1992:1) it is close to the value at the beginning of the recession.

The recent increase in M2 velocity can be traced to the behavior of the small time deposit component of M2. Small time deposits outstanding are plotted in Figure 6.6, and it can be observed there that they have declined dramatically and steadily since the beginning of the 1990 recession.

The decline in small time deposits is not unprecedented. While such deposits grew almost continuously throughout the 1960s and 1970s, there have been three periods in the 1980s during which the outstanding volume of these deposits declined. Two of these incidents occurred long before the thrift crisis became everyday news or a public concern. The reason for these declines does not seem particularly mysterious. In Figure 6.7 the rate on small time deposits of six-month maturity (as collected by the staff of the Board of Governors) is plotted with the three-month Treasury bill rate. It is evident that over the decade the small time deposit rate has tracked the path of the Treasury bill rate quite closely.[4] This rate clearly is *not* sluggish in response to changes in market rates. In Figure 6.8 the spread of the six-month small time deposit rate over the rate paid on other checkable deposits (OCD) is plotted. The three periods during the 1980s in which the outstanding volume of small time deposits declined correspond to the three periods in which this spread fell. Over the past year to 18 months, this spread has been below 1% consistently and close to the historical lows observed in 1986. The only question is why the decline in small time deposits in the recent past has been so dramatic relative to the decline in 1986. The most frequently cited explanation for the extent of the recent decline in these deposits is the thrift crisis, because the decline in small time deposits at thrifts is much larger than the decline in such deposits at commercial banks. This is part of Chairman Greenspan's rationalization of the recent behavior of M2.

It is probably premature to jump to the conclusion that this behavior of small time deposits represents a unique portfolio restructuring. The major difference in the behavior of the rate spread shown in Figure 6.8 in 1991–92 compared with 1986 is that the spread rebounded quickly from its minimum in 1986, whereas at the present time it has remained near the 1986 minimum for almost a year and a half. Given the long maturity of a large portion of the outstanding small time deposits (Poole, 1991) and the "substantial penalty for early withdrawals," the potential exists for rolling a much larger fraction of the outstanding balances over into other assets in response to the present lower rate spread than existed during the short-lived decline of the spread in 1986. The declines in outstanding small time deposits in 1986 and 1991–92 are quite similar to the declines in outstanding large time deposits in 1968 and 1970, when Reg Q ceilings were allowed to become binding. In those

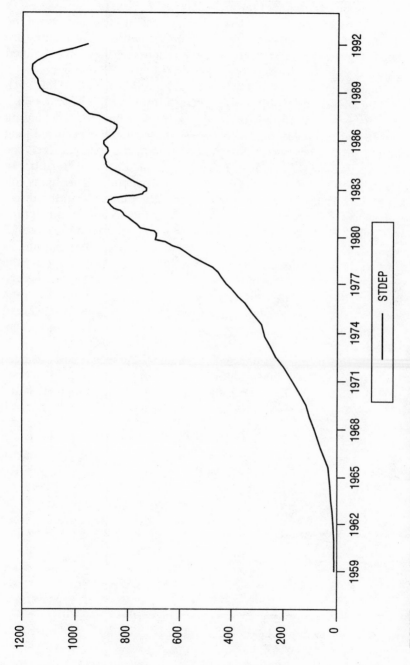

FIGURE 6.6 Small Time Deposits *Source:* Federal Reserve System.

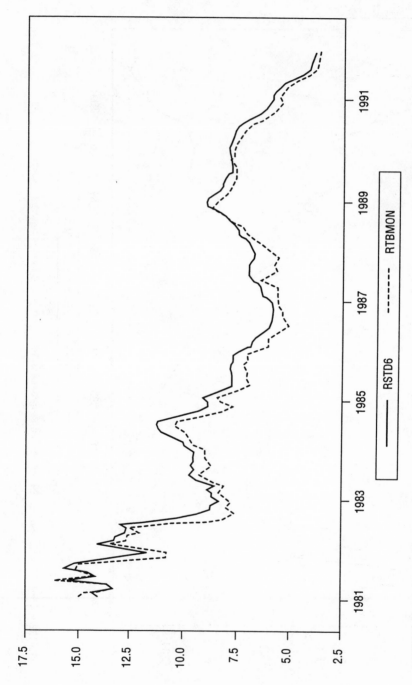

FIGURE 6.7 Six-Month Small Time Deposit Rate and Treasury Bill Rate   *Source:* Citibase and Federal Reserve System.

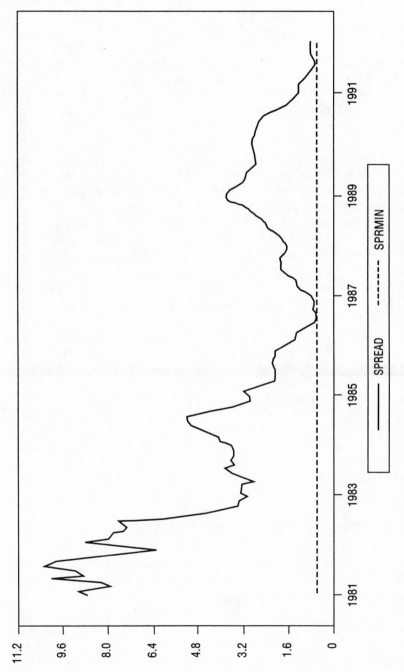

FIGURE 6.8 Six Month Small Time Deposit-OCD Rate Spread *Source:* Citibase and Federal Reserve System.

two cases, the size of the "runoff" in large CDs was directly related to the length of time that the Reg Q ceiling remained effective. A second factor is the difference in the shape of the yield curve in the recent past compared with 1986. In May 1992 the yield on five-year Treasury bonds was 6.69%; in December 1986 it was 6.67%. However, in December 1986 the spread between the two-year and five-year Treasury rates was only 40 basis points; in May 1992 this spread was 166 basis points. If the yield curve on small time deposits has a shape similar to that in the Treasury market, then in recent months there is considerably more incentive to roll maturing intermediate maturity small time deposits over into longer-term nondeposit assets. Therefore a reasonable alternative hypothesis is that the recently observed behavior of small time deposit balances is a normal portfolio adjustment in response to the prevailing structure of interest rates, and would have occurred regardless of the severity or existence of the thrift crisis. Discriminating between these two alternative views of the recent behavior of small time deposits (and M2) will take a considerable amount of careful research, and a definitive answer may not be possible at the present time, given the short history of small time deposit behavior in the absence of interest rate regulation.

If the view that the decline in small time deposits is a normal response to changes in the structure of interest rates, proposals that advocate additional Fed intervention to lower short-term interest rates must be examined with considerable caution. Further reductions in the funds rate target are not likely to have much impact on the spread between small time deposit rates and rates offered on other checkable deposits, since banks will not find it profitable to bid aggressively for such deposits when short-term lending rates are low. Increasing the funds rate in an effort to improve the yield on small time deposits relative to longer-term maturity nondeposit assets and stimulate the growth of M2 is not a policy that will be considered in the present circumstances. Under these conditions it is possible that short-run manipulation of M2 growth by the Fed may be difficult or impossible.

The Velocity of Zero-Maturity Money

The M2 aggregate as currently defined is available in official published sources only back to January 1959, though unofficial estimates exist for the period since January 1948. This definition is *not* the "broad money" whose long-term historical relation to nominal income was investigated by Friedman and Schwartz (1963). The inclusion of small time deposits in the current concept appears inconsistent with the rationale that Friedman and Schwartz use for their concept of "broad money" and inconsistent with their argument for the exclusion of large negotiable certificates of deposit at commercial banks after 1960:

The component added to the narrower total [M1] to get this total [M2] is termed "time deposits" through January 1961, and "time deposits other than large negotiable certificates of deposit" thereafter. These terms are something of a misnomer. In practice, these deposits have almost always been available on demand. The only important exceptions are periods during and after banking panics when there have been restrictions on convertibility of deposits into currency. However, such restrictions applied equally to all deposits at commercial banks, whether termed demand or time deposits. The distinction between demand and time deposits at commercial banks, at least since 1933, has typically been that demand deposits were, and time deposits were not, transferable by check.

The large negotiable certificates of deposit . . . that are excluded after 1961 are a recent development that have no counterpart earlier. We are inclined to regard them as more nearly comparable to market instruments such as commercial paper than to the items earlier classified as "time deposits." (Friedman and Schwartz, 1970, p. 80)

It is my judgment that exactly the same argument made about large negotiable certificates of deposit in the above passage can be made about small time deposits, with Treasury bills as the comparable market instrument to such deposits. Therefore, the monetary aggregate that at present is most closely related to the "broad money" concept advocated by Friedman and Schwartz is the zero-maturity money (MZM) proposed by Poole (1991). Zero-maturity money is constructed by subtracting the small time deposit component from the official measure of M2 and adding the institution-only money market fund balances that are included in the official measure of M3.

The velocity of zero-maturity money (VELMZM) is plotted in Figure 6.1 along with the velocity of M1. There are many similarities between these two measures. Both show positive trends throughout the 1960s and 1970s, negative trends in the 1980s, and much larger amplitude fluctuations in the 1980s compared with the previous decades. The velocity of zero-maturity money has declined relative to the decline in M1 velocity since the beginning of the 1990 recession in about the same relationship that occurred during 1986. The trends in zero-maturity money velocity before and after 1980 appear to be smaller in absolute value that those in M1, and the fluctuations of the former measure have much smaller amplitude than those of the latter measure during the 1980s.

Some additional information that is helpful in understanding the difference in the behavior of M1 and MZM velocities on the one hand and M2 velocity on the other is contained in Figure 6.9. The solid line (RTBMON) in this figure is the monthly Treasury bill rate from January 1980 through June 1992. The broken line (SPREADM1) is the difference between the

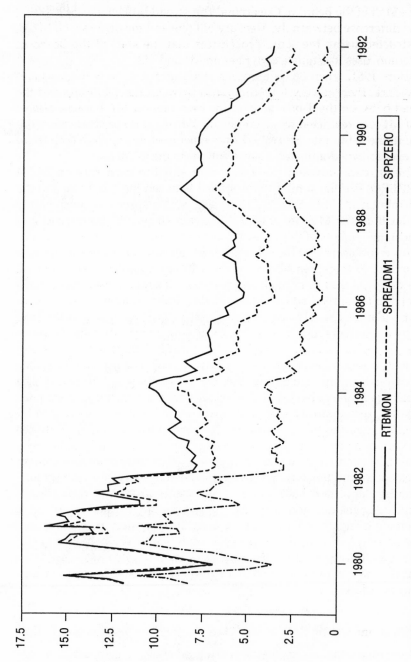

FIGURE 6.9 T-Bill Rate and T-Bill Rate Spreads, 1980–92 *Source:* Citibank and Federal Resserve System.

Treasury bill rate and the own rate of interest on M1 balances as estimated by the staff of the Board of Governors. The second broken line (SPRZERO) is the difference between the Treasury bill rate and the own rate on MZM, constructed using the same procedures that the staff of the Board of Governors uses to estimate own rates on M1 and M2.

Before 1981, when NOW accounts were limited to New England and New York, there is very little difference between the T-bill rate and the spread between the T-bill rate and the own rate on M1, because almost all of M1 was restricted to a zero rate. In 1981-82 this spread declines relative to the T-bill rate. Since 1982, movements of this spread, both trend and cyclical, are dominated by movements in the T-bill rate.

The spread between the T-bill rate and the own rate on MZM (SPRZERO) is quite similar to the spread between the T-bill rate and the own rate on M1 (SPREADM1). The size of this spread is considerably smaller than the M1 rate spread, but again since 1982 both trend and cyclical movements of this spread closely parallel those of the T-bill rate.

This characteristic of the M1 and MZM rate spreads stands in dramatic contrast to the spread between the T-bill rate and the rate on small time deposits that is implicit in Figure 6.7. There the two rates move closely, so the spread between them shows little variation.

At a glance it would appear that if M1 velocity is driven in the long run by a relatively high interest elasticity (Figure 6.2), then the long-run behavior of zero-maturity money velocity could be similarly explained, but with a much lower interest elasticity. I have been unable to isolate such a relationship statistically. The reason seems straightforward. The problem is in the behavior of this velocity measure in the 1978–82 period, when zero-maturity money deposits were substantially affected by Req Q ceilings and other deposit regulations. In the late 1970s VELMZM rose very quickly, but this increase was completely reversed in the 1981-82 period, when banks were authorized to issue insured money market deposit accounts. Separating shifts in the demand curve for zero-maturity money deposits from the impact of changes in interest rates (movements along the demand curve for these deposits) during this period is extremely difficult and will require considerably more research than I have accomplished to date. Until we understand the behavior of the velocity of this aggregate in the absence of regulatory changes, my judgment is that it is premature to make it a significant factor in monetary policy decisions.

Implications for the Role of Monetary Aggregates in Monetary Policy

Several conclusions about the role of monetary aggregates in monetary policy can be drawn from the above discussion. First, with respect to M2, it is important to distinguish between the transitory nature of shocks to M2 velocity and the variance of those shocks. The fact that M2 velocity has returned to its mean during the postwar period implies nothing about the variance around that mean. In fact, that variance is considerable. The coefficient of variation of M2 velocity (standard deviation relative to sample mean) in quarterly data is 2.9%. Therefore, from quarter to quarter large changes can occur in nominal GDP independent of changes in M2. The collapse of the economy is not guaranteed by any short period of slow M2 growth any more than an explosion in inflation is guaranteed by a similarly short period of high M2 growth. Second, there may be market conditions, such as have been experienced recently, in which Federal Reserve actions to lower short-term interest rates have no impact on increasing the growth rate of M2, and indeed may be counterproductive in that objective.

With respect to narrower monetary aggregates such as the base or M1, policy has to be designed to cope with permanent changes in trends such as occurred around 1980. My conclusion is that the change in velocity trend in these aggregates can be attributed to changes in interest rate trends. My view is that the most plausible cause of the change observed in the early 1980s in interest rate trends is a change in inflation expectations. Under these conditions, changes in monetary policy regimes that affect inflation expectations will in turn affect nominal interest rate trends and velocity trends.

Monetary rules that do not allow for feedback from velocity changes are not going to work very well under these conditions if the objective of monetary policy is the stabilization of nominal income or its rate of growth. For example, suppose that inflation, expected inflation, nominal interest rates, and velocity have been drifting upward. Further suppose that with these initial conditions the monetary authority desires to stabilize the inflation rate and sets a growth objective for a narrow definition of the monetary aggregate equal to a projected growth rate for natural output plus a desired stabilized inflation rate, minus the historically observed drift in the velocity of the monetary aggregate. If this money growth rate is maintained after expected inflation is stabilized, the drift in nominal interest rates will have disappeared and the actual steady rate of inflation will prove to be lower than the planned rate.

Meltzer (1987) and McCallum (1988) propose alternatives to a fixed money (base) growth rule that allow feedback from velocity onto the planned growth in money (base). These rules are designed to account for permanent shocks to velocity, but not to respond to transitory velocity shocks. The rules set the growth rate of the monetary base equal to a desired growth of nominal income less a moving average of the drift in base velocity. McCallum's rule provides an additional adjustment to base growth as nominal income is observed to deviate from nominal natural output. These rules establish base growth consistent with the planned stable inflation once stabilization is achieved and adjust base growth to compensate for the declining velocity drift during the transition period to the stabilized inflation rate.

However, the above result depends critically on the credibility of the monetary authority. As long as private agents believe that the monetary authority is following the feedback rule consistently, inflation expectations should adjust either in anticipation of or with the observation of falling inflation over time and the feedback mechanism will adjust base growth as desired. Both the Meltzer and McCallum rules are deterministic. In practice, stochastic fluctuations around such deterministic rules will be observed that may make direct verification of the rules difficult. If the monetary authority lacks credibility, feedback rules such as these could prove unstable. Suppose the rule is implemented by the monetary authority and inflation, and inflation expectations begin to stabilize. This lowers the drift in velocity, and the feedback rule calls for base growth to be adjusted upward. The McCallum rule, which ultimately restores nominal income to a specified path of nominal potential income, requires that base growth and nominal income growth overshoot equilibrium base growth and equilibrium income growth during the transition period in order to produce the larger equilibrium real balances that are consistent with the lower equilibrium nominal interest rate. The required overshooting is greater the higher the elasticity of the long-run demand for real balances. If the rule is not well understood by private agents, or if the increase in base and nominal income growth is interpreted by such agents as an abandonment of the rule, then inflation expectations could start adjusting upward. This would change the drift of velocity and the rule would then call for reductions in base growth. It is not difficult to conceive of a situation where the monetary authority lacks credibility, in which the Meltzer-McCallum rules suffer from instrument instability (Holbrook, 1972) if the observed behavior of the monetary base affects inflation expectations, and through this the drift of base velocity. Under these conditions the rule could produce explosive oscillations in money (base) growth. Therefore, a prerequisite of the success of these types of monetary rules is a good and convincing explanation by the monetary authorities of their objectives and how they are seeking to obtain those objectives.

Some analysts object to the implementation of monetary policy through the monetary base, because the base is largely currency, and large quantities of currency may be held by foreigners and/or are held as a result of illegal activities. From time to time, the level of the base outstanding has changed considerably as major currency exports occurred.

These arguments strike me as a basis for devoting additional resources to obtaining better data on the holdings of base money in the domestic economy, not for ruling out monetary policies implemented through the monetary base.

Finally, why not ignore monetary aggregates altogether and pursue a strict Funds rate target? A fatal problem with such monetary regimes is that they fail to supply information to private agents on the longer-run outcomes of the policy procedure. Current conditions provide an excellent example of this flaw. Inflation has fallen steadily since the end of 1990 and is now about 1.5% lower than the period preceding Operation Desert Shield if measured by the CPI, and has fallen even more if measured by the PPI or GDP deflator. Nevertheless, long-term Treasury bonds continue to trade in the 7.25-7.50 range, not much below the 1987 low (7.62 in March 1987). Consensus estimates of inflation for 1992–93 are higher than current experience and not much below the average observed inflation rate from 1982–89 (3.4% versus 3.7% measured by the CPI). Even the Bush administration (*Economic Report of the President*, February 1992) and the CBO (*The Economic and Budget Outlook: Fiscal Years 1993–1997*, January 1992) projected long-term (five-year) inflation in the 3.2% range. It is difficult to find convincing evidence that longer-term inflation expectations have dropped *significantly* below the 4% level. The Funds rate operating procedure of the recent past has not provided a basis to support major downward revisions in long-run inflation expectations, without which actual inflation will not remain at current levels throughout the coming decade.

Notes

1. The data used in the current estimation are the 1992 Federal Reserve revised measures of the money stock for 1959–92 and my (1987) estimates of an M1 series consistent with current definitions of M1 for the earlier years. GDP for 1959–92 are the current Bureau of Economic Analysis revisions. For the earlier years the older (pre-1991) revisions of GDP and real GDP were used. These were adjusted to the 1959 annual levels of the current revisions.

2. There are two ways of testing for the temporary nature of these deviations. The first is one of the several "unit root" tests, where the null hypothesis is that the deviations are permanent and the alternative hypothesis is that they are transitory. The second is a class of tests in which the null hypothesis is that the deviations are transitory and the alternative hypothesis is that they are permanent. Using a Phillips-Perron test to implement the first approach, we reject the null hypothesis of permanent deviations. Using a KPSS (Kwaitkowski, Phillips, Schmidt, and Shin, 1991) test as adapted by Shin (1992) to implement the second approach, we fail to reject the null hypothesis of transitory deviations.

3. Here we have tested deviations of M2 velocity from its mean using Phillips-Perron tests for which the null hypothesis is that the deviations are permanent

and using KPSS tests for which the null hypothesis is that the deviations are temporary. In the former case we reject the null hypothesis; in the latter case we fail to reject the null hypothesis. Thus the results of both types of tests are consistent and support the conclusion of Hallman et al. (1991) that deviations of M2 velocity from its mean in the postwar period are transitory.

4. It would be interesting to observe the entire term structure of rates on small time deposits. I have looked at a few of the weekly Banxquote Money Markets (published in the *Wall Street Journal*) for average CD yields offered through leading brokers. The term structure of savings CDs appears to track the term structure of Treasuries quite closely out to five years at the present time. I am told that it is difficult to obtain consistent data series for other maturities. The rate on six-month deposits is used by the staff of the Board of Governors as the yield on all small time deposits in the construction of an effective yield on M2.

References

Citibase. (1991). New York.

Federal Reserve System. (1992). Division of Monetary Affairs, Money and Reserves Projection Section. Washington, DC.

Friedman, B. M. (1988). "Monetary Policy without Quantity Variables." *American Economic Review, 78,* 440–445.

Friedman, B. M., and Kuttner, K. K. (1992). "Money, Income, Prices and Interest Rates." *American Economic Review, 82,* 472–491.

Friedman, M., and Schwartz, A. J. (1963). *A Monetary History of the United States, 1867–1960.* Princeton, NJ: Princeton University Press.

Friedman, M., and Schwartz, A. J. (1970). *Monetary Statistics of the United States: Estimates, Sources, Methods.* New York: Columbia University Press.

Hallman, J. J., Porter, R. D., and Small, D. H. (1991). "Is the Price Level Tied to the M2 Monetary Aggregate in the Long Run?" *American Economic Review, 81,* 841–858.

Hoffman, D. L., and Rasche, R. H. (1991). "Long-Run Income and Interest Elasticities of Money Demand in the U.S." *Review of Economics and Statistics, 78,* 665–674.

Holbrook, R. S. (1972). "Optimal Economic Policy and the Problem of Instrument Instability." *American Economic Review, 62,* 231–255.

Judd, J. P., and Trehan, B. (1992, September 4). "Money, Credit and M2." *Weekly Letter* (Federal Reserve Bank of San Francisco).

King, R., Plosser, C. I., Stock, J. H., and Watson M. W. (1991). "Stochastic Trends and Economic Fluctuations." *American Economic Review, 81,* 819–840.

Kwaitkowski, D., Phillips, P. C. B., Schmidt, P., and Shin, Y. (1991). "Testing the Null Hypothesis of Stationarity against the Alternative of a Unit Root: How Sure Are We That Economic Time Series Have a Unit Root." Unpublished manuscript, Michigan State University, Department of Economics.

Lucas, R. E. (1988). "Money Demand in the United States: A Quantative Review." *Carnegie-Rochester Conference Series on Public Policy, 29,* 137–168.

McCallum, B. T. (1988). "Robustness Properties of a Rule for Monetary Policy." *Carnegie-Rochester Conference Series on Public Policy, 29,* 173–203.

Meltzer, A. H. (1987). "Limits of Short-Run Stabilization Policy." *Economic Inqui-ry*, 25, 1–14.

Poole, W. (1988). "Monetary Policy Lessons of Recent Inflation and Disinflation." *Journal of Economic Perspectives*, 2(3), 73–100.

Poole, W. (1991). "Choosing a Monetary Aggregate: Another Look." *Shadow Open Market Committee, Policy Statement and Position Papers* (Bradely Policy Research Center Public Policy Studies Working Paper Series, PPS 91–02) 91–104.

Shin, Y. (1992). "A Residual-Based Test of the Null of Cointegration against the Alternative of No Cointegration." Unpublished manuscript, Michigan State University, Department of Economics.

Comment

George Horwich

I think this session should have been entitled "Velocity Matters." Both presenters and one of the discussants have long been identified with monetarist positions during their careers. Since they have always believed that *money* matters, if only in the negative sense that irregular and unpredictable variations in its supply cause endless economic mischief, they have sought to design policies that would assure steady nondiscretionary growth of money in any and all circumstances.

As a Chicago student, I could scarcely fail to be sympathetic to that effort, and I still am. Nevertheless, there were numerous influences in my early training, along with monetarist doctrine, and I pursued what I personally regarded as a more economically, if not politically, correct path to the formulation of monetary policy. At first, I did not use the term *velocity* in my fledgling endeavors, as that word was as acceptable to my dissertation adviser, Lloyd Meltzer, as the term *privatization* is to the old guard of the present Chinese Communist party. It reminded him too much of the discredited equation of exchange and relics of a pre-Keynesian decadent era. But *I* knew that all the wondrous Keynesian relationships were incorporated in the velocity component of the equation, along with dependent variations in the stock of money.

As luck would have it, the Friedmanite monetarists at Chicago also did not care much for the velocity concept, because if velocity were anything other than a toothless and passive variable, it would make control of money and the economy difficult, if not impossible, to achieve. I was truly loved by no one.

It was thus with special pleasure, even excitement, that I read Bob Rasche's and Allan Meltzer's chapters. These authors forthrightly, unabashedly, and unashamedly confront the instability of velocity in their attempt to define a rule for monetary policy. Rasche even prefaces his study with a devastating reduction of recent velocity behavior to movements along an old-fashioned liquidity preference schedule, which is as intact, elasticity and all, as one might possibly expect it to be. Jim Tobin, who first constructed such a schedule post-Keynes, had it right the first time, which, I think, was in 1947. It is, of course, the liquidity preference schedule, the interest-elastic demand for money, that generates all those Keynesian multipliers.

I want to emphasize that my use of the word *Keynesian* refers to a theoretical or analytic framework characterized in textbooks as the IS-LM model, and not at all to policies of tax and spend, which I generally loathe as much as the next student of Milton Friedman. That point takes on a special force for me, because I believe that Fridrich Hayek contributed importantly to the development of IS-LM dynamics in his *Pure Theory of Capital* in the early 1940s.

Where does all this velocityism lead? I think, having thrown ourselves at the mercy of liquidity preference and the nonvertical LM schedule, inevitably we must dig a little deeper and ask why and how velocity varies in that world and what, if any, implications these variations might have for a monetary rule. We may find most of these implications without practical significance at the present time, but we should at least know what they are and establish what is doable and what is not. Having introduced the Keynesian demand for money as the counterpart to velocity, we cannot in conscience close the door to Keynes, Hicks, Robertson, Robinson, Wicksell, Hayek, Lange, Lutz, and the Lord knows who else.

I will try to run through a velocity exercise quickly, using IS-LM as the general framework and the equation of exchange as the money/velocity counterpart. The use of IS-LM to identify a rule for monetary policy goes back to Martin J. Bailey's 1960s text, *National Income and the Price Level*, my 1964 study of money and capital and a 1966 conference paper I presented in Los Angeles, and, I believe, to one or more papers by Bill Poole. (My access to an English-language economics library to confirm these sources has been severely restricted by my residence this fall at the People's University in China.) The idea of this policy perspective is simply that shifts at full employment in, say, IS, up or down, whether due to I, investment, or S, saving, are offset by corresponding upward or downward shifts in money (or its rate of change) and hence LM. The net effect would be to keep the intersection of IS and LM at the same real and nominal income level. Undesired increases in the price level or decreases in both prices and output are headed off—prevented from happening—in a process that takes no longer than the time for interest rate changes caused by the monetary changes to spread through the money and capital markets. Granted that our econometric models were good enough to tell us what is happening to IS—and I doubt that they are—the only lag in the effect of monetary policy would be in its implementation and the transmission process through the financial markets. There would be no necessity to alter the rate of expenditures in the goods market, and hence, no lag in reaching it, because the policy, if successful, would prevent undesired changes in expenditures from occurring in the first place.

In terms of velocity, which is the ratio of nominal income, Y, to the stock of money, M, the changes in velocity under the policy occur not because P, the price level, and hence Y in the numerator, goes up following, say, an increase in investment, but because P and Y are constant and M in the denominator goes down via the policy move. The idea is to create the kind of velocity changes we want—caused by changes in the nominal stock of money and not by changes in nominal income—unless, at below full employment, we want to let IS shift up and cause both real and nominal income and velocity to increase without interference.

Another variety of velocity change we would not want to impede would be the increase that tends to result from a negative supply shock. The associated loss of output would tend to raise velocity by reducing real income and saving and thus raising the rate of interest, which reduces the quantity of money demanded, thereby raising velocity and nominal income, including both output and the price level.

I think negative supply shocks occur more frequently than is commonly supposed. They originate not only in dramatic reductions in energy supply (or its rate of growth), but in more ordinary occasional concentrations of resource reallocations caused by clusters of demand shifts or supply-side innovations. As such adjustments take place, significant temporary losses of aggregate output can occur. Michael Bernstein (in *The Great Depression*) writes convincingly of such occurrences in the late 1920s and early 1930s and in the 1970s.

What all this suggests to me is that simple rules altering the growth rate of money in response to ex post changes in velocity leave a lot to be desired and may even do a great deal of harm, perhaps more than would result from simply ignoring velocity. I think we are better advised to pursue econometric efforts at identifying the underlying structure of the macro system and its parametric shifts. It may not be as difficult as it sounds if we know exactly the policy context we are aiming for. I think the abysmal forecasting performance Allan Meltzer documents so well may in large part be the result of an inadequate theoretical framework on the part of the forecasters. The period covered by Meltzer also encompasses a number of significant historic developments that made forecasting particularly hazardous and may not recur with the same frequency in the nirvana that lies ahead. I refer to the development of peacetime inflation and inflationary expectations in the 1960s for the first time in U.S. history; the occurrence of supply-side shocks, one of which, at least, the energy crisis, was massive in its effects; and the innovations in the monetary system caused by deregulation. Before drawing any final conclusions on the ability to forecast, I would also like to see controlled tests of forecasting conducted under well-specified alternative theoretical frameworks.

Meltzer writes persuasively of the desirability of accommodating—by which he seems to mean not reversing the price level effects of supply shocks, both positive and negative. But I cannot fathom how reversal will not occur under his rule for the growth of the monetary base. That rule places the growth of the base as the difference between the growth of output and the growth of velocity, both measured as moving averages. A negative supply shock causes output to contract and, for reasons noted above, velocity to increase. Both of these responses reduce the difference between output and velocity and call forth, under the rule, a reduction in the monetary base. That monetary tightening is the very opposite of what I think constitutes good policy and hardly seems consonant with the accommodation that Meltzer himself says he favors. Although a several-quarter moving average of the indicator variables will moderate the reduction in the growth of the base, any amount of slowing down strikes me as a perverse reaction to a disturbance that should absolutely be left free to work itself out without the inhibiting influence of monetary stringency. It was, of course, the failure of central banks worldwide to distinguish between demand-induced and supply-induced inflation in the 1970s that led to excessive monetary restraint following the energy shocks and to economies far weaker than they would have been under the energy shocks alone. That perverse policy response, which Meltzer's rule seems to incorporate, is by far a greater threat to economic stability than any inflation caused directly by supply-side disruptions.

Comment

David I. Meiselman

Allan Meltzer's chapter is a very useful survey of some important issues in monetary economics and related public policy issues. Wisely, Meltzer does not attempt the impossible task of covering all the issues. Instead, he focuses mainly on three issues: first, the relation of money to economic growth; second, the important role of forecasts in the conduct of discretionary monetary policy and the related hazards of relying on forecasts, even the best of which are notoriously flawed and unreliable; and finally, his proposal for a monetary rule that would substitute for the current discretionary policies an adaptive rule to target the monetary base. One purpose of the rule is to achieve a stable price level by means of adjusting the monetary base to actual changes in productivity and/or in the income velocity of the base. This rule proposal is discussed in detail later in this comment.

Money and Growth

Meltzer's discussion of the relationship of money and economic growth starts with his citation of one point, perhaps the only point, on which essentially all economists agree: money is neutral in the long run under certain highly specific analytical assumptions. These analytical assumptions include flexible prices, wages, and interest rates, and that essentially all other real variables, including preferences, are given and fixed. Usually, perfect foresight is also assumed. There is no uncertainty. A once-for-all change in the nominal stock of money has no real effects under these static conditions. The real value of the stock of money remains unchanged whatever the short-run transitional effects. Similarly, other real variables, such as real income and relative prices, also remain unchanged. Only the price level changes in response to the change in nominal money. (Money and the printing press cannot create real goods.) Nominal money, under these assumptions and for this analytic exercise, affects only nominal prices, but not relative prices or real variables. By the same analysis, repeated, rather once-for-all changes in nominal money known in advance will affect the real quantity of money demanded because the resulting inflation and/or deflation alters the cost of holding money.

The resource cost of creating money is zero—the cost of printing money or expanding bank reserves is essentially zero. Given the productivity- and utility-enhancing properties of money, some economists have concluded that the optimal quantity of money is one where people have so much real money that, at the margin, its private yield is also zero—that this is, there is satiety (see Friedman, 1969). This would make money essentially a free good, equal to the marginal resource cost of producing more units of money. The theoretical optimum can be achieved by deflation equal to the real rate of return on other capital. Nominal interest rates would be zero because the inflation premium in nominal interest rates would be negative, and a perfect offset to the real interest rate, which is always positive. Each unit of money would therefore have a real yield apart from the money services it provides, the yield equal to the rate of deflation, which would be the rate at which each nominal unit of money would appreciate in value. This would be one way of effectively paying interest on money, which would induce people to hold more money. Money would be a composite good, part of which yields real asset returns equal to the deflation and part of which yields monetary services. At the margin, the monetary yield on money is driven to zero, its real resource cost. There is no opportunity cost to holding money in this regime.

Nonspecialists may not see the relevance of this exercise in formal theory. To monetary theorists, however, this abstract theorizing is very interesting, in part because it helps analyze and isolate some of the essential long-run *static* characteristics of money and of monetary change, particularly under conditions of no uncertainty.

In this connection, Meltzer, summarizing various surveys of the literature, states, "A common conclusion is that the direction of any effect of inflation or money growth on output is ambiguous" (p. 168). As noted, my own impression of the theoretical literature is that money is long-run neutral. The empirical records, or other circumstances, may yield other conclusions.

Meltzer correctly notes that the services of money include saving transaction and information costs and that "the meaning of *money* . . . should include the set of institutions that permit the public to develop optimal payment schedules—schedules that minimize the costs of carrying out current and intertemporal transactions" (p. 168–169). I strongly agree. Focusing on fully anticipated monetary change and related rates of inflation,[1] Meltzer makes no reference to the important role of uncertainty about both absolute and relative prices, including uncertainty about interest rates and asset values generated by discretionary monetary policies, and uncertainty about changes in the stock of money or in the demand for money. Uncertainty about inflation and monetary policy are central and pervasive features of essentially all national economies. These uncertainties, largely avoidable, contribute to short-period real effects of monetary change, to so-called business cycles and to large-scale deadweight loss of output, wealth, and employment during cyclical downturns and recessions and during inflation surprises. Meltzer's essential neglect in his chapter of short-run real effects of monetary change is, in my judgment, a serious deficiency that calls into question the validity and relevance of much of his theoretical and policy analysis, as well as his conclusions.

Meltzer goes on to examine the relations between inflation and growth, citing empirical results from his recent study that relies on World Bank data for 100 countries. The study uses three subsets of countries for the years 1965–88, each subset at a different level of income.

There is, on average, a negative simple relation between growth and inflation for the group as a whole and for each subset of countries. More inflation is associated with less growth; less inflation is associated with more growth.[2] Meltzer cites these results as consistent with and an implication of Milton Friedman's (1969) theoretical analysis, summarized above. But Friedman's analysis is about the world of perfect foresight, and flexible wages and prices that abstracts from uncertainties about inflation, monetary change, and other real variables. In the real-world economic experience of the 100 countries, uncertainty is surely a large and ever-present part of the drama.

I would suggest three explanations for the negative association between growth and inflation. One is that growth per se reduces prices on average. Given aggregate nominal demand or nominal GNP, which is largely determined by the nominal stock of money, the more output, the less inflation, and vice versa.

A second reason is an implication of the optimal quantity of money literature. Because inflation, even anticipated inflation, increases the cost of holding money, it induces people to hold less of it. One effect is the loss of the services of money not held, which would result in the loss of those money services and thereby in a decrease in income and growth.

The third reason for the negative association of growth and inflation is related to uncertainty. It results from the consequences of inflation, especially the surprises of unanticipated inflation, the only kind of inflation that essentially has any real effects. These surprises effectively destroy information and thereby impair the efficiency of markets, in part by increased information and search costs to replace impaired information, and in part by the decreased efficiency of existing ways of transacting, monitoring, and doing business. The inflation surprise environment increases the uncertainty under which decisions are made and the outcomes of those decisions (Meiselman, 1976), and leads to the adoption of different, more costly contractual and exchange arrangements.

I would agree with Meltzer that averages of inflation for the period studied may not be the relevant rates for these analyses because the averages ignore the variability of inflation rates. Although variability of inflation tends to be related to the level of inflation, the two should be treated explicitly and separately. Averages also ignore the element of inflation surprises and anticipations gone wrong that are cost enhancing and efficiency diminishing.

These data, in my judgment, probably do not have any bearing on the question of the optimal inflation rate in a hypothetical surprise-free world of no uncertainty, perfect foresight, and flexible wages and prices, which are the assumptions of the optimal inflation and growth literature cited above. Nevertheless, for these and for other reasons, I would agree with Meltzer's conclusions that "the choice of monetary policy must continue to rest on considerations other than those stressed in the theoretical literature on optimal policy" (p. 170–171).

However, I would take exception to his reading of the literature when he states, "Results from theory and data analyses about the optimal rate of inflation or rate of money growth are inconclusive. It is not clear whether there is a unique, optimal monetary policy in the sense used in this literature," Here Meltzer begs the question and pays no heed to the costs and chaos of undependable, unforecastable, and hence destabilizing monetary policies. These repeated failures and costs present a strong case for a dependable, forecastable price level and for not imposing inflation and deflation surprises on the economy. Whatever that surpriseless, or surprise-minimizing, price level happens to be seems to me to be less important than reducing the uncertainty, costs and distortions of the present anchorless discretionary regime. Or, as Meltzer, himself, later states, "A main objective of economic stabilization policy should be to reduce the uncertainty faced by consumers and producers to the minimum inherent in nature and trading arrangements" (p. 172). But if there is no secular advantage to any specific inflation rate provided it is essentially certain, why not settle for a stable price level and zero inflation, which would have the added virtue of facilitating intertemporal contracting and exchange, and the pricing of securities discounting future payments. A stable price level regime would also avoid the costs and distortions of the present tax code that effectively taxes nominal capital gains even when assets values in real terms decline.

Discretionary Monetary Policy: Why Forecasts Fail[3]

Meltzer then goes on to the relationship between discretionary policy and forecasts. His excellent survey of various studies of the accuracy of forecasts shows that all forecasts are poor, even with respect to the direction of the economy. This poor forecasting record includes government forecasts derived from access to presumed superior or privileged information. One important item missing from the survey regards the forecasting of turning points. Even though there is no reason to believe that any of the forecasters would be better at forecasting business-cycle turning points than other events, it would be worthwhile knowing, if only to complete the record. In any event, Meltzer concludes, "forecast errors are so large relative to the mean rate of change that forecasts cannot distinguish slow growth or recession from a boom. Similar conclusions hold for forecasts of inflation . . . . No single method or model seems to be superior to others" (p. 172).

Meltzer lists several explanations for the poor performance of all forecasts. One is that forecasting errors "reflect . . . . unpredictable, random shocks that hit the economy" (p. 172), either from real events or from unanticipated or misperceived policy actions. He cites a 1985 study by Litterman that indicates monetary policy actions account for a large part of the uncertainty and variability experienced during the sample period. I agree with Meltzer that "holding monetary policy constant, or otherwise making policy more predictable, would reduce this source of variability" (p. 178).

This raises several questions about forecasts, including why they have been, and continue to be, so poor. Inability to forecast is one reason for the closing of so many bank, brokerage house, and business economics departments that were mainly devoted to forecasting. The forecasts were not worth their costs. Given the years of serious analysis and research on business cycles, macroeconomics, money, and Federal Reserve behavior by the best and the brightest of the world's economists, including Nobel Prize winners and highly paid Fed watchers, and the potentially huge payoffs for successful forecasting, how come no one of them can do a consistently good job of forecasting? Moreover, how come much of the economics profession and many of their students use an analysis of the effects of monetary change that is derived from the assumption that the Fed cannot surprise them because the public knows in advance what the Fed will do (even though the Fed itself may not know)? One implication is that Fed policies have little or no impact on real variables. This is the so-called policy ineffectiveness analysis of the rational expectations approach. If the best and the brightest cannot forecast, how can the rest of the public? A related and intriguing question is why people have not discovered how to forecast, including how to forecast Fed policies.

I have one explanation for some of these related puzzles. Recent research in monetary economics emphasizes the crucial importance of policy surprises on economic outcomes. It is unanticipated money growth that alters interest rates and the real variables that cause real effects, including business cycles. This is how the rational expectations analysis leads to an emphasis on a money supply rule, especially a rule consistent with stable prices. But such a rule would then limit, even eliminate, the Federal Reserve's ability to affect financial markets and real economic outcomes such as employment and output precisely because the rule would not permit any monetary surprises.

To protect and enhance their power as well as the role of their institutions and their personnel, the Federal Reserve and other discretionary authorities *cannot* and *will not commit institutional suicide by adopting a fixed strategy*, including any stabilization or monetary policy rules. Indeed, the Federal Reserve will *not* adopt such rules and will fight, as it has fought, any attempt to have rules or fixed strategies imposed that would make its actions predictable. Instead, the Fed's institutional incentives are to adopt a strategy that permits it to continue imposing surprises on the public, and thereby to retain its power. That power largely stems from the Fed's ability to pursue actions that have real effects in the short run on income, employment, interest rates, and so forth. One further important by-product of this strategy is the impairment of accountability, thereby also protecting the Fed from having to answer for its actions and its errors.

The changing and changeable Fed policies and operations are intended to keep Fed policies and behavior essentially hidden from the public. The result is that Fed policies and operations are essentially unforecastable. Expectations of Fed policy may be "rational" in the sense that they are not systematically biased, but such expectations are typically so far off the mark that large numbers of people typically, consistently, and inevitably make large forecasting errors. Even the best and the brightest experts who devote much of their professional lives to studying the Fed have poor records when it comes to forecasting Fed actions. If Nobel Prize winners, or others, become able to forecast Fed policies, the Fed can easily change its policies to keep itself unforecastable and still capable of creating surprises, thereby remaining both powerful and effective in imposing surprises.

Thus, analogous to the Heisenberg principle in physics, when the public observes the Fed, as it surely does, it causes a change in Federal Reserve behavior. Similarly, when the public goes on to use those observations to anticipate Fed actions, it changes the public's behavior, too. The results are unstable, dynamically inconsistent expectations of each other held by both the Fed and the public. Policies and actions chosen today as optimal, given today's expectations about tomorrow, may no longer be optimal when tomorrow comes. For one thing, even good forecasts go awry, one reason policies, actions, and anticipations may frequently change in unpredictable, essentially unforecastable ways. One result is *bilateral dynamic inconsistency*, which is a process of sequentially shifting anticipations, behavior, and uncertainties of *both* the public and the Federal Reserve stemming from discretionary and essentially unconstrained monetary policy. One irony is that the Fed cannot hope to be credible if it fails to make itself effective in achieving stabilization goals, and the Fed cannot be consistently effective in achieving stabilization goals if it makes itself unpredictable. The Fed cannot avoid the genuine dilemma.

Discretionary policy essentially generates a two-person rather than a one-person game. Because the Fed cannot know what expectations the public holds or how the public's expectations will respond to its actions, the Fed's policies, too, are unavoidably subject to error in achieving Fed goals. Interest rate targeting, central to Fed procedures, adds to the accident-prone and unstable characteristics of the system. Because the public cannot know current and future policies, the public, too, has more uncertainty and makes more errors in evaluating present and future markets and in making appropriate choices and decisions. Discretionary monetary policy cannot be rendered wholly ineffective by the public à la the rational expectations policy/policy ineffectiveness/dynamic inconsistency literature, because the public cannot determine with confidence what current policies are, or what future policies will be.

Discretionary monetary policy thereby generates uncertainty and deadweight losses, real effects. These considerations argue for the creation and adoption of monetary rules that, if feasible, would largely reduce the uncertainties and the associated costs resulting from discretionary policies—rules that could have self-stabilization properties and eliminate the need for depending on forecasts.

The Base Is the Wrong Target

The last part of Meltzer's chapter is devoted to a discussion of his preliminary work on developing just such an adaptive or adjustable monetary rule, similar, but not identical, to the adaptive or adjustable rules of his Carnegie colleague, Ben McCallum. In order to achieve a stable price level, Meltzer proposes a rule to target the monetary base to offset either a change in base income velocity or "permanent changes in productivity or other one-time changes in output" (p. 182). (How could one tell if changes in output were one-time only?) It is as if the monetary base is substituted for the stock of money in the income variant of the Irving Fisher equation of exchange, $MV = Py$. The result is in a new identity, $BV = Py$, where B is the average quantity of the monetary base in the period; V is the income velocity of the base, the average number of times B is spent for current output (real income), y; and P is the relevant price index or average price per unit of output, y. The price stabilization mechanism of the rule to keep P essentially constant is to adjust B to offset any changes in V or y.

Such rules, if properly constructed, are highly desirable. I would be very pleased if such an effective rule could be successfully developed and adopted. Meltzer himself is realistic and cautious, as he notes, "The public must have confidence that the policymaker knows these magnitudes. Such confidence would be misplaced" (p. 183). For now, the work is so preliminary that we must wait for better and tested results.

However, I do wish to comment on the use of the monetary base as the target of monetary policy. Some of my comments are directly relevant to current and recent Fed policies and to the prolonged recession and slow growth of the past several years of the Bush administration and of the Greenspan Fed.

There are several virtues to the monetary base as the target of monetary policy or of Fed policy actions. Data on the base are available daily to the Fed because the base is essentially composed of two Fed liabilities: (1) Federal Reserve notes used by the public as currency, plus (2) bank deposits at Federal Reserve banks, which are essentially the reserves of the banking system. Data on the monetary base are available on a daily basis because they are taken directly from the Federal Reserve's own books. The fact that data are available day by day is surely inconsequential, especially given the huge amount of noise in the daily changes in the data.

A more appealing feature of the base is the potential for simplifying much of the conduct of monetary policy and for avoiding the hazards and complications of the variability of the money multiplier, the ratio of the money stock to the monetary base. In fact, under some monetary rules, including a fixed percentage increase in the stock of money each week or each month, a base rule and a base target rather than a money stock rule and target would simplify the operation of monetary policy. The enormous trading and churning of the Fed's portfolio would be eliminated, as would the various "defensive" operations designed or intended to offset currency drains, float, and other factors that alter the base money multiplier. Also, a base target and a base rule would eliminate moment-to-moment changes in the base required to peg in the federal funds rate, now the primary target of Federal Reserve policy.

Despite these appealing characteristics, the base may well be the wrong target, wrong in the sense of the relative instability of the base with respect to the goal of either nominal GNP or a price index, especially when the base is compared with an alternative money stock intermediate target such as M2. Moreover, the theoretical link between the base, itself mostly a component of money, and nominal GNP or prices is less well grounded than is the money stock itself. Indeed, I know of no extensive literature or validated hypotheses on the demand for the base per se. Thus, the relationship of the base to real or nominal income or other variables cannot be analyzed. At most we may have an empirical rule of thumb for a ratio not derived from the body of economic analysis.

Most of the base is composed of currency. It is well to recall that during the banking and monetary collapse of the early 1930s, the M2 money stock fell 35% but the monetary base actually increased in every year from 1930 through 1933, largely as a result of the increase in the currency component of the base. Currency in the hands of the public increased 45% between the end of 1929 and March 1933, as bank depositors ran from the collapsing banking system to the safety of currency, also appreciating in real value because of sharply falling prices.[4]

For many years, currency, which is essentially demand determined, has been rising relative to bank reserves, M1, and M2. Part of the reason for the relative increase in the currency-deposit and currency-reserve ratios is the apparent significant and growing use of U.S. currency in foreign countries, possibly for illegal tax evasion, possibly for drug-related uses, possibly for flight purposes, or possibly to conceal assets and to protect them from confiscation. I use the word *apparent* because virtually nothing is known about who holds U.S. currency or where it is held, making it essentially impossible to analyze or to understand much about demands for or uses of U.S. currency, including how much is held and used abroad. There are small bits of information—for example, that Federal Reserve notes of the Federal Reserve Bank of Chicago rose sharply several years ago during the liberation of Eastern Europe, suggesting that the large Slavic communities in Chicago and the Midwest were sending cash to their relatives behind the fallen Iron Curtain—but this is a far cry from any quantitatively or analytically relevant measures.

Despite the secular rise in the ratio of currency to deposits, monetary base velocity, the ratio of GNP to the base drifted *up*,[5] from approximately 12 in 1959 to 20 in 1980. It has generally been falling since 1985. In 1991, base velocity was approximately 18.5. Base velocity fell even more up to the time of this writing in 1992. The monetary base, largely

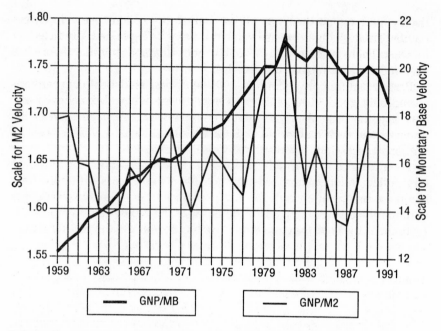

FIGURE 1 M2 Velocity and Monetary Base Velocity, 1959–91 (Annual Averages of Quarterly Figures)

currency, continues to grow rapidly, but nominal GNP has been rising slowly (see Figure 1).

In contrast, M2 velocity is essentially trendless. Except for the rapid rise during the inflation and interest rate surges in the late Carter years and its decline to earlier norms in the early Reagan years, M2 velocity essentially remained within the range of 1.6 to 1.7 between 1959 and 1991, with a mean value of 1.65, the midpoint of the range. The mean annual change is –0.01%, which is essentially zero. This is hardly surprising, given that M2 velocity in recent years—for example, during the Bush presidency since 1989—is essentially identical to the M2 velocity of the late 1950s and early 1960s. On an annual basis, for the 33 years from 1959 through 1991 the mean of M2 velocity is 1.65 and its standard deviation is 0.046. Its coefficient of variation, the ratio of the standard deviation to the mean, is 2.79%.[6]

For base velocity between 1959 and 1991 the mean is 17.46; the mean annual change is 1.35%; the standard deviation is 2.68, or 15.35% of its mean. This is 5.5 times the corresponding coefficient of variation for M2. Not only is the relative and absolute variability of the monetary base many times greater than the variability of M2, but there is no tested theory, perhaps no theory at all, to analyze or explain base velocity behavior. Thus, changes in base velocity cannot be explained, predicted, or forecast. There is some analysis of currency demand, but that theory has been most unsatisfactory for decades.

Perhaps more convincing than these *ex post* statistical comparisons would be a good, clear real-world experiment, where M2 behaved one way and the base clearly behaved another way. We have been in the midst of one such real-world experiment since at least 1990, the onset of the recent recession. The results of the test are in.

The evidence is clear. M2 has been a dependable indicator of monetary policy; the monetary base has not. For several years, while the base has been rising, often rapidly, M2 has grown very slowly, with some variability (see Figure 2). Since the onset of the recent recession in mid-1990, the growth of the monetary base has been high and mostly rising,

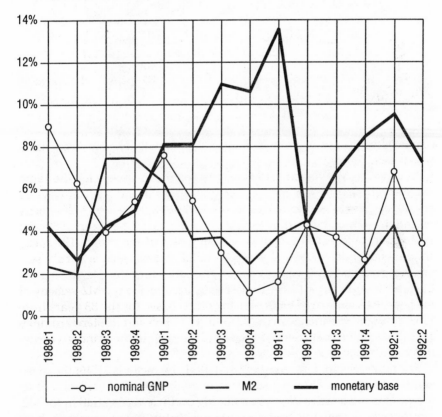

FIGURE 2 Growth of M2, Nominal GNP, and Monetary Base, Quarterly, 1989-92:2 (Quarterly Percentage Change at Annual rates)

often exceeding its growth in the period before mid-1990. In fact, as Figure 2 shows, the growth of the base speeded up prior to the onset of the 1990 recession and continued to grow even more rapidly as the recession deepened in late 1990. In addition, because GNP or GDP has not responded proportionally to the rapid increase in the base, base velocity has fallen sharply: 2% in 1990, 6% in 1991, and about another 6% (at annual rates) in the first half of 1991. Indeed, forecasts and related public policy prescriptions derived from the base, including concerns about imminent inflation stemming from double-digit percentage increases in the base, have also been wide of the mark. Another forecast that failed!

The Recent Record

By contrast, M2 velocity in recent years, especially since George Bush became president, has been relatively stable. During the recession year of 1990, M2 GNP velocity was virtually constant, declining only six one-hundredths of 1%, which rounds to zero. In 1991, M2 velocity declined 0.4%. In the first half of 1992, M2 velocity rose at about a 2.5% annual rate. There may be some puzzles about M2 components such as small time deposits, but it is total M2 and its velocity that are important.

It is little wonder that the sharp slowdown of M2 growth starting in early 1990 led to the 1990 downturn, that slow or no M2 growth in the spring and summer of 1991 was followed by the "double dip" in the fall of 1991 as the expansion faltered, and that 1992's slow or no M2 growth between February and July preceded the subsequent sluggish GNP growth. In my judgment, both the slow and the stop-go money growth have been a major, perhaps even *the* major, factor in the poor economic performance that seems likely to have resulted in the political demise of George Bush.[7]

Other policies, such as the increases in taxes, spending, and regulation during the Bush administration, hobbled efficiency and economic growth. But the long period of cyclical recession and the lack of recovery from it have seen the Fed responding to signs of recovery by imposing periods of still further monetary restraint, periods when the Fed repeatedly failed to reach even the bottom of its own M2 growth target range. It is almost as if the Fed were fighting to stem or turn back imminent growth. This pattern of M2 growth indicates that excessively tight money first created a recession and then prevented, or at least impaired, recovery.

Nominal money cannot systematically and permanently generate real GNP. But we certainly know from many episodes of monetary history and business cycles that shortfalls of money growth initially have real effects resulting in shortfalls of real income, output, and employment; only later does inflation slow down. For given or stable velocity, as recently, when there is a change in the stock of money, there is a corresponding change in nominal GNP. Although we cannot dependably tell how much of a given change in nominal GNP will be composed of prices and how much will be made up of real output, we do know that real GNP tends to be affected first, and prices later. There may be no permanent output effects of monetary change, but there surely are initial real effects within the time frame of the business cycle.

Although we have recently been through a long period of slow or no M2 money growth, the Fed has little or no credibility with respect to its long-term monetary targets or discipline. This is why the long-term interest rate has declined so little relative to the sharp fall in short-term rates and why the long-term rate adjusted for current inflation remains so high. The Fed has a long and dreary history of episodes of rapid, too rapid, money growth and inflation that have followed, sometimes almost as a reaction to, periods of monetary reduction and economic recession. Indeed, I recall Allan Meltzer saying to me some years ago, "The Fed only knows two speeds—too fast and too slow!" Perhaps the Fed's lack of credibility in the eyes of the public reflects a reality-based set of expectations derived from historical experience as well as the absence of a monetary rule and the lack of statutory or administrative monetary constraints, commitments, or accountability that would guarantee a noninflationary monetary policy. With no such guarantees, why should the future differ from the past?

One result of this lack of credibility and commitment is that the Fed policy of squeezing down the rate of M2 money growth, especially in the face of relatively stable M2 velocity, has meant not only a corresponding slowing down of the growth of nominal GNP, but also that there has been relatively more real output response and less price level response to tight money than would be the case in a regime where the Fed had better credibility. This mirrors the sharp fall in short-term rates and the sluggish decline in long-term rates.

Another ironic result of the Fed policy has been that Bill Clinton and the Democrats have certainly had a powerful, if unintended, assist from all the Reagan and Bush appointees at the Fed. By contrast, in the Eisenhower, Nixon, and Reagan Republican administrations, each incoming administration endured a restrictive Fed policy in the first year of each presidential term that led to a recession that lasted until the second year of the term. The Republicans lost congressional seats in each off-year congressional election, but by the end of the four-year term, inflation rates were down and the economy was growing well. All earlier Republican presidents were reelected. In the Bush presidency, perhaps the tight money started too late—and lasted too long.

Obviously, George Bush, who majored in economics at Yale, never read Irving Fisher, Yale's great economist of an earlier era, or took the lessons of Fisher to the White House. Nor did the other Ivy Leaguers—Baker, Brady, and Darman. Otherwise, they might have known what the Federal Reserve did to them (and to the rest of us) in time to have saved their administration.

Notes

1. Meltzer notes, "The choice of a wealth-maximizing rate of inflation requires analysis of how this institutional structure evolves *under different known and fully anticipated rates of inflation*" (p. 3; emphasis added).

2. In a paper I wrote some years ago, I described essentially the same evidence for the United States (see Meiselman, 1976).

3. This discussion depends on the analysis developed in Meiselman (in press).

4.

	Money Stock (M2)	Monetary Base	Currency Held by Public	Commercial Bank Reserves
October 1929	48,155	7,345	3,832	3,513
December 1929	45,867	6,978	3,800	3,178
December 1930	44,054	7,125	3,809	3,316
December 1931	37,339	7,735	4,604	3,131
December 1932	34,031	8,028	4,830	3,198
March 1933	29,970	8,414	5,509	2,905
December 1933	30,807	8,302	4,839	3,463

Source: Friedman and Schwartz, (1963, Appendix A). *Note:* The monetary base (or high-powered money) is the sum of currency held by the public outside banks and commercial bank reserves. Figures are in millions of dollars.

5. For given income velocity of money (the ratio of GNP to the stock of money), a rise in the currency-deposit ratio would result in a decline in base velocity.

6. The coefficient of variation is a measure used to facilitate comparison of the variability of two or more series by deflating the standard deviation of a series by its mean to adjust for differences in the level or scale of the series involved.

7. This was one forecast that did not fail.

References

Friedman, M. (1969). "The Optimal Quantity of Money." In M. Friedman, *The Optimal Quantity of Money and Other Essays*. Chicago: Aldine.

Friedman, M., and Schwartz, A. (1963). *A Monetary History of the United States, 1867–1960*. Princeton, NJ: Princeton University Press.

Litterman, R. B. (1985). "How Monetary Policy in 1985 Affects the Outlook." *Quarterly Review* (Federal Reserve Bank of Minneapolis), *9*, 2–13.

Meiselman, D. I. (1976, January). "More Inflation; More Unemployment." *Tax Review* (Tax Review Foundation, Inc.).

Meiselman, D. I. (in press). "Rational Expectations and the New Classical Microeconomics." *Cato Journal*, *12*(1).

PART FOUR

Government Spending and Taxation

Introduction

The consumption and reallocation of resources perhaps constitute the very essence of government, achieved in the main through its powers of taxation and spending. That such fiscal activity by the public sector yields both benefits and costs is beyond doubt, but the measurement of those effects remains difficult, despite much research effort over many years. This difficulty does not reduce the need for qualitative and quantitative analysis of the benefits and costs of fiscal activity, as government consumes and redirects a substantial proportion of national output in most of the world.

But for market economies, in which prices are assumed to reflect the value and cost of resources, the value of government output in national accounts generally is measured as (or is assumed to be equal to) the cost of the inputs used by government; those costs usually do not reflect secondary but important effects of taxation and spending. If government is "too big"—that is, if aggregate wealth would be increased were some resources shifted away from government back to the private sector—then the national accounts are likely to overstate the value of government spending. And the secondary effects of fiscal activity imply that the government budget would understate the true economic cost of taxation and spending.

Notwithstanding the existence of a vast literature on the demand and cost of public services, much work remains to be done in terms of both conceptual and empirical analysis of public sector spending and taxation, and attendant effects upon aggregate economic well-being. William A. Niskanen reports empirical findings on the effect of several types of fiscal activities upon three alternative measures of economic growth. He finds that government spending increases real GNP significantly, whereas taxes and deficit spending (i.e., future taxation) have significant negative effects. Interestingly, Niskanen finds that the economic benefits of nondefense spending not used for transfer payments—loosely, public sector nondefense investment—may be greater than the economic costs of the taxes and debt needed to finance the additional spending, at least as the benefits are measured in his econometric analysis. One possible problem with this finding is that some or much government investment could be undertaken by the private sector, and it is at least plausible that costs would fall. If that is true, it may suggest that the actual net effect of some government spending upon growth and productivity is negative, but not captured by the data.

Norman B. Ture notes that recognition of the importance of investment and saving in the process of economic growth has grown in policy circles, but that the disincentives for investment and saving yielded by various public policies usually are ignored or discounted heavily. Ture notes that a subtle effect, for example, of the erosion of property rights, is a reduced incentive to save, that is, to acquire capital. Various taxes and regulations have similar effects; Ture emphasizes in particular the multiple taxation of saving and capital.

More generally, Ture outlines several features of the U.S. tax system that represent hindrances for economic growth, and then turns to a detailed discussion of ways to increase the neutrality of the tax system. One potential problem with the quest for greater neutrality in the tax system may be inherent in democratic processes: to the extent that representative democracy yields incentives for government to bestow benefits upon concentrated interest groups at the expense of diffused majorities, a tax system with many "loopholes" and high tax rates may represent a political "equilibrium" inconsistent with neutrality.

The general discussion following presentation of the work in this section centered, interestingly, upon the design of taxes as a system of user fees, in a fashion similar to the use of gasoline taxes as an approximate method of imposing the costs of highway construction and maintenance upon the respective beneficiaries in rough proportion to the benefits received. This concept of "optimal" taxation is reflected in a large literature extending over many years, and it differs substantially from the more mainstream "neutrality" objective emphasized heavily by Ture. To put it differently: the very meaning of *neutrality* is more obscure in a world in which the benefits of government spending vary among individuals and voting groups. As long as the total amount and the composition of the government budget are not independent of the tax system and resulting political pressures, neutrality actually may yield reduced national wealth in the form of a government budget too small or too large and inappropriately configured.

7

Fiscal Effects on U.S. Economic Growth

William A. Niskanen

Most empirical studies of the fiscal effects on economic growth are of two types. One set, the focus of most applied public finance, estimates the partial effects of changes in specific government expenditures or tax provisions, based on the data from one country (for example, see Aschauer, 1990; Jorgenson and Yun, 1990). The other set, the focus of several recent studies, estimates the effects of changes in highly aggregated fiscal conditions, based on cross-country data (for example, see Barro, 1989; Barth and Bradley, 1987; Grier and Tullock, 1987; Kormendi and Meguire, 1985; Landau, 1983).

These two types of studies are subject to different limitations. The microstudies invite concern about whether the estimated effects may be partly due to omitted variables. The aggregated studies invite concern that the effects of different types of government spending and receipts may be quite different; in addition, there is reason to question whether the estimates based on cross-country data sets reflect the effects of fiscal conditions in any one country. Both types of studies, in addition, have characteristically assumed that changes (or differences) in fiscal conditions are exogenous.

Some of the results of these studies are also inconsistent. For example, Aschauer (1990) finds a strong positive effect of public capital on U.S. output, but Barth and Bradley (1987), in a study based on a cross-country data set, find no significant effect of government investment. Some of the studies based on cross-country data sets find a negative effect of various measures of government consumption expenditures on economic growth; others find no significant effects.

This chapter summarizes the results from a study of data somewhat intermediate between the above two types. The data set comprises annual U.S. observations for the period 1950–89. Economic growth is measured in three dimensions: real GNP per working-age adult, output per hour worked in the business sector, and hours worked in the business sector per working-age adult. Combined government sector (federal, state, and local) expenditures are aggregated in three groups—defense expenditures, other government purchases of goods and services, and transfer payments plus net subsidies—without any a priori identification of these expenditures as consumption or investment expenditures. Government revenues are aggregated in only two groups: total tax revenues and the net deficit. The test equations do *not* control for the level of private saving and investment, because these conditions are clearly endogenous to changes in fiscal conditions. In this sense, the test equations are reduced form equations in a larger model in which the effects of fiscal conditions operate, in part, through the level of private saving and investment. The effects on each of the three dimensions of economic growth are estimated simultaneously by the iterative three-stage least squares technique.

The advantages and limitations of this approach are also obvious. One advantage is that there is no clear a priori basis for separating government expenditures into investment (or property rights-enhancing) expenditures and consumption expenditures. A second advantage is that this study, to my knowledge the only one of its type, recognizes that economic growth and the fiscal variables are jointly determined. Another advantage is that the study is based only on U.S. data, at least reducing the omitted variables problem specific to cross-country tests. The major limitation, of course, is that the government expenditures and revenue variables are still highly aggregated, both by type and across the three levels of U.S. government.

Some (Minimal) Theory

Robert Barro (1990) has recently developed a characteristically elegant model of the effects of government spending on economic growth that is an adequate basis for selecting the test equations and interpreting the results presented in this chapter. Barro's model, like most other recently developed growth models, assumes constant returns to scale in producing total output. In his model, however, the production function exhibits constant returns to scale in the combination of private capital and the level of government investment services, but diminishing returns to each component separately.

$$y = \phi(k,g) = k \cdot \phi(g/k),$$ [1]

where y is output per worker, k is the private capital stock per worker, and g is the level of government investment services per worker. There are two reasons government investment services are imperfect substitutes for private capital. Some government services, like defense and the maintenance of law and order, are not efficiently excludable. And for some government services, user fees are not efficient because the services either are nonrival in consumption or have positive external effects.

In the simple case where governments produce only investment services and finance these services entirely by a flat tax rate,

$$g = t = \tau \cdot y = \tau \cdot k \cdot \phi(g/k) \qquad [2]$$

For this case, the rate of growth of consumption expenditure per worker is

$$y = \dot{c}/c = 1/\sigma [(1 - \tau) \cdot \phi(g/k) \cdot (1 - \eta) - \rho], \qquad [3]$$

where σ is the (constant) marginal utility of consumption, η is the elasticity of y with respect to g, and ρ is the (constant) rate of time preference of the representative worker. Further, if the production function is Cobb-Douglas, η is also constant. For this case, there is a unique optimum level of g that maximizes both the growth rate and the utility of the representative worker. At lower levels of g, the positive marginal effect of g is higher than the negative marginal effect of τ; the opposite is the case at higher levels. Because private saving is a function of $(1 - \tau)$, k is endogenous (in a closed economy) and the private saving rate peaks at a level of g lower than the optimum; in the region near the optimal level of g, thus, the partial effect of g on private saving is negative.

In the more complex (and realistic) case, governments supply both investment and consumption services. For this case,

$$t = (\tau g + \tau h) \cdot y, \qquad [4]$$
$$y = 1/\varepsilon \cdot [(1 - \tau g - \tau h) \cdot \phi(y/k) \cdot (1 - \eta) - \rho], \qquad [5]$$

where the new term τg is g/y, τh is h/y, and h is the level of government consumption services. In this case, the rate of economic growth and the optimum level of government investment services are both a negative function of the level of government consumption expenditures, and the combination of private and government decisions does not maximize the utility of the representative worker.

For this chapter, this model implies that the test equations should express the several dimensions of economic growth as a logarithmic function of the level of real government expenditures and the combined *after*-tax rate; the parameters σ, η, and ρ are each assumed to be constant. For test purposes, there are several problems with this formulation. First, there is no a priori basis for identifying the type and amount of government expenditures that provide investment services or consumption services (to either the population or a self-serving government). Second, governments finance part of their expenditures by borrowing. For this reason, the test equations summarized in the next section include each of the major types of government expenditures and test for the effects of both taxes and borrowing.

Test Results

Structure of the Test Equations

As in any time-series analysis, the appropriate form of the test equation depends on whether the variables are stable in the level or in the first or some higher-order difference of these variables. For this reason, each of the test variables was subject to the augmented Dickey-Fuller unit root test. The results of these tests indicate that none of the dependent variables is trend stable but that the first difference of each of these variables (with a trend) is stable. The first statistical implication of these tests is that each of the test equations should be expressed in first difference form with a trend term. The second implication is that the standard error of forecast of the *level* of these variables is unbounded. The important economic implication of these tests is that shocks to each of the dependent variables are permanent. A shock that reduces productivity in one year, for example, reduces the level of productivity in each subsequent year; in other words, there is no evidence that productivity growth will return to its prior trend. This is the primary reason economic forecasts for more than one period ahead are subject to such large errors.

Sample and Test Variables

The samples for each of these tests are annual observations for the period 1950 through 1989. The economic and fiscal data are based on the July 1992 revision, but the population data for 1981–89 are subject to revision based on the 1990 census. All of the economic and fiscal data are from the 1988 and 1992 issues of the *Economic Report of the President* and the July 1992 *Survey of Current Business*. The data on oil prices and net imports were provided by the American Petroleum Institute.

Each test equation includes the same list of independent variables. The dependent and common independent variables are described below:

Dependent Variables
D(LRGNP)   first difference, natural log of real GNP per working-age adult

D(LPROD)   first difference, natural log of output per hour in the business sector

D(LHOUR)   first difference, natural log of hours worked in the business sector per working-age adult

Independent Variables

C   constant

YEAR   50–89

D(UER)   first difference, civilian unemployment rate

D(NDEPY)   first difference, real defense expenditures as a percentage of (prior year) real GNP

D(LROGE)   first difference, natural log of real other government purchases of goods and services per working-age adult

D(LRTRP)   first difference, natural log of real transfer payments and net subsidies per working-age adult

D(LOMTR)   first difference, natural log of $(1 - TAX/GNP)$, where TAX is the total government tax receipts

D(LOMDR)   first difference, natural log of $(1 - DEF/GNP)$, where DEF is the net total government deficit

D(OIEPY)   first difference, domestic price of oil times the level of (prior year) net oil imports as a percentage of GNP

Some minor additional explanation is necessary. The number of working-age adults is the population age 20 through 64. Real national security expenditures are based on a price index of my construction, splicing the implicit price deflator for total federal purchases of goods and services through 1971 to the implicit price deflator for defense expenditures since 1972. Some experimentation indicated that the marginal effects of defense expenditures are more significant in the linear form than in the logarithmic form. Real other government purchases of goods and services are the total real purchases of goods and services minus (my estimate of) real national defense expenditures. Real transfer payments and net subsidies are based on the implicit price deflator for personal consumption expenditures. Among the independent variables, C, YEAR, D(NDEPY), D(LROGE), and D(OIEPY) are exogenous. Variables D(UER), D(LRTRP), D(LOMTR), and D(LOMDR) are treated as endogenous.

Instrumental variables used in the system estimates include the included exogenous variables, one-period-lagged values of both the dependent variables and the included endogenous variables, and several excluded exogenous variables that specifically affect D(UER) and D(LRTRP). The several additional instrumental variables are the next-year armed forces overseas share of the working-age population, the first and second lagged ratios of the corporate (Aaa) bond rate to the commercial paper rate, the population age 65 and over as a share of the working-age population, and the relative price of consumer goods. (More information on all variables and data sources is available from the author on request.)

The Estimation Procedure

The three test equations were estimated by the iterative three-stage least squares procedure. This procedure yields more efficient estimates than from two-stage estimates of the separate equations if there is any correlation among the residuals of the several equations. Estimates from this procedure are asymptotic full-information maximum likelihood estimates.

Test Results

Table 7.1 presents the systems estimates of the fiscal effects on real GNP, productivity, and hours worked. (The numbers in parentheses are the standard errors of each coefficient.) This table also presents two other columns, where D(LRBDP) is the first difference of the log of real (gross) business domestic product and D(LRNBP) is the first difference of the log of real nonbusiness product (the sum of government payrolls and output originating in nonprofit institutions, households, and abroad). The coefficients in these columns (but not the standard errors) can be calculated from the estimates in the other columns. Given that real business sector output is the product of productivity and hours worked in the business sector, the coefficients in the second column are the sum of the coefficients in each row of the third and fourth columns. In addition, as real GNP is the sum of real business domestic product and real nonbusiness product, the coefficients in each row of the first column are the weighted sum of the coefficients in the second and fifth columns, where the weights are the respective shares of business and nonbusiness product in real GNP. At the sample means, real business domestic product was .831 of real GNP, and real nonbusiness product was .169 of real GNP. The coefficients of the fifth column, thus, are calculated by solving for the effects on real nonbusiness product from the coefficients in the first and second columns. This procedure provides estimates of the fiscal effects on all of the components of real GNP without solving a more complicated five-equation model with interequation coefficient restrictions. The primary disadvantage of this procedure is that it does not provide estimates of the standard errors of the coefficients in the second and fifth columns.

At this stage, it is useful to discuss the effects of each of the independent variables on the several dimensions of economic growth based on the estimated coefficients presented in Table 7.1.

TABLE 7.1
System Estimates of the Fiscal Effects on Economic Growth

Independent Variables	Dependent Variables				
	D(LRGNP)	D(LRBDP)	D(LPROD)	D(LHOUR)	D(LRNBP)
C	.03789 (.0092)	.0359	.0503 (.0140)	−.0144 (.0083)	.0477
YEAR	−.0003 (.0001)	−.0003	−.0005 (.0002)	.0002 (.0001)	−.0005
D(UER)	−.0060 (.0032)	−.0076	.0086 (.0048)	−.0162 (.0029)	.0019
D(NDEPY)	.0162 (.0025)	.0127	.0139 (.0038)	−.0012 (.0022)	.0332
D(LROGE)	.2647 (.0526)	.2698	.2235 (.0805)	.0463 (.0476)	.2396
D(LRTRP)	.0623 (.0351)	.0614	.1173 (.0537)	−.0559 (.0318)	.0667
D(LOMTR)	1.1286 (.3055)	1.0622	.4778 (.4673)	.5844 (.2763)	1.455
D(LOMDR)	1.7636 (.2722)	1.9514	1.4727 (.4164)	.4787 (.2462)	.8396
D(OIEPY)	−.0031 (.0050)	−.0154	−.0211 (.0077)	.0057 (.0045)	.0574
R^2	.9985		.9977	.9803	
S.E.R.	.0077		.0117	.0069	
D.W.	2.0004		1.8461	2.1554	

Note: Standard errors in parentheses.

The first and second rows present estimates of the annual exogenous increases in the several dimensions of economic growth. The primary lesson from these estimates is that the "natural rate" of increase of real GNP, productivity, and hours worked has changed substantially over the postwar years. Table 7.2 summarizes the estimates of these natural rates over this period. The exogenous contributions to productivity growth are declining, but the exogenous decline in hours worked per member of the working-age population was reversed in the late 1960s.

The third row presents the effects of an increase of one percentage point in the civilian unemployment rate. Such an increase reduces real GNP by 0.6%, with a somewhat larger effect on the business sector. An increase of one percentage point in the unemployment rate increases productivity in the business sector by 0.9% but reduces hours worked by 1.6%.

TABLE 7.2
Exogenous Annual Changes in Economic Conditions (in percentages)

Variables	1949	1969	1989
RGNP/Population	2.3	1.6	1.0
Productivity	2.6	1.5	0.5
Hours/Population	−0.4	0.1	0.5

The fourth row presents the effects of changes in real defense expenditures. An increase in defense expenditures by 1% of GNP, for example, appears to increase real GNP by about 1.6%, primarily by increasing productivity in the business sector and expenditures in the nonbusiness sector. This result, however, should be interpreted with caution, because defense expenditures are valued at cost—not at market value. The effect of defense expenditures on real GNP should be considered a benefit, of course, only if these expenditures are worth at least what they cost.

The fifth row in Table 7.1 presents the elasticities of the dependent variables with respect to the real level of other government purchases of goods and services—most of which are for education, physical infrastructure, police, fire protection, and the like. A 10% increase in real expenditures for these services increases real GNP by about 2.6%, primarily by increasing productivity in the business sector—suggesting that the services financed by most of these expenditures are complementary to inputs in the business sector.

The sixth row presents the elasticities of the dependent variables with respect to real transfer payments and net subsidies. A 10% increase in real transfer payments increases real GNP by about 0.6%, the net effect of an increase in productivity and a reduction in hours worked in the business sector.

The seventh row presents the elasticities of the dependent variables with respect to the *after*-tax rate. The proportional effect of a change in the average tax rate, in turn, is $-b(1 - TR)^{-1}$, where b is the estimated elasticity on the after-tax rate and TR is the ratio of total tax receipts to GNP. An increase in the average tax rate has a large significant negative effect on both real GNP and business sector output and, interestingly, an even larger negative effect on expenditures by the nonbusiness sector. The elasticity of real GNP with respect to the after-tax rate b can also be used to estimate the revenue-maximizing tax rate (t^*), where $t^* = 1/(1 + b)$. The estimate of b indicates that the revenue-maximizing average tax rate in the United States is about 47%.

The eighth row of Table 7.1 presents the elasticities of the dependent variables with respect to the *after*-deficit rate. The proportional effect of a change in the deficit rate, in turn, is $-b(1 - DR)^{-1}$, where b is the estimated elasticity on the after-deficit rate and DR is the ratio of the net total deficit to GNP. An increase in the deficit has a large significant negative effect on real GNP, reflecting significant negative effects on both productivity and hours worked in the business sector. The effect of deficits on expenditures by the nonbusiness sector appears to be smaller than the effect of taxes.

The ninth row presents estimates of the effects on each of the dependent variables of changes in expenditures for oil imports. An increase in expenditures for oil imports by 1% of GNP reduces productivity in the business sector by about 2.2%, but appears to increase hours worked and expenditures in the nonbusiness sector. The net effect on real GNP is not significant.

In summary, the sign, level, and significance of most of the estimates from these tests are satisfactory, and the statistical characteristics of the three test equations are quite satisfactory.

Further Implications of the System Estimates

The partial effects of a $1 billion increase in any of the fiscal variables depends on the form of the variable. For this test, real defense expenditures are expressed as a percentage of real GNP in the prior year. The partial effects of a $1 billion increase in defense expenditures, thus, is

$$\frac{\partial Y}{\partial X} = b[Y/\text{RGNP}(-1)],$$

where b is the estimated coefficient, Y is the level of the economic variable, and RGNP(-1) is the level of real GNP per member of the working-age population in the prior year. This is the only fiscal variable for which the partial effects are independent of the level of the variable.

The estimates of the other fiscal variables are expressed in terms of constant elasticities. The partial effects, for example, of a $1 billion increase in these fiscal variables, however, are a function of both the level of the economic variable and the level of the fiscal variable. Specifically,

$$\partial Y/\partial X = b(Y/X), \qquad \frac{\partial Y}{\partial T} = -b(Y/(Y - T)),$$

where b is the estimated elasticity, Y is the level of the economic variable, X is the level of the expenditure variable, and T is the level of tax receipts or the deficit.

Table 7.3 presents the partial effects of an additional $1 billion of each of the fiscal variables, given the level of the economic and fiscal variables

TABLE 7.3
Partial Effects of the Fiscal Variables in 1989 (in billions of dollars)

	Total	Business	Other
Defense	1.6	1.3	0.3
Domestic	2.1	1.8	0.3
Transfers	0.5	0.4	0.1
Taxes	−1.6	-1.3	−0.3
Deficit	−1.8	-1.7	−0.1

in 1989. An increase in defense expenditures appears to increase GNP by about the same as the negative effects of the taxes or deficit necessary to finance these additional expenditures. At the margin of current conditions, additional defense expenditures are not a good investment in terms of the marketed output of the business sector. One cannot judge whether the United States underinvests in national security without estimating the security value of the additional expenditures. The above estimates are not sufficient for making that judgment.

Some increase in other government expenditures, however, may be worth the additional taxes or deficit. At the margin of current conditions, the positive effects on GNP of additional expenditures of this type appear to be somewhat higher than the negative effects of the additional taxes or deficit. This result is consistent with but more general than the conclusion of Aschauer and others that the United States underinvests in physical infrastructure.

An increase in transfer payments, however, appears to be a bad economic investment. The increase in GNP is much smaller than the negative effects of taxes or the deficit. The value of additional transfer payments, like additional defense expenditures, must be judged on other grounds.

Additional taxes and borrowing have roughly similar negative effects on GNP. The most important implication of these estimates is that government spending for any program should be constrained to a level for which the marginal value of additional spending is equal to 1.6 times the incremental budget cost if financed by taxes or 1.8 times the additional cost if financed by borrowing. The effects of taxes on the business sector are somewhat lower and on the nonbusiness sector are somewhat higher than the corresponding effects of government borrowing.

In summary, the aggregate fiscal package of U.S. governments does not appear to maximize economic growth. At the margin of current conditions, defense expenditures and transfer payments appear to be consumption expenditures, which may be valuable on other grounds but reduce economic growth. The United States, however, appears to underinvest in other government expenditures. A fiscal strategy that reduced national security expenditures and transfer payments, increased other government expenditures, and reduced taxes and the deficit would almost surely increase U.S. economic growth.

An Omitted Variable

One other variable was included in prior versions of these tests: the number of lawyers in active practice. There is reason to believe that the increase in the number of lawyers in active practice reflects conditions that reduce U.S. economic growth, particularly the increase in litigation, lobbying, regulation, and other forms of rent-seeking and rent-defending activity. Stephen Magee (1991), for example, estimates that the average lawyer reduces U.S. GNP by $1 million, based on a cross-country study of economic growth that included, as one variable, the number of lawyers as a percentage of white-collar workers. For this reason, I included the following variable in some prior tests:

$$LOMLS = \log(1 - L/N),$$

where L is the number of lawyers in active practice and N is the working-age population. This variable is not measured very accurately; only 10 consistent observations at different intervals on the number of lawyers in active practice are available in the postwar years, and the other data points were estimated by exponential smoothing around the available observations. The results of these tests were striking but not conclusive. As of 1989, the conditions that led to the employment of the marginal lawyer appeared to reduce GNP by $2.5 million(!), with an even larger proportional effect on business sector productivity; moreover, in prior tests based on the levels of the dependent variables, this variable was quite significant. In the first difference form of the test equations, however, the significance of this variable was reduced, and deletion of this variable did not much change the estimates of the fiscal variables. This is an important issue and a striking estimate, however, and merits further research.

Next Steps

This chapter is the first report of a larger study. One part of this continued research will be to refine the estimates of the policy effects on U.S. economic growth. More attention to separating the effects of peacetime and wartime national security expenditures is merited. It may be useful to divide the large aggregate of other government purchases of goods and services into education expenditures and an "other expenditures" variable. The effects of transfer payments may be better measured in the (1 – transfer rate) form, consistent with the treatment of the tax and deficit rates, for which the marginal effects are increasing. The tax variable should be expressed in terms of the effective average marginal rates, rather than average rates, but I do not know whether there is an adequate time series on average marginal tax rates. I am compelled to find an adequate index of the level of regulation and litigation activity. Suggestions are welcome.

The other part of this research will use the data base to estimate jointly the demand functions for government services, the tax and deficit function, and real GNP. From some prior estimates, some further refinement of the variables in these functions is probably necessary. This study, to my knowledge, will be the first to estimate jointly the several fiscal functions and the effects of fiscal conditions on real GNP.

References

American Petroleum Institute. (1990). Washington, DC.

Aschauer, D. A. (1990). "Is Government Spending Stimulative?"*Contemporary Policy Issues, 8*, 30–46.

Barro, R. J. (1989). "Economic Growth in a Cross Section of Countries." NBER Working Paper 3120.

Barro, R. J. (1990). "Government Spending in a Simple Model of Economic Growth." *Journal of Political Economy, 98*, (supplement), S103–S125.

Barth, J., and Bradley, M. D. (1987). "The Impact of Government Spending on Economic Activity." Unpublished manuscript, George Washington University.

Grier, K. B., and Tullock, G. (1987). "An Empirical Analysis of Cross-National Economic Growth, 1950–1980." Unpublished manuscript. California Institute of Technology.

Jorgenson, D. W., and Yun, K. Y. (1990). "Tax Reform and U.S. Economic Growth." *Journal of Political Economy, 98* (supplement), S151–S193.

Kormendi, R. C., and Meguire, P. G. (1985). "Macroeconomic Determinants of Growth: Cross-Country Evidence." *Journal of Monetary Economics, 16*, 141–163.

Landau, D. L. (1983). "Government Expenditure and Economic Growth: A Cross-Country Study." *Southern Economic Journal, 49*, 783–792.

Magee, S. P. (1991, January/February). "The Negative Effect of Lawyers on the U.S. Economy." *International Economic Insights*, pp. 34–35.

United States. (1988, 1992). *Economic Report of the President Transmitted to the Congress*. Washington, DC: U.S. Government Printing Office.

United States. (1992, July). *Survey of Current Business*. Washington, DC: Department of Commerce.

8

Capital Formation, Economic Growth, and Jobs: A Heretical Tax Strategy for Economic Growth

Norman B. Ture

Public Policies and the Costs of Growth-Generating Activities

Promoting economic growth has long been a byword of public policymakers of all ideologies and party affiliations. For the most part, however, the concept of growth as a public policy goal has not been carefully articulated, nor have the criteria to guide progrowth policies been spelled out and subjected to critical examination. It is not surprising, therefore, that even as the emphasis on growth as a policy goal has increased over the past several years, few, if any, public policy initiatives have effectively pursued that objective. Indeed, many policy developments have added new impediments to achievement of this goal. A cynical observer may be forgiven for viewing policymakers' self-proclaimed dedication to economic growth as mere rhetoric masking undeviating pursuit of their own agendas.

In fact, however, there has been some modest advance in the policy community's grasp of the concept of economic growth, its sources, and the way in which public policies affect growth. In the past decade and a half, for example, there has been a growing consensus that increasing the rate of national saving is a key to achieving more rapid growth. There remains, to be sure, a sharp division of views about the means by which public policy can achieve any significant increase in saving as a share of national product—whether the focus should be on aggregate fiscal-budgetary policies to reduce the budget deficit or on changes in the tax structure and spending programs to moderate the saving disincentives facing household and business decision makers.[1] Nevertheless, the broad consensus that increasing saving contributes to growth is a significant advance over the notion prevailing not so long ago that saving deterred economic progress.

Implicit in the emphasis on increasing saving is recognition that the essence of the growth process is expansion of production capability. Policymakers tend to focus narrowly on saving as the means of financing additions to the stock of physical capital, which they deem to be the critically important element in economic growth. I do not mean to deprecate this emphasis. Increases in such capital contribute directly to potential output, and increases in the capital/labor ratio are needed to help maintain or increase the rate of advance in labor's productivity. In turn, the higher level of labor's productivity is equivalent to an increase in the demand for labor services that when implemented results in increases in employment, output, and real wage rates.

This perception of the importance of saving in this connection, a commonplace in today's policy forum, represents a huge advance in policymakers' thinking about growth over the view, prevailing in much of the postwar era, that growth is generated by increases in aggregate demand and that growth and associated increases in employment have to be weighed against the increases in inflationary pressures allegedly resulting therefrom. Largely overlooked by public policymakers, however, is that growth entails real costs—that increasing production capability requires forgoing alternative uses of time, talents, energies, and other resources. For any person or business, the pace of growth depends on how much additional income and wealth can be obtained by incurring any given amount of these opportunity costs and how much of these costs one is willing to incur today for the gains in future well-being that may be obtained thereby. In a free society, growth of the economy as a whole is determined by the aggregation of these decisions. Because they tend to overlook the opportunity costs of growth-generating activities, policymakers ignore how policy initiatives affect these costs, and hence are not mindful of the growth implications, often adverse, of the policies they promote.

This failure to identify the opportunity costs of growth-generating activities accounts for the inconsistency—indeed, the incoherence—of public policies. Examples abound, particularly in the area of so-called social policy, where many legislative initiatives have overlooked their effect in raising the cost of labor services, thereby limiting employment gains and the associated increases in output potential. The Civil Rights Act of 1991 and the 1990 Americans with Disabilities Act are prime examples of legislation in the development of which no consideration was given to how these laws would affect employment costs and the employment even of those for whose benefit the legislation ostensibly was intended.

In a similar vein, the many and varied legislative initiatives to raise taxes on upper-income individuals either disregard the resulting increases in the opportunity costs of productivity-enhancing efforts or assume that such efforts are substantially unresponsive to their costs. This assumption implies that large shares of the compensation and other income that affluent people receive represent quasi-rents—receipts in excess of the costs incurred to produce them. In some—the most dramatic—cases, this must surely be true.[2] But the compensation of most highly paid people closely approximates the opportunity costs they have incurred to achieve the levels of productivity reflected by their rewards.

Also ignored by policymakers are the consequences for other suppliers of production inputs of any curtailment of efforts or less productive uses of resources by those subjected to high marginal tax rates. The compensation of these individuals is not earned in economic isolation, but by the combination of their efforts with various other production inputs. Unless the laws of production have been repealed, any reduction in the inputs of the highly paid reduces the productivity of these other inputs and the incomes of their suppliers.

Given the near-universal conviction that we save too little, it is ironic that in no other case is the failure to consider opportunity costs more blatant and more damaging than with regard to the impact of public policies on private saving. Tax and other policies that raise the cost of saving not only tend to curtail capital formation, but have more far-reaching antigrowth consequences. Saving—the reservation of current income and production resources from consumption uses to acquire sources of income—is essential if wide-ranging growth-generating activities are to be undertaken. Research, mineral exploration and development, enhancement of educational attainments and skill training, reorganization of production arrangements, and other activities that add to the productivity as well as the amount of production inputs require reserving the use of production inputs and income from current consumption. Important as it is in expanding production potential, capital formation in the usual sense of additions to the stock of physical production facilities is not the uniquely important use of saving or source of growth. Depressing saving by raising its cost, therefore, has far-reaching antigrowth consequences.

Although tax policy is a prime culprit, other public policies as well raise the cost and depress the amount of private saving. Recognizing that saving is the acquisition of sources of income—of property or rights to property—any public policy that erodes property rights or limits their exercise increases the risk of holding them and reduces the risk-adjusted returns for doing so. Clearly, this must raise the cost of saving and reduce the share of income used for this purpose. Income taxes, of course, directly erode the value of property rights by taking some of the returns thereto; less obviously, so do regulatory policies and government mandates that constrain the acquisition, use, or disposition of property. All such public policies, accordingly, must be seen as inhibiting private saving. That the effects of such policies on the cost and volume of saving are almost entirely ignored in policy formulation is obvious and regrettable.

Taxes and the Costs of Growth-Generating Activities

As indicated, the barrier to growth imposed by taxes stems from their raising the relative cost of growth-generating activities. Every tax, taken by itself, exerts an excise effect, that is, raises the cost of the thing that is taxed relative to the costs of other things. A perfectly neutral tax system would raise the cost of all private sector activities in the same proportion relative to the cost of public sector activities and uses of resources. Such a tax system would to the same degree raise the costs of personal "effort" and of "leisure," of consumption uses of income in the same proportion as saving, of any one consumption product or service in the same proportion as any other, of labor services in the same proportion as the services of capital, of any one sort of labor or capital service in the same proportion as any other, and so on. A neutral tax system, in short, would impose a uniform excise on all private sector economic choices and behavior.

The existing federal tax system, far from imposing a single excise on private sector activity, levies a bewildering array of differential excises. The most obvious examples are the explicit excises imposed on the manufacture or sale of a wide variety of products and services. These excises, however, account for a relatively small fraction of the total amount of federal tax revenues. In fiscal 1992, they are estimated to have produced $46.0 billion in budget receipts, only 4.3% of total receipts of $1,073.6 billion. Vastly larger and of far greater consequence for the economy's performance and growth are payroll taxes, amounting to $410.4 billion, 38.2% of total estimated receipts. However else one might wish to characterize them, payroll taxes are fundamentally selective excises on the supply of and demand for labor services. Individual and corporate income taxes, estimated to have raised $566.3 billion in fiscal 1992, are a bewildering array of differential excises, imposing widely varying marginal tax rates, depending on a mind-boggling number of variables pertaining to taxpayer attributes and the activities in which the taxpayer is involved.

The overall effect of these differential excises is to raise the costs of growth-generating activities relative to the costs of other uses of resources.

Clearly, imposing income and payroll taxes on the taxable compensation of labor services while not taxing the nonpecuniary returns of "leisure" uses of time and resources raises the cost of the former relative to the latter.[3] With a combined federal payroll and income tax marginal rate of between (roughly) 30% and 43% for the vast majority of employed individuals, these taxes raise the relative opportunity cost of labor by between 43% and 75%. Accounting for state and local income and payroll taxes, the tax-induced increase in the opportunity costs of labor ranges between 54% and 92%. The higher the marginal tax rate, clearly, the greater the impact of these taxes in raising the opportunity cost of effort that is rewarded by taxable income, hence, the greater the cost of productivity-enhancing effort. Graduation of the rates of tax on such income is the equivalent of imposing a system of increasing selective excises on productivity advances.

Even more pronounced is the tax bias against saving compared with consumption uses of income. The prototype income tax includes in the tax base the portion of current income that is saved and the returns on that saving when realized. Some saving by individuals, to be sure, is excluded from the tax base under the existing tax provisions; employer contributions to employee retirement and health insurance plans are the principal examples. And some returns on saving, principally interest on municipal bonds, are exempt from federal income tax. Notwithstanding, most private sector saving is included in the income tax base; so, too, are most of the returns earned by that saving. In addition, most of the saving and its returns is also included in the bases of state income taxes; a significant part of those returns is subject to both individual and corporate income taxes; the capitalized value of much of those returns is subject to state and local property taxes; and some of the accumulated saving is subject to death and gift taxes. In contrast, income that is used for consumption is subject to federal and, with some exceptions, state income taxes and relatively modest sales or excise taxes, but the satisfactions provided by consumption, analogous to the returns on saving, are not taxed.

The differential tax treatment of income that is saved and income that is used for current consumption raises the cost of the former relative to the latter.[4] With the current tax structure, taxes raise the cost of saving relative to consumption roughly two and a quarter times. Because saving is required for a wide range of productivity-increasing activities, from adding to knowledge and production skills to additions to the stock of capital, its treatment in the existing tax system is the equivalent of an extraordinary excise on a major source of progress.

Particularly significant in the global context of economic activity are the barriers the existing U.S. tax system erects to the movement of saving, particularly that embodied in business capital, and business ventures across national borders. The federal income tax treatment of the costs and earnings of American multinational companies in their foreign business operations is more protectionist than the prevailing trade policy. The North American Free Trade Agreement, while falling short of providing truly open trade borders, reflects a major policy thrust toward removing trade barriers. Nothing comparable is to be seen on the tax front; indeed, many of the tax policy initiatives in this area, from the Tax Reform Act of 1986 (TRA86) on, have aimed at further impeding American businesses' undertaking business in foreign jurisdictions and at deterring investment and business undertakings by foreign companies in the United States.

The inventory of antigrowth features of the existing tax system could be extended at length, but the features described above suffice to indicate how steeply that system is stacked against growth-generating initiatives in the economy's private sector. How consequential is the antigrowth thrust of these features? A widely held view is that neither personal effort nor saving is significantly affected by the perverse excise effects of the existing tax system. In this view, the so-called income effect of increases in real rates of compensation tends to offset—if not, indeed, to outweigh—the incentive effect; by the same token, the income effect of cuts in real compensation rates at least offsets the adverse incentive effect. This view is a very fragile basis on which to formulate public policy. The notion that, with a given level of wealth, an increase in the marginal rate of tax on the rewards for personal effort, hence an increase in the opportunity cost of that effort, will not reduce the quantity of effort supplied implies something very peculiar, indeed, about the utility systems of the affected individuals.[5]

A similarly perverse view, reflected in the emphasis many public policymakers place on tax increases to reduce the federal budget deficit, holds that saving, too, is unaffected by the impact of taxes on its opportunity cost. The presumption on which this view appears to rest is that tax increases reduce only consumption uses of current income, so that private sector saving is substantially unaffected by tax increases, whereas the public sector's "saving" rises or its dissaving falls by the amount of the additional taxes. In the usual exposition of the argument for tax increases, no distinction is drawn regarding which taxes should be raised.

The rationale for this peculiar view is that saving is "interest inelastic." Of course, if this is the case, it must also be true that saving is also inelastic with respect to its opportunity cost, the amount of current consumption that must be forgone to obtain a dollar of additional income.

But if the cost of saving is raised by increasing the tax on its returns, then the cost of consumption clearly must be reduced. Then if one maintains that a tax-induced increase in the cost of saving and concomitant decrease in the cost of consumption reduces consumption but not saving, one must hold that the higher the cost of consumption, the greater its amount. The implication of this notion for individuals' utility functions is challenging, to say the least.

Essentially, this view about individuals' work and saving responses to tax changes is equivalent to asserting that the demand for income is positively sloped—that the greater its cost in terms of forgone leisure or forgone consumption, the greater the amount of income people will seek to obtain. By the same token, this view implies that the lower its opportunity cost, the lower the amount of income people want. It is difficult to conceive of a more unappealing view of how people pursue satisfaction.

There is method in the madness of this view. The insistence that saving is unresponsive to changes in its opportunity cost, for example, allows policymakers to give priority to so-called tax fairness without perceiving any conflict with the growth objective they espouse. Implementing tax fairness, or "make the rich pay their fair share," calls for tax changes that for the most part increase the real marginal rate of tax on saving or the returns thereto. By disregarding the effect of income tax rate increases in raising the cost of saving or by holding that saving is unresponsive to changes in its opportunity costs, tax fairness proponents are free to pursue their redistributive goals without bearing the onus of being antigrowth.

It may not be possible to assess confidently the weight of the antigrowth thrust of the tax system, but surely one can comfortably assert that the economy's growth path is lower than it would be if the tax system conformed more closely to the neutrality standard.

Moving toward Tax Neutrality

Focusing on how public policies affect the costs of growth-generating activities provides the basis for a progrowth tax strategy. The objective to be pursued by using this strategy is not to promote jobs, saving, capital formation, or any other specific growth-generating activity. It is, instead, to seek out the provisions of the existing tax laws that raise the relative costs of these activities and to modify these provisions in order to moderate their excise effects. The key element of this strategy, in other words, is to seek to make the tax laws more nearly neutral—to reduce to the greatest possible extent their distortion of the cost and price relationships that would prevail in efficiently operating markets in the absence of taxation. The strategy eschews the pick-and-choose approach that is the essence of industrial policy. It does not seek to provide incentives (read "subsidies"), but to moderate the disincentives in existing tax laws.

What can and should be done to moderate the distortional features of the present tax system? An agenda of major tax changes to this end should focus on reducing the tax-elevated opportunity costs of the activities that contribute significantly to economic progress.

Moderating the Tax Bias against Labor

In view of the fact that labor services account for the preponderant share of total production, moderating the differential cost of labor compared with leisure clearly should be given a high priority on a progrowth reform agenda. One heroic step, obviously, is to eliminate payroll taxes, and hence the existing social security and unemployment insurance systems. Another is to moderate the antieffort, proleisure bias in the income tax.

Reduction of Payroll Taxes. The socialization of provision for retirement income surely must have eroded private retirement income provisions. Payroll taxes do not finance the acquisition of additional capital facilities the returns on which might provide future retirement annuities. The notion of "social security wealth" is, accordingly, entirely fanciful. So, too, is the rationale for payroll taxes that so heavily burden the supply of and demand for labor services.

It is time, therefore, to initiate a major privatization of social security's retirement system by (1) reducing payroll tax rates without raising the cap on taxable wages and salaries, (2) reducing the rate of growth in initial benefits of future retirees, and (3) including only the net return on social security "contributions" in the income tax base, and providing more nearly neutral income tax treatment of personal saving, whether undertaken by the individual or by employers on behalf of employees. Ultimately, what remains of social security should be a means-tested welfare system, clearly of vastly more limited scope than the tax transfer system now in place.

Much the same fate should befall the other elements of the social security system. It is surely timely to move toward dismantling the existing Medicare system, the operations of which are probably the single weightiest source of escalation in medical care costs. It is difficult to find a tenable rationale for requiring people aged 65 and over, irrespective of their income or wealth, to benefit from subsidized medical care, provided primarily by younger people by virtue of their participation in the labor force. Converting Medicare into a component of a means-tested welfare system and providing neutral tax treatment of saving, including that devoted to the purchase of health insurance, would permit substantially eliminating the hospital "insurance" component of payroll taxes.

The unemployment insurance component of payroll taxes, an excise on the use of labor services, also should be scrapped. Unemployment is surely a privately insurable event. The premiums employers would pay for such insurance as part of their employees' compensation would be highly useful inputs in employees' decisions about the kinds of jobs they seek and would improve the functioning of labor markets by more accurately pricing the real costs of alternative uses of labor inputs.

Income Tax Adjustments. One of the principal distortional elements of the income tax treatment of personal compensation is that it makes no allowance for the opportunity costs incurred to produce taxable income. In effect, all compensation is identified as quasi-rents, whereas in truth a substantial part of the compensation represents recovery of the costs of providing the services for which the compensation is received. The supply prices of these services, therefore, are higher than they would otherwise be, with adverse consequences for the amount of them that is employed.

To address this distortion, a deduction should be allowed for recovery of these opportunity costs. Their precise identification and measurement for each individual would be virtually impossible, but partial and rough justice could be done by allowing deductions for education and training associated with one's employment, including the explicit costs incurred to secure promotions or higher-paying positions.

Beyond this, all graduation of *marginal* tax rates, whether by explicitly statutory provision, phaseouts of deductions, or other tax base provisions, should be eliminated. Overt or disguised marginal rate graduation defies justification in terms of any meaningful social policy objectives. It is, at best, a suboptimal means for reducing income or wealth inequality, even ignoring its adverse effects on the levels of overall income and wealth. It is, moreover, an ethically repugnant way to strive for wealth redistribution, because it announces that one's property rights are less secure the more productive one is. If, notwithstanding, it is believed that tax liabilities should be graduated with income, this result would be better achieved with a flat rate of tax imposed on a correctly defined tax base, with a zero-rate bracket large enough to produce whatever is the desired graduation of *average* tax rates.

Moderating the Tax Bias against Saving and Investment

Neutral tax treatment of saving implies that the tax does not change the opportunity cost of obtaining the additional income that saving provides relative to the cost of current consumption. The opportunity cost of saving, simply put, is the amount of current consumption that must be forgone to obtain any given stream of additional income, whereas the opportunity cost of any given amount of current consumption is the additional income that is forgone by not saving that amount. With an income tax, these opportunity costs that would prevail in the absence of taxes are not altered if either (1) income that is saved is excluded from the tax base and all returns on the saving, including the gross proceeds from the disposition of the property rights acquired with the saving, are fully taxed or (2) income that is saved is currently taxed but the returns are not subject to tax.[6]

Expensing Saving and Capital Outlays. As indicated earlier, the tax treatment of some personal saving satisfies these requirements for tax neutrality. The part of personal compensation represented by employer contributions to qualified retirement plans is not included in the employees' current taxable income, but the subsequent withdrawals by the employee of the accumulated earnings and principal are taxed. The tax treatment of individual retirement accounts (IRAs) meets the neutrality standard for the limited amounts of deductible saving by eligible persons committed to these accounts. Saving committed to the purchase of tax-exempt municipal bonds similarly receives neutral income tax treatment. A few other forms of saving receive partially or fully neutral tax treatment. These are exceptions, however. The generally applicable income tax treatment of saving fails the neutrality test by taxing both the income that is saved and the returns on the saving.

The income tax bias against saving could be overcome through universalization and elimination of the limits in existing IRAs. Indeed, retiring Congressmen Richard Schulze and Ed Jenkins, toward the end of the 102nd Congress, introduced a bill that would allow every individual to deduct any and all amounts contributed to an IRA; withdrawals could be made at any time and would be fully included in taxable income, but no penalty tax for early withdrawal would be imposed.

Not all personal saving would receive this treatment. Payments to reduce mortgage indebtedness, a substantial portion of personal saving, would fall outside the purview of the proposed treatment. So, too, would saving channeled into the purchases of "collectibles." Nevertheless, implementing the universal IRA would go a long way toward eliminating the existing tax bias against personal saving. It would, moreover, substantially eliminate the existing differences in the tax treatment of various saving channels—the so-called second-level differential excise effect.

In essence, the universal IRA approach to providing neutral tax treatment of saving calls for expensing—immediate deduction from taxable income—of outlays for the purchase of property or property rights that produce income of a character that is subject to the income tax. The same principle should apply in the case of business taxpayers' purchases of any and all kinds of production facilities, intangible as well as tangible, as well as to all expenses incurred in research and experimentation, in mineral exploratory and development activity, and so on. With expensing, all of the gross income produced by the facilities, as well as proceeds from their sale or other disposition, would be included in taxable income. Equivalent tax treatment would be to require the write-off of such outlays against taxable income over a number of years, provided that the inflation-adjusted present value of the deductions equaled the amount of the outlays. Senators Robert Kasten and Malcolm Wallop and Congressmen Tom DeLay and Vin Weber have repeatedly urged the latter approach to reducing the existing income tax bias against investment in depreciable property.

Expensing or its equivalent would confine the income tax on the returns to capital to the quasi-rents, if any, included in those returns. If the present value of the gross returns produced by the property just equaled the outlay for the property, by definition no quasi-rents would be produced. In this case, the present value of the taxes on the income produced by the property would be just equal to the taxes forgone by expensing of the outlays to acquire it. Only if the present value of the gross returns exceed the capital outlay would the present value of the taxes on those returns exceed the tax forgone by expensing.

Under either of the approaches described above, the income tax would not affect the cost of saving relative to consumption uses of current income or the cost of using existing production capability to produce consumption goods and services compared with production facilities. Because taxes account for a very substantial fraction of the total returns to saving and capital, the result of moving to neutral tax treatment would be a significant reduction in the service price of capital.

Integrating Personal and Corporate Income Taxes. A significant part of the tax-induced escalation of the service price of capital is attributable to the multiple layers of tax imposed on the earnings of property. One of these extra tax layers, the corporate income tax, imposed on income generated by corporate businesses, is in addition to the individual income tax on (1) the income that was saved and invested in corporations by their owners and (2) the corporate earnings distributed to the shareholders or the capital gains shareholders may realize upon the disposition of their equity interests in the corporations. The corporation income tax, therefore, is appropriately perceived as a selective excise on the corporate form of organizing business activity.

It is difficult to identify any justification for the tax—any significant social purpose that requires it. No useful purpose is served by making it more costly to do business in corporate than in unincorporated form, nor is there constructive purpose served by raising the service price of capital used by corporations relative to that of unincorporated firms. Moreover, because the market mechanism tends to equalize returns on saving and capital relentlessly in all uses, the tax-induced increase in the price of corporate capital services results in a higher service price of capital for all businesses.

The principal rationale that used to be offered for the corporate income tax is that in its absence, individual shareholders would seek to shelter their earnings from the individual income tax by having these earnings retained by the corporation. Preventing shareholders from deferring their tax liabilities on their shares of the earnings generated by the corporations they own—if this is deemed to be an appropriate objective—can be accomplished without the adverse effects of the corporate income tax by allocating corporate-generated earnings to individual shareholders as the earnings are generated. The mechanics of this attribution were detailed in a Treasury study published in 1977 and have again been examined in the 1992 Treasury study of the issues of separate taxation of corporate income (see Bradford et al., 1984; U.S. Department of the Treasury, 1992).

The basic objective of integration is to eliminate a separate, additional income tax levy on corporate business-generated income. This objective is often misconstrued in the public policy forum; the focus more often than not is on equalizing the tax treatment of dividends and interest payments in order to eliminate the tax bias in favor of the latter. To this end, the solution that is generally proposed is to allow corporations to deduct dividend distributions as well as interest payments or to allow shareholders to credit against their taxes on the dividends they receive the amount of the corporate income tax deemed to be attributable to the dividends. An allegedly equivalent approach is to deny the deductibility of interest payments but to exclude both dividends and interest from the taxable incomes of their recipients.

Although any of these alternatives would be a step in the right direction, all fall short of fully satisfying the neutrality requirement. Also needed would be to exclude from the taxable income of shareholders any gains realized on the disposition of their shares to the extent that these gains equaled the accumulated earnings retained by the corporation. The difficulties of implementing this treatment of capital gains on corporate shares constitute a major stumbling block to the approaches derived from focusing on the bias against equity financing under present law.

Irrespective of the method for effectively eliminating the corporate income tax, achieving neutrality also requires expensing, or its equivalent, of all business purchases of property for the correct measurement of corporate-generated taxable income. Failing this, although the tax on the returns on saving channeled into corporate businesses would be less punitive than at present, a substantial tax bias against saving and investment would remain.

Substituting Value-Added Taxes for Business Income Taxes? The proposal to replace the present business income taxes with a value-added tax has received increasing attention in recent years. In large part, the recent interest in the proposal stems from notions about the allegedly favorable effect of the substitution on the competitive position of American manufacturers in both domestic and foreign markets, but some of the most vigorous VAT proponents emphasize its neutrality with respect to saving and capital formation compared with consumption.[7]

Irrespective of the method of assessing and collecting the liabilities they impose, all so-called consumption-based VATs are imposed on the same base—the difference between a business's total sales revenues and its purchases from other businesses. The base of the VAT, therefore, is the sum of the business's payroll and its net capital income—the gross returns to the capital it uses less its capital outlays. The VAT treatment of capital conforms with that called for by the neutrality standard and would, therefore, be free of the bias imposed by the income tax against business use of capital. As a *substitute* for the income tax on business income, therefore, the VAT would reduce the overall tax bias against saving and capital. It would not, however, eliminate the personal income tax penalty on saving resulting from taxing both the income that individuals save and the returns on that saving that they receive. Introduced as an *additional* tax, on the other hand, the VAT would not abate the bias against saving, although it would intensify it less than if additional tax revenues were sought from the present income taxes.

Unless the VAT were to substitute for the personal income tax as well as business income taxes, its favorable effect in reducing the bias against saving would be countered by its intensifying the tax bias against labor. The largest component, by far, of the VAT base consists of compensation for labor services—payroll and employee fringe benefits, most of which are also taxed under the individual income tax. In contrast, the base of business income taxes does not include employee compensation. Substituting the VAT for business income taxes and leaving the personal income tax in place would subject labor income to both taxes and enormously increase the opportunity cost of personal effort relative to leisure.

A standard argument on behalf of substituting a VAT for business income taxes is that this would lead to substantial increases in the stock of capital and in the capital/labor ratio, resulting in an increase in labor's productivity, and hence in the demand for and use of labor services, and in output and real wages. Overlooked is that by increasing the opportunity cost of labor, the substitution would reduce the supply of labor services. The resulting decrease in capital's productivity would offset, in some part, at least, the decrease in the service price of capital resulting from the substitution. The use of capital services would, therefore, increase less than otherwise and might even decline, resulting in a contraction in total output. In short, the progrowth implications of the substitution of a VAT for business income taxes requires far more careful examination than its proponents ordinarily undertake.

Revising the Tax Treatment of Foreign Source Income. Over the past three decades, but particularly as a result of the TRA(86), the tax treatment of the foreign source income of U.S. multinational companies has become extraordinarily complex and has persistently raised the costs of the foreign business operations of these companies. The overall thrust of these changes in the foreign tax provisions of the federal income tax has been to accelerate the payment and thereby increase the effective rate of tax on U.S. businesses' foreign-source income, to curtail the effective deductibility of costs incurred in the production of that income, and, through an ever-increasing array of rules for allocating expenses and sourcing income, to erode the credit of foreign tax against U.S. federal tax liabilities, thereby raising the cost of capital committed to foreign operations. During much of this period, in contrast, the tax treatment accorded by many foreign governments to the foreign operations of their multinationals moved in the opposite direction. The consequence has been that as economic borders have widened, with the resulting expansion of the growth opportunities that market expansion affords, U.S. businesses have been at an increasing disadvantage compared with foreign companies in responding to these opportunities.

The current trend in U.S. foreign tax policy is precisely opposite to that called for by neutrality. Recent legislative initiatives would seek to restrict expansion of U.S. business operations abroad, presumably in the interests of confining these operations to the domestic economy. Whether public policymakers subscribe to the principle of comparative advantage in the area of trade policy, they tend to be highly mercantilist in tax policy. The notion on which tax protectionism is based, that the foreign operations of U.S. businesses are at the expense of the operations these companies otherwise would undertake at home, are both bad economics and at odds with actual experience. Indeed, to the extent tax protectionism prevails, it impairs the efficiency and productivity of the domestic economy and lowers its growth path.[8]

The neutrality standard precludes taxing both a business and its owners on the income generated by the business. The implementation of this standard would eliminate the U.S. federal corporate income tax, no matter in what jurisdiction the corporation produces the income. It would not, of course, go beyond this to cancel any taxes that a foreign jurisdiction might impose on the income produced within its jurisdiction by a U.S. business. Application of this "source rule" or territoriality principle, moreover, would remove the results of U.S. businesses' foreign operations completely and permanently from the purview of the federal income tax.

The inventory of tax changes to conform the tax system more closely than at present with the requirements of neutrality encompasses a very large number of other issues and provisions of existing law. The preceding discussion should suffice, however, to indicate very clearly the basic strategy that is proposed to deal with any of these other issues, to wit, to identify the features of the tax system that disproportionally raise the costs of growth-generating activities and the changes in those provisions that would mitigate, if not eliminate, their excise effects.

Implementation of any substantial part of the agenda outlined above would, in all likelihood, result in significant reductions in the flow of tax revenues to the Treasury. This result should be identified as a plus, not a minus. For one thing, if the agenda were adopted and implemented, it would reveal a preference among the majority of public policymakers for shifting resources from the public sector's to the private sector's use; by the same token, it would reflect a decision to cut back federal outlays. Second, adoption of the agenda would reflect policymakers' judgment that the principal objective of economic policy is to allow the economy to operate more efficiently, to permit the operation of the market system to reflect more accurately the preferences of market participants.

It may well be that even if policymakers were to embrace the agenda and its objectives, they might believe it to be imprudent to implement any changes until the level and growth of federal spending could be decreased sufficiently to prevent significant increases in annual budget deficits. The agenda nevertheless should serve the highly useful purpose of providing policymakers with guides for future policy initiatives. As such, the agenda might help to deter enactment of additional antigrowth provisions and to permit a better balanced consideration of budgetary and growth considerations.

Progrowth Strategy: A Neglected Issue

How effective would the implementation of this strategy be in raising the growth path of the U.S. economy? For policy activists, this is always the bottom-line question. How big a bang we get for the bucks we have to "spend" on this or that progrowth policy initiative appears to be the principal criterion applied in policy formulation. It should not be. It implies, mistakenly, that the "resources" whose use is to be economized in a progrowth policy are federal tax revenues. The implementation of that policy also implies acceptance of subsidizing some activities that contribute to growth, with or without recognition of the fact that doing so necessarily raises the opportunity cost of one or more other activities. At bottom, this approach is industrial policy.

Most simply put, the issue is whether good public economic policy should identify specific measures of aggregate economic performance as appropriate policy goals and craft public policies that give priority to the attainment of those goals. Or should public policy instead be guided by perceptions of the basic attributes of a good society and of the institutional arrangements consistent with these attributes? Should public economic policy formulation be guided by the specific outcomes that are desired and expected, or should it rather be guided by some set of principles and criteria that define goodness of policy, divorced from likely outcomes?

It must be avowed that the latter position is far less widely held than the former. Across virtually the entire political spectrum in the United States—indeed, in most of the Western world—the former view is a given; policy debates are framed on the implicit assumption that government can and should use its policy tools to produce desirable economic outcomes.

Overlooked, as a consequence, is the more basic question concerning where responsibility for economic progress should reside. The fundamental, but neglected, reservation about policy activism concerns the desirability of efforts, irrespective of their philosophical or analytic orientation, to manage the economy's performance. Even if we could be far more confident than experience warrants about our ability to design policies that will have the desired economic consequences, do we want to assign that function to government? Industrial policy is government control of economic behavior, no matter its objectives.

Nor is the issue properly framed as whether one set or another of demand management policies is more "effective" than one or another mode of supply management in accelerating economic growth, expanding jobs, and so on. Industrial policy, in either case, means that public policymakers, not market participants, are supposed to shape market outcomes and the economy's performance. The issue is not whether policymakers are up the challenge; it is whether they should be asked to accept it.

Rejecting the control approach identifies a different responsibility for public economic policy. It should be addressed to identifying and eliminating the encumbrances that government imposes on markets. Government responsibility should not extend beyond creating the least distortional set of policies and institutional arrangements. Having done this, government should then get out of the way.

Suppose government's presence in our daily lives were much reduced, sufficiently so that market price signals and outcomes were little affected by government policies and activities and much more than now reflected the preferences and the opportunity cost constraints of its participants. Given those suppositions, on what basis should the market's outcomes be a matter of public policy concern? If, under those circumstances, the trend rate of growth of total output were to be, say, 2%, what would be the justification for government's adopting policies seeking to raise that rate to, say, 3%? The government's doing so necessarily would entail costs that, clearly, market participants chose not to incur. In a free society, it is difficult, at the least, to identify any basis for government's overriding market-determined preferences regarding the trade-off of future versus present states of affairs.

The role that I suggest for public policy is not a minor one, given the extent and variety of intrusive policies now burdening the economy, nor is it a negative one. It is a different role, however, from that articulated or at least implied by policy activists, be they Keynesians, monetarists, supply-siders or whatever. It calls for identifying fundamental principles and criteria that are to guide and constrain the relationship of government to private sector entities—to set a framework that will maximize the opportunity for the market system to perform the basic economic functions in a free society as efficiently as possible.

The question, therefore, about how effective the agenda of tax changes discussed above would be in raising the economy's growth path should be treated as substantially irrelevant. In the contemporary, highly growth-repressive public policy setting, these policy changes are likely to be quite effective indeed, but their desirability should be determined not on the basis of what bang they will give for the buck, but, instead, on whether they will allow the market system to perform more effectively.

Notes

1. Little attention is given, on the other hand, to the effects of regulatory policies and legislated mandates on saving behavior, possibly because these policies are viewed in different terms from those in which the effects of fiscal measures are assessed.

2. It is also true in these cases that their compensation falls short of their actual contributions to the total value of output, the more so the rarer their talents and the more highly specialized their arts or skills.

3. Designating the opportunity cost of an hour of labor services as the forgone value, w, of an hour's leisure and the combined marginal payroll and income tax rate as t_w, these taxes raise the cost of labor relative to leisure by $1/(1 - t_w)$.

4. In the absence of taxes, the optimum division of current income between saving and consumption uses would be such that a marginal dollar of income could purchase a dollar of consumption (C) or an income stream with a present value of (R^*), equally valued by the income recipient. With an income tax of the present configuration and sales taxes, a marginal dollar of income can purchase $\$(1 - t)$ of consumption (where t = the overall marginal income plus sales tax rate). With no change in the real yield per dollar of saving, the same marginal dollar of current income obtains a pretax income stream with a present value of $R^*(1 - t)$. But that income stream is also taxed, so that a marginal dollar of current income can obtain a net of tax income stream of only $R^*(1 - t)^2$. Hence, the existing taxes raise the cost of saving relative to consumption by $(1 - t)/(1 - t)^2$, or by $1/(1 - t)$.

5. This is not to gainsay that a change in wealth has no effect on the conditions of supply of personal effort. It may well be the case that, other things being equal, the higher the level of one's wealth, the lower the amount of effort provided at a given rate of real after-tax compensation.

6. With a tax imposed at rate t, a marginal dollar of consumption requires current income = $\$1/(1 - t)$. If saving is deductible and the income stream produced by the saving is taxable, to acquire an income stream with a present value of $\$1$ also requires $\$1/(1 - t)$ of current income; no tax is paid on the income that is saved, but tax is paid on the income stream it produces. In the alternative treatment, an income stream with a present value of $\$1$ is not reduced by the income tax, but because no deduction is allowed for its purchase, $\$1/(1 - t)$ of current income is needed.

7. The allegedly favorable trade effects are naively ascribed to the border tax adjustments that are widely but erroneously perceived to be inherent features of value-added taxes. Applying the VAT to imports would not favor sales of domestically produced products (also subject to the VAT) over imported products. Remitting VAT on exports would not affect the terms of trade for products sold at world market prices, although it would permit producers of significantly differentiated products to reduce their export prices, if they deemed this to be an effective marketing strategy. In either case, rebating the tax on exports would increase profit margins on export production relative to production for domestic markets and would induce a shift in the composition of output from the latter to the former. The border adjustments are predicated on the view of a VAT as a tax on consumption rather than, in fact, the equivalent of a proportional income tax on labor and capital incomes. For a discussion of these VAT features, see Ture (1979).

8. For a discussion and exploration of the issues in this area, see Ture (1975) and Ture and Carlson, (1991).

References

Bradford, D., and Staff of the U.S. Treasury Office of Tax Policy. (1984). *Blueprints for Basic Tax Reform*. Arlington, VA: Tax Analysts.

Ture, N. B. (1975). "Taxing Foreing Source Income." In *U.S. Taxation of American Business Abroad*. Washington, DC: American Enterprise Institute for Public Policy Research.

Ture, N. B. (1979). *The Value Added Tax: Facts and Fancies* (Fiscal Issues 1). Washington, DC: Institute for Research on the Economics of Taxation and the Heritage Foundation.

Ture, N. B., and Carlson, G. C. (1991). "Tax Policy to Address the Challenges and Opportunities of the Growing World Marketplace." In *U.S. Foreign Tax Policy: America's Berlin Wall* (Conference proceedings, Institute for Research on the Economics of Taxation). Lanham, MD: University Press.

U.S. Department of the Treasury. (1992). *Integration of the Individual and Corporate Tax Systems: Taxing Business Income Once*. Washington, DC: Government Printing Office.

Comment

Robert Eisner

I can attest personally to Bill Niskanen's well-known courage and boldness. In the issues he raises and conclusions he reaches in this chapter, he confirms his courage and boldness. Alas, although some of his policy prescriptions please me, I do not find his analysis convincing.

In his conclusions, Niskanen would have us increase economic growth by cutting defense expenditures, transfer payments, taxes, and the deficit, while raising other government purchases of goods and services. And he would also reduce the number of lawyers or the government practices that generate their activity! In fact, his basic regression results, presented in Table 7.1, do not clearly support his conclusions. Further, it would appear very unlikely that his estimated parameters are in any way measures of the contributions of his variables to economic growth.

Essential problems with Niskanen's statistical work relate to murkiness in the distinction between exogenous and endogenous variables, the assumption that contemporaneous relations among year-to-year changes in the variables tell us about growth rather than cyclical factors dominated by short-term demand considerations, and a particular problem with the use of the actual deficit/GNP ratio as a measure of fiscal stimulus.

Niskanen's regressions would suggest that, in each case, holding other variables constant, each dollar more of defense expenditures adds $1.62 to GNP and that increasing transfer payments per working-age adult also adds to GNP. But surely both of these variables, in contemporaneous first differences, are reflecting an aggregate demand and multiplier relation with changes in output.

It would appear too that changes in nondefense government expenditures for goods and services, also positively related to changes in GNP, are manifesting a short-term demand phenomenon. This would appear all the more likely in view of the fact that no distinction is made, in Niskanen's measure, between government expenditures for investment and consumption. It is hard to believe that year-to-year changes in government expenditures for goods and services have much to do with contemporaneous changes in supply or productivity. They will, given the fact that GNP is almost never at its upper bound or fixed, almost certainly show a positive relation with changes in GNP if only because they are a component of GNP.

Niskanen's taxes variable indicates a substantial negative impact on the change in GNP contributed by the ratio of taxes to GNP. This may reflect a corrective for misspecified nonlinear relations among the other variables or, again, a cyclical factor in which in recessions, as GNP falls, many taxes, especially those on property and some excise taxes, do not fall proportionately. Thus the tax/GNP ratio may rise when GNP is falling.

The oil price imports variable also reflects a demand factor. When the cost of imported oil rises, this operates precisely as a tax on the U.S. economy, thus reducing aggregate demand and purchasing power and driving GNP down.

Perhaps my biggest problem is with the presumed finding that changes in the ratio of the total government budget deficit to GNP are negatively related to changes in GNP. Niskanen's measure of the deficit here is not cyclically adjusted (let alone adjusted for inflation to arrive at what I call a "real deficit"). It is clear, however, that this actual deficit/ GNP ratio goes up in recessions and down in recovery, as tax revenues move cyclically while transfer payments move countercyclically. The relation between changes in GNP and simultaneous changes in the actual deficit must certainly be overwhelmingly one in which changes in GNP cause changes in the deficit, rather than vice versa, as Niskanen infers. I might add that my own regressions relating changes in GNP to lagged, cyclically adjusted, real federal deficits are clearly positive. Larger deficits have been associated with greater increases (or lesser decreases) in subsequent GNP growth.

I might also call attention to some implausible estimates coming out of Niskanen's regressions. He indicates, for example, that a 1% increase in unemployment generates a 0.6% decline in GNP. Although not viewing original or modified Okun's Law numbers as sacrosanct, the data most generally show each percentage increase in unemployment to be associated with some 2% less GNP. Further, Niskanen reports that one percentage point increase in unemployment is associated with an *increase* of 0.9% in productivity. This flies in the face of fairly overwhelming data that indicate a kind of labor hoarding in which, as hours and employment decline in recessions, output declines more, and productivity therefore declines.

Niskanen's final conclusions stem from assumed interrelations among variables. For example, he sees a cut in defense expenditures as *increasing* GNP, despite the positive coefficient of his defense variable in his regressions, because it would imply either an increase in other government expenditures for goods and services or cuts in taxes and/or in the deficit that would increase GNP. But surely these are not one-to-one relations. Indeed, Niskanen declares that transfers, taxes, and the deficit are endogenous variables, although he seems to treat them as exogenous in inferring effects on the dependent variable, GNP change, stemming from changes in their magnitudes. A more informative exercise might involve the use of vector autoregressions, which would track the impact of the "shock" to any one of the variables for interrelations among all of them.

Finally, as to that negative finding about the impact of lawyers, are we really supposed to take this seriously? Where is the evidence? Even if the number of lawyers is a proxy variable for, say, regulatory intrusion, what are the specific relations involved? In fact, after all, even costly and undesirable regulations may bring about an increase in measured GNP by forcing expenditures for final product necessary to meet the regulations. And anyway, some of my best relatives are lawyers.

Norman Ture is also bold in his policy prescription for economic growth. He has a set of measures that he thinks will do good, unlike Niskanen, however, advanced here with no statistical support. For some, as he suggests, they may seem "heretical." For others, they may appear as an amalgam of a usual conservative agenda of less government and a perhaps somewhat self-serving agenda of those who would benefit from government where they can but generally avoid the bill.

Ture puts forth in various places a view to which I subscribe: that government should no more undertake the role of promoting economic growth than of promoting motherhood and apple pie, desirable as all of these seem to some. We do not need Big Brother to tell us to sacrifice now so that our children or grandchildren should be better off, or to save more now so we can have more later. We might each better be free to look after our own futures and balance our own needs and those of our children.

Ture takes the position, which I share, that government should not be preventing growth or, for that matter, doing anything to reduce real product below the preferences of its people. To those ends, he looks to eliminate inefficiency-breeding taxation.This, unfortunately, raises the issue of whether we can change our tax structure to make it more neutral or must simply eliminate formal taxes and dismantle government or finance it by inflation and seignorage. Since, as Ture fairly knows, there is no fully neutral tax—even a "head tax" may be taken to discourage childbearing and to encourage emigration or suicide—the ultimate implication of his goal is the dismantling of government.

This may appeal to some on basic ideological grounds, but does raise questions for many of us as to the provision of essential public goods, reaction to externalities, and, indeed, fulfillment of the basic requirements for the functioning of a market economy.

Let us get down to a number of specifics in issues raised in Ture's chapter.

1. Ture picks up the widespread view that national saving is the key instrument of economic growth. He largely recognizes that contribution to growth comes from much more than the usual measure of private capital formation. Correctly defined, national saving should indeed the include the research and enhancement of educational attainment and skill training to which he refers, but his proposals on reduced taxation and government spending do not always seem consistent with his recognition of this broader measure of saving. Private saving would and should in any event be encouraged to reach its maximum potential by providing the framework for a fully employed private economy with maximum income.

2. This relates to Ture's standard assertion that more growth must impose real costs. This is in principle true only if an economy is on its production possibility frontier. If it suffers considerable unemployment, excess capacity, or other inefficiencies, keeping it at an interior point, it is indeed possible to increase output and, at least in the short term, economic growth without imposing additional current costs.

3. Ture objects, along with others, to the Civil Rights Act of 1991 and the 1990 Americans with Disabilities Act as "prime examples of legislation" that may impede growth by imposing added employment costs. He ignores the possibility that in a society that will (properly) not allow its jobless to starve to death, forcing business to hire or hire at full potential people it might otherwise avoid will add to the net product of society if the additional product of those hired exceeds the additional imposed costs. Ensuring that the disabled can work may indeed prove optimal, whatever the complaints of self-interested individual employers forced to assume costs that would replace the larger costs of public "welfare" payments.

4. We all like to believe that in a well-functioning market economy compensation generally equals opportunity costs. Ture, however, goes pretty far out in implying that this is necessarily always true, or so close to being true that there is clearly never any point for the government, through taxation or otherwise, to alter the distribution of income. Has compensation really been equal to opportunity costs for Madonna, or Ross Perot?

5. Ture is concerned with protection of property rights, and that is certainly vital in a market system. But certainly that general role does

not give all the answers to complex problems. Do we want to protect all property rights? How about the rights to ownership of human capital? Before the American Civil War many argued that the property rights in slavery had to be protected. Since human capital is indeed critical, should we not protect the right to human capital owned by individuals in a free society? And in that case, how do we react to such issues as the rights of firms to replace strikers permanently? Would this not destroy *their* human capital?

It might also be recognized that whereas government regulations and taxes may reduce the value of property rights, government services may well enhance them. It is certainly clear that much of private property would be worthless without public infrastructure. And government regulations—zoning restrictions, for example—may well enhance property values.

6. Ture is concerned with taxation of "saving" and is inclined toward a consumption tax. A consumption tax also discourages labor, however, and encourages nonmarket activity and leisure. It is thus clearly nonneutral in these regards. Further, if consumption includes expenditures for education and other investment in human capital, a consumption tax will bias the economy against human capital accumulation.

In fact, most private sector saving is not taxed now. Saving in the form of pension fund accumulations and, especially, accrued capital gains is not taxed. How much in the way of taxes has ever been paid by Mr. Perot in building his reported net worth of $3 billion? And how much of his continued saving is being taxed now? It might also be acknowledged, of course, that human capital accumulation in the form of public school education does not come out of taxable income.

7. Ture states at one point that the cost of saving versus the cost of consumption is raised two and a quarter times by taxes. But according to his own formulation, the relative cost is $1/(1 - t)$, which, unless t, the rate of taxation on saving, is greater than or equal to $5/9$, is surely less than 2.25.

8. Ture makes much of taxes discouraging efforts in saving. He seems generally to ignore, however, widely accepted economic theory and analysis that income and substitution effects may go in opposite directions, so that the net effect of taxes on saving is in general ambiguous. High taxes on the income from saving suggest a substitution effect against saving. But income effects might increase saving to the extent that people find they have to abstain from more current consumption in order to provide the future consumption they wish.

Further, taxing the rich more and the poor less does not hurt saving in the permanent income theory of Milton Friedman or the life-cycle consumption model of Franco Modigliani. In any event, even if higher taxes were shown to reduce income, it does not follow that they reduce the rate of growth of income. They may simply put us on a lower, but parallel, growth path.

9. Social insurance contributions are not necessarily a tax on labor. Whether part of a public or private insurance system, if the contributions (taxes) are entitlements to pensions of equal present value, and are so perceived, they should not generally be viewed as discouraging labor. Many workers may want to get jobs precisely in order to pay for an actuarially fair pension. In general, both publicly operated and private insurance may be expected to have similar implications in terms of payments that reduce current consumption, thus saving resources for saving investment out of which future benefits will come.

All insurance, of course, involves costs of moral hazard. Substituting private unemployment insurance for government insurance, as Ture suggests, raises some very serious additional questions, however. Not only does unemployment involve the kind of social risk that private insurance may be utterly unable to meet in the face of a widespread recession or depression, it also invites serious dangers in terms of discrimination and exclusion. Given, for example, whatever the reasons, greater incidence of unemployment among blacks, employers buying private unemployment insurance may well find costs higher if they employ more blacks. The lack of ability to determine which blacks are likely to have greater bouts of unemployment creates a cost differential for all blacks and hence encourages discrimination against their employment.

10. Ture would also do away with Medicare. I would submit, however, that Medicare offers advantages both as insurance and in provision of horizontal equity. It has been commonplace in recent years to argue that the elderly do not deserve special treatment because their incomes are no longer generally less than those of the young. But if medical costs are taken to be a necessity and are much greater, as they certainly are, for the elderly, then provision of equal income for the elderly net of medical costs may well require substantial subsidization of these costs.

11. Ture is all for expensing business capital expenditures. But, despite the hullabaloo about reducing taxes on capital gains, we currently have little in the way of real taxation of capital gains because gains are taxed not upon accrual but only upon "realization," and taxation of gains is completely avoided when wealth is passed on at death. Along with the existence of tax deductibility of nominal interest payments, we have a situation where substituting expensing for reasonable economic depreciation as a tax deduction would make the tax system usually nonneutral, and rather bias it in the direction of borrowing to finance capital accumulation.

12. Integration of personal and corporate income taxes is something that I also have long advocated. But Ture reminds us that corporations do have special advantages bestowed upon them by government, particularly limited liability and the general protection of public authority. The corporate tax, further, is not properly viewed as a tax on capital. Rather, it is a tax on the corporation and the income of the corporation from whatever source it is earned—physical capital, intangible capital, labor, management, advertising, monopoly, and the like.

13. Excluding dividend and interest payments from taxation would surely bias the tax system in favor of property income, as well as make it regressive. Why should we want to exclude dividend and interest payments from taxation while continuing to tax labor? This would give people an incentive to abandon labor production to work on maximizing the dividends and interest from their investments.

14. Ture would reduce total taxation as a means of increasing economic growth, but is it likely that he can do this without also reducing public investment and the provision of public services necessary for the functioning and growth of the economy? One could make the argument, of course, that public investment and the services provided by government might, in at least some cases, be provided by private enterprise and the market system. But would this always, or as efficiently, be the case?

15. Finally, Ture seems appalled by government intervention in the form of "demand management" and "industrial policy." But surely these are not identical. Many of us look with skepticism at industrial policy as an attempt by the government to pick winners and losers better than the market. But we also recognize that, at the least, government has a major role in providing a monetary and fiscal framework, along with investment in infrastructure and human capital, such that a complex, modern market economy can indeed function with maximum efficiency and all of the growth that may result from the mass of choices and decisions made by millions of free individuals.

Comment

William Poole

Norm Ture's contribution to this volume is totally impractical, which is one of the reasons I like it. His aim is to lay out the principles underlying a tax system consistent with real economic growth at a rate determined by the preferences of the private sector. Subject to amendments I will offer below, I applaud his insistence that we should not think in terms of promoting growth per se; rather, the goal of public policy should be to let the private sector make undistorted choices among leisure, goods today, and goods tomorrow. He and I agree that adopting a tax policy consistent with this principle would yield a considerably higher growth rate, at least for a period of some years, than the U.S. economy is capable of achieving under its present tax policy; neither of us knows how much higher.

Ture has provided us with a comprehensive statement of the principle of tax neutrality and the implications of the principle for most of the major areas of U.S. tax law. Having this comprehensive review in one place is very useful; I cannot possibly discuss his entire chapter, and so must pick and choose.

Despite the breadth of Ture's chapter, several important topics are missing. The one that concerns me most is whether an efficient, nondistorting tax system would be likely to lead to a larger government. The answer is that it probably would unless some kind of constitutional constraints are in place on the size of government and the range of activities it can pursue. The political equilibrium in which the squawks of plucked taxpayers just balance the glee of beneficiaries of larger government spending would be likely to occur at a higher average rate of tax when marginal tax rates on various activities are equalized and as low as possible given the revenue raised. For this reason, I am not prepared to buy into Ture's tax program until I see some mechanism to constrain the size of government.

The second topic missing from Ture's chapter is an analysis of the substitutability of tax incentives for government spending where a government role is justified. I accept the traditional case, based on public goods and externalities, defining the appropriate and necessary role of government. Once we accept a role for government, the logic leads to the question of whether in any given area the government's intervention should take the form of government provision of services; subsidies, tax incentives, or penalties; or regulation. Because government bureaucracies are so often inefficient, I believe that tax incentives or penalties are often more efficient than direct government provision of services.

For example, should a pollution problem be handled through government spending or through departures from tax neutrality that induce changes in private behavior? Tax neutrality is an important principle, but it cannot be our only principle. Compared with regulatory approaches, effluent taxes promote more efficient resource allocation, are less intrusive, and are less subject to administrative abuse.

The example of effluent taxes constitutes a foot in the door that opens up other issues. Benefit-cost analysis may provide the framework to set the level of effluent taxes, but the benefits and costs themselves are in part matters of preference. Consider aircraft noise. High noise levels are hazardous, but medium and low levels are just a nuisance. Different people have different aesthetic reactions to noise, and there is no economic principle we can use to tell us what the "right" reaction is. Analysis of property rights helps, but does not take us very far. Suppose I buy a farm in the country to provide a weekend escape from the city, but find that a change in flight patterns imposes low-level aircraft noise on me. Is this simply one of the risks of living in a modern society, or should I be able to sue someone for compensation? How loud does the noise have to be for me to be able to sue? How many people have to be affected? Should redress come through private actions in the courts or should the government impose taxes on noisy airplanes? How far should any of these remedies go in reducing noise? If we strengthen property rights to handle externalities problems, will we produce an excessive litigation burden on society?

I doubt that any sweeping generalizations are possible in these sorts of cases. What I do know, or think I know, is that taxes and subsidies are sometimes the preferred approach. Moreover, we will have to rely on the political system to resolve many issues of preferences. Some communities (or some societies) will be willing to accept more noise than other communities. A community with a preference for a low amount of noise will want to tax noise more heavily than will other communities even if doing so reduces growth. Ture emphasizes that individuals make saving-consumption decisions based on how much growth they individually want; what I am arguing is that some similar decisions are inevitable at the level of the community. It is simply not true that the government can or should place all growth decisions with individuals by adopting a nondistorting tax system.

Tax neutrality, then, is the baseline starting point for analysis of the ideal tax system. We should modify these baseline taxes, and introduce subsidies, to handle public goods and externalities where dealing with these problems through the tax system is efficient.

This brings me to the subject of tax-exempt activities, which Ture barely mentions except in the context of individual saving decisions. The tax-exempt or tax-favored sector in the United States is very large. Most educational services, services provided by religious organizations, and many medical services are quantitatively significant examples. Would society be better off if we wiped out all these tax preferences, including those that benefit institutes such as the one Ture directs? Should church property be taxed just like industrial property? Should universities attract capital and pay returns to capital providers as for-profit corporations do?

Present arrangements certainly create many problems; tax rates on property subject to tax must obviously be higher than would otherwise be the case, and therefore more distorting, to offset the zero rate on tax-exempt property. Tax-exempt property is often used inefficiently. Communities containing tax-exempt property bear the costs, whereas some of the benefits go to users of the property from other communities. Tax-exempt firms try to take advantage of their tax-exempt status to expand into taxable activities. These and many other disadvantages of differential tax rates make a strong case for ending the practice of exempting certain activities from one or more major taxes.

On the other side of the ledger, however, is the fact that charitable voluntary activity is a source of great strength for the United States. Tax-favored firms perform many public or quasi-public activities that might otherwise be performed by government. Reliance on tax-favored firms has the advantages of decentralization and exposure to market forces. Consider higher education. Public subsidies for higher education may well be excessive; most of the benefits of university education are private and not public. But putting that argument aside and accepting for present purposes the judgment of the voters that subsidies for higher education are desirable and worth paying for, there is no doubt in my mind that providing the subsidies through tax preferences is far more efficient than raising revenues to support public universities as our states and most European countries do, even if the taxes were nondistorting.

Would we, however, be even better off under a system of universal student vouchers but without the tax preferences universities enjoy? I'm not sure. Charitable deduction promotes a healthy involvement of givers in university affairs. Perhaps it would be better if for-profit universities obtained capital from providers seeking a return rather than from donors under today's system; perhaps not. What I do know is that the answers are not simple and not obvious. I think the U.S. system of higher education is much better than the European system because the U.S. system is much more decentralized and competitive. We do not have a good example of how an educational system organized on for-profit principles would work. U.S. educational firms and other not-for-profit firms have an economic structure shaped by their tremendous tax preferences. Ture is silent as to whether all these tax preferences should be swept away, although the logic of his chapter seems to say that they should be. There are a lot of deep issues here having to do with the ways in which voluntary decentralized activities shape our society. I am not prepared, therefore, to say that universal student vouchers for higher education would work better than our current system. A decentralized system of determining who gets aid and who does not has great advantages over a uniform national system. I would rather have my university supported by a diversified group of tuition-paying families and donors than by tuition from a single national voucher system.

I have argued that some decisions are inherently societal; we cannot think of the tax system solely as a device to raise revenue through neutral taxes. Social insurance is the most pressing issue today. I share Ture's view that we rely far too much on social insurance. He would scrap the social security system, except for a minimal means-tested program. But he and I and others much more eloquent than either of us have as yet been unsuccessful in making this case. We should not give up trying to make the case, but in the meantime should also provide additional analysis that points to improvements in the efficiency of taxation within the current system.

Ture discusses the incentive effects of taxes on provision of labor services and on saving. I think the former issue is more important quantitatively than the latter one. The effects are large and not properly appreciated. Assuming that all social insurance taxes fall on labor, whether collected from employees or employers, social insurance taxes plus personal taxes were 21% of personal income in 1991; the transfers component of personal income was 18% of disposable personal income that year. In 1948, total personal taxes were 12.5% of personal income and transfers were 6% of disposable income. These are averages; marginal rates are much higher, as Ture rightly emphasizes. It is reasonable to believe that work disincentive effects of taxes and transfers are larger the closer a person is to retirement age. A young person needs to work to accumulate rights to both public and private pensions. Once eligibility is established, today's marginal tax and transfer rates, which tend to be higher for older workers than for younger ones, create a substantial incentive to take early retirement and an overwhelming incentive to retire once age 65 reached.

Figure 1 documents what has happened to labor force participation since World War II.[1] We know that life expectancy has risen and that improvements in medical care have lengthened the productive life spans of most people. Yet men have been increasingly dropping out of the labor force while still young enough that their accumulated experience and skills could make an enormous contribution to national output. Labor force participation of men aged 55–64 has dropped from about 90% in 1948 to less than 70% today. Participation of men 65 and over has dropped from about 45% to less than 20%. There has even been some decline in participation by men aged 45–54, from about 95% to about 90%. We are in danger of a downward spiral as slower economic growth resulting from withdrawal of productive labor from the labor force reduces tax revenues, requiring higher tax rates, which will further increase incentives for early retirement.

The bottom panel of the figure shows that labor force participation of women has risen for all age groups, except for those 65 and over. Here we have a growth success story; an increasing number of women have found productive careers during the past 40 years. However, the net result of women entering the labor force has not been higher national output. Instead, for society as a whole, the extra output produced by higher employment of women has served to finance retirement for men, including early retirement. Many women have complained in recent years that they feel compelled to work to "make ends meet," but few understand that the burden of personal income and payroll taxes is so high in part because men are leaving the labor force to live off the fat of the land. Do radical feminists understand what is going on?

Ture offers a vision of tax reform on a massive scale, but does not say where he would start. So, I will finish my discussion of his chapter paper with a few comments on this issue. We need to target first tax reforms that have an early effect on U.S. output, because raising output will generate tax revenues and will help to provide political support that will make further reforms possible. The two most important distortions, it seems to me, arise from the taxation of income from capital and the taxation of labor income of older workers. I am relatively less concerned about tax disincentives for saving, both because I believe the effects have been relatively smaller and because in our integrated world capital market increased U.S. saving may have little impact on U.S. investment. Saving will simply flow abroad if U.S. investment returns are inadequate.

I turn now to Bill Niskanen's chapter, about which, I must admit, I have a hard time knowing what to say. Quite frankly, I do not believe that the statistical results tell us much about the subject at hand, because practically all the variance in the first differences of annual data reflects cyclical and temporary factors. Niskanen's estimates of the effects of

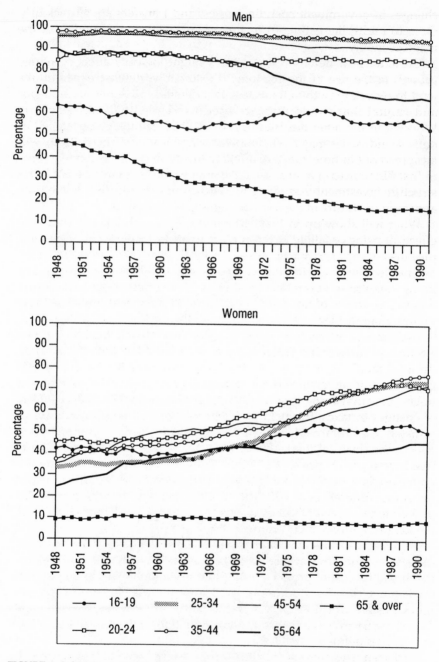

FIGURE 1 Labor Force Participation by Gender and Age, 1948–91 *Source:* Data are from the U.S. Department of Labor, Bureau of Labor Statistics.

changes in government spending, taxes, and transfers are suspiciously close to multiplier estimates in Keynesian econometric models of the macroeconomy.

Consider how defense expenditures might logically affect economic growth in the rest of the economy. Presumably, defense expenditures tend to reduce growth to the extent that defense industries absorb labor and capital that would be more productively employed elsewhere. Working in the other direction is the fact that technology developed in defense industries may have nondefense applications. These effects will be spread out in time; they are unlikely to rise above measurement error in first differences of annual data. Another example is government infrastructure investment. Assuming infrastructure is productive, the returns appear in the future in the form of higher private output.

What will show up in first differences of annual data are short-run effects of rising or falling government purchases. Defense cuts, for example, may temporarily depress GDP while resources released from defense industries are finding employment in nondefense industries. We know something about this process in New England and California today. The effects of nondefense government purchases probably show up in similar fashion.

Estimates of effects from taxes, transfers, and deficit finance might be a bit more trustworthy. These items do not affect GDP directly, but only through their effects on behavior of private agents. To the extent that private agents understand the long-run effects of changes in government policy, they may bring forward some of the long-run and delayed effects of changes in taxes, transfers, and deficits. For example, an increase in transfers may depress labor supply and saving. Understanding those effects, the financial markets may bid interest rates up, depressing current investment. However this process might work, to be convincing the paper needs a model to explain how long-run effects on growth show up in first differences of annual data. I suspect that the time-trend term in the model, which Niskanen labels "exogenous," is capturing most of the long-run effects of government policy on growth.

Niskanen cautions that we must not take his estimates of the effects of defense expenditures at face value because the national accounts value defense at its cost of production. This observation applies to all government purchases. I am quite prepared to argue that some government purchases are worth zero cents on the dollar, or even less, even though they show up in his estimates as contributing to GDP because that is the way GDP is defined.

Niskanen uses some words in his chapter that need to be interpreted carefully. He says that "some increase in other government expenditures, however, may be worth the additional taxes or deficit" (p. 20).

That is simply a matter of reading the estimated effects in Table 7.3; per billion dollars of a government policy variable, the partial effect on total output of domestic government spending is $2.1 billion and of taxes –$1.6 billion. Suppose I take those estimates at face value and apply them to proposals for more infrastructure investment. Perhaps building more highways in certain places would be a good investment. However, the return might be far higher if we would price highway use properly. In contrast, if we uncovered high returns in a particular industry in the private sector we would be justified in assuming that the private sector had allocated capital to projects with the highest prospective returns, given the information available. We have too much information about government behavior to accept that proposition with regard to government capital.

Is there a way to extract information of the type Niskanen is seeking from time-series data? There ought to be some way to use data on relative prices and returns to examine the questions Niskanen wants to address. For example, if defense expenditures on aerospace have valuable technology spin-offs, perhaps we should observe a high return to capital in civilian aerospace, which is getting lots of technology at below its cost of production. There is evidence that government research has boosted agricultural productivity, and I suspect that only through detailed studies will we learn what government expenditures are genuinely productive.

Niskanen says that, "a fiscal strategy that reduced national security expenditures and transfer payments, increased other government expenditures, and reduced taxes and the deficit would almost surely increase U.S. economic growth" (p. 21). I know Bill Niskanen too well to infer that he recommends proportional increases in all areas of nondefense government purchases, from staffs of congressional committees to regulatory agencies to Commerce Department trade promotion, and so forth. Clearly, detailed studies are needed to draw policy implications from Niskanen's estimates, even accepting them at face value.

In sum, Bill Niskanen has asked a number of interesting questions and has emphasized that we need a better empirical base to judge the effects of government on economic growth. Unfortunately, his chapter is not in the end successful in providing the estimates we seek.

Notes

1. I acknowledge with thanks research support from Data Resources, Inc. in the form of access to its data bank.

PART FIVE

Concluding Thoughts

9

Economic Literacy and Economic Growth

Lewis C. Solmon

I would like to offer a few thoughts on the relationship between economic understanding on the part of the public and economic growth. In particular, I would like to focus upon the links between such general economic literacy and growth in a nation in which both market and political processes affect the level and structure of economic activity.

Adam Smith pointed out more than two centuries ago that it is not the altruism of the baker that yields our daily bread. Instead, it is the baker's self-interest. In this age of mass communication—and, to a considerable degree, mass misinformation and disinformation—individuals are subjected to a constant torrent of advice and argument about paths that purportedly will further their interests. But we still can observe that private incentives are the engine of economic growth and prosperity. It is fair to conclude that individuals know their interests and how to further them; and ordinary people who never have heard of a demand curve, but manage somehow to survive nonetheless, seem able to pick and choose among the myriad bits of advice emanating from "experts" and other assorted kibitzers.

Thus, in a narrow sense the general state of economic literacy or understanding is or ought to be irrelevant in terms of the advance of human well-being. After all, humanity never has been a mere collection of economists, but somehow we have managed nonetheless to advance from caves to condominiums, from finger counting to computers, and from superstition to laser surgery. Indeed—I know some of you are smiling at this—the thought of a world of economists seems less than wholly appealing, at least at an intuitive level.

Of course, I am being a bit disingenuous. The issue is not whether everyone ought to be an economist; it is instead whether basic economic literacy among the electorate matters. Historically it seems not to have

mattered, as the long-term growth in human wealth has not been correlated very closely if at all with advances in the general state of economic
understanding. Indeed, however we might attempt to measure the
degree of economic literacy among the general population, it is not clear
that it has increased much over, say, the past 50 or 100 years.

But let us now consider a more modern world or economy in which
government has considerable power over resource use, and in which
political processes are the predominant mechanism through which government decisions are made. To some substantial degree, then, the magnitude and pattern of economic growth now is determined not only by self-
interest pursued in markets, but also by self-interest pursued through
political processes. Under our institutions of representative democracy,
government derives its powers with the consent of the governed, more or
less, and so voters must be convinced after a fashion to support one set of
policies over others.

It is that process of persuasion that is so fascinating. What I think I see
consistently is a quest for political support grounded in the promotion
of economic arguments that are highly questionable at a minimum. An
increase in the minimum wage will help the poor. Price controls will
reduce prices and inflation. Protectionism will save jobs. National health
insurance will increase something called "access" to health care. And on
and on, *ad infinitum*.

This political use of questionable arguments is hardly news, but the
long-term *viability* of that technique is very interesting. Why is it that
politicians seeking public office find it advantageous consistently to
make poor arguments, and to refute their opponents' bad arguments
with retorts that are hardly better?

At least two hypotheses can be mustered to explain this phenomenon.
Perhaps there is a self-selection process at work: people who are good at
getting elected for some reason uniformly are bad at economic analysis.
Now, I just do not buy that argument. It is true that few politicians are
intellectuals, and it may be true that economic analysis is common sense
made difficult. But I do not think it is *that* difficult, and I can think of
several professional politicians whose understanding of basic economic
analysis is not at all bad.

My hunch is that the answer lies in a different direction. Ordinary
people have powerful incentives to know their interests as they make
choices in markets, but their interests may be far more difficult to discern
in the choices presented by political processes. And the negligible impact
of a single vote leads powerfully in the direction of rational ignorance:
as the vote of a given individual does not matter, the time and effort
needed to discover one's true interests are better applied elsewhere.

Let me make the point a bit differently: most policy serves particular interests or coalitions but necessarily imposes losses upon other interests. The losers often do not know that they are losers, particularly if the losses are diffused over a large number of people, and another way to reduce the effective political opposition of the losers is, bluntly, to confuse them. Such obfuscation is facilitated by low general levels of economic literacy.

On the other hand, some politicians may not have a point of view on a particular policy issue; even if they do have a view, pursuit of office makes them willing to support the position favored by the majority of the public. In that case, some organization takes a poll to determine the views of voters. Then, the policymakers develop or support policies and programs that reflect voter prejudices. Hence, if capital gains tax cuts are viewed by the majority as "unfair," such cuts are dead in the political water. If high executive pay is disturbing to the majority, riders are added to bills in Congress to limit executive pay. If banks are likely to fail, surely we need to raise limits on deposit insurance. Unfortunately, the public "view" is generally influenced by special interests who have a stake in directing public opinion. And the public's economic illiteracy prevents them from discerning what is in their self-interest.

A low level of economic literacy for many years has been a concern of mine, and at the Milken Institute, we are focusing on this issue as well. We have devoted considerable time and effort reflecting on this issue, particularly as we peruse the economic news reports each day. Accordingly, we decided to examine public views on some specific job creation issues in the United States, and so in May 1992 we commissioned Princeton Survey Research Associates to conduct a national survey on the current status of U.S. employment. The results were not encouraging.

More than two-thirds of the respondents understood correctly that from 1983 to 1990, most new job creation took place in relatively small firms rather than in firms in the Fortune 500. On the other hand, after being told that during the 1981–82 recession about 15.5 million people were employed at Fortune 500 companies, the respondents were asked whether that figure had increased, decreased, or stayed the same. The actual figure is a decrease of more than 3.5 million, but, only 14% of the respondents knew that employment at Fortune 500 firms today is lower by at least 1 million (Princeton Survey Research Associates, 1992).

More disturbing still are the reasons deemed important by the general public for U.S. job losses over the past 10 years. On a scale ranging from "no importance" to "greatest importance" among 33 alternative causes, the factor rated highly important by the greatest number of respondents (77%)—believe it or not—was "corporate executives being paid too much." The gap between that factor and the second factor cited most frequently was greater than that between any other pair of factors among our 33. As a footnote, I might add that much of the news media that reported the results of our survey proved incapable even of reporting the results correctly; for example, the front page of the *Wall Street Journal* reported, "A survey by the Milken Institute for Job and Capital Formation . . . *concludes* that high executive pay is the leading factor for U.S. job losses (emphasis added)." It is not too difficult to discern some sources of public confusion.

I do not want to bore you by listing all the responses to our survey. Let me just say that various dimensions of foreign competition ranked right behind high executive pay as causes of job loss in the public's view. Some 66% blamed job loss on "greed," 53% felt inadequate regulation of financial institutions was a very important factor, and only 40% blamed excessive workers' compensation costs, inability of firms to get financing, and excessive corporate taxation.

Now, most of us here this evening probably would rank the 33 factors somewhat differently. But I doubt that any of us would rank excessive executive compensation at all highly as a source of U.S. job losses; and an isolationist or protectionist foreign economic policy, seemingly supported by most of our respondents, is not something with which most economists would agree. And I believe that the importance of the U.S. regulatory environment is underestimated by our respondents.

Now, there is little doubt that politicians and policymakers both shape and respond to public attitudes. This effort to pander to public misperceptions is mischievous; a relatively minor example is the growing effort to limit executive compensation or to limit the favorable tax treatment of purportedly excessive executive compensation through legislation. More important is the trade protectionism given added impetus during hard times, or the political popularity of mandated benefits by employers. Moreover, attention spans are limited; attention paid to minor, irrelevant, and counterproductive issues must detract from efforts to address such real problems as monetary and tax policy, the regulatory burden, artificial capital market constraints, and so on.

There is additional survey evidence of poor economic literacy on the part of the public. The National Council on Economic Education issued in mid-September 1992 a press release titled "Everybody Talks about the Economy, but Gallup Survey Shows That the Public Knows Little about It." The press release points out that "the nation's economy has become the main issue in the presidential campaign and a heated topic of conversation everywhere from board rooms to backyards." Steven Buckles, president of the National Council on Economic Education, one of the group of organizations that sponsored the Gallup survey, comments that "economic illiteracy is rampant. It has the potential to misshape public opinion on economic issues and lead to policies that have perverse effects on the economy."

Similarly, William H. Donaldson, chairman and CEO of the New York Stock Exchange, says in the press release, "This Gallup survey sounds an alarm. The economy is a pivotal issue in this year's elections, yet many Americans lack even fundamental knowledge about economics. As a result, we find ourselves as a nation groping in the dark about personal and national choices."

What did the Gallup survey find? Only 36% of the respondents knew the central purpose of profits in a market economy. Only about a third could identify the most widely used measure of inflation, namely, the consumer price index. Just 40% recognized that economic growth is measured by a change in the gross domestic product; the other 60% thought that economic growth is measured by changes in the producer price index, the money supply, the balance of payments, or something else. Half understood that an increase in the exchange value of the dollar would lead to a decrease in U.S. exports. A bit less than half—47%—understood that increasing trade barriers (quotas) on imported goods would not increase employment in domestic industries in the long run.

And there was a clear awareness of personal deficiencies in economic literacy. About half of the respondents rated their own understanding of economics and economic issues as fair, and one-third rated it as poor, on a scale that ranged from excellent to good to fair to poor. Only 29% of the general public, 50% of high school seniors, and 44% of college seniors reported taking steps over the previous six months to understand economic issues.

Unsurprisingly, the major source of current information about the economy is the news media. The source cited most often by all groups in roughly equal proportions (70–79%) was television. The second major source was newspapers, read more by the general public (77%) and college seniors (78%) than by high school students (62%). Magazines (14–27%) and radio (9–16%) were cited less often.

There is nothing surprising about these patterns, and I believe that many of us would agree that the quality of economic analysis available from such sources is not reassuring. And it is more than merely plausible that public attitudes are influenced in important respects by these sources of information on economic news. On the other hand, the United States has more college-educated people than any other nation in the world. Economic issues are addressed by the media every day. Recent economic sluggishness has affected a wider cross section of the population than have previous slowdowns. Why is the American public seemingly so poorly informed on economic issues?

Part of the problem, clearly, is that the dismal science—or, perhaps more precisely, the art of dismal thinking—is difficult to explain in ways practical within typical individuals' attention spans. That may even be the major explanation. But I think that there is more to it. Our graduate economics training, and even our undergraduate economics education—let's face it—have become sorely deficient in terms of the application of theory, critical thinking, and resulting policy implications. The profession is becoming more aware and concerned about this trend, as illustrated, for example, by an essay in the recent *Journal of Economic Literature*, in which Bradley Bateman (1992) discusses recent committee reports on this problem.

Moreover, it is no secret that our academic system discourages top academic economists from explaining the policy implications of their research findings. The prospect of promotion, tenure, and the award of the Nobel prize is not affected by the frequency with which an economist appears on the op-ed page or on television interviews. And many of our best scholars probably derive greater personal satisfaction from the development of a new model or technique than from popularization of basic principles.

Obviously, there are important exceptions. Several participants in this conference devote considerable time to the policy implications of their work. Allan Meltzer is a member of the *Los Angeles Times* Board of Economists, and chairs the Shadow Open Market Committee. Robert Barro serves as a contributing editor of the *Wall Street Journal*. Bill Niskanen is the chairman of an institute devoted entirely to public education on policy issues. Glen Yago and Ben Zycher are frequent op-ed writers. Allan Reynolds and other participants pursue similar activities. Regular columns appear in newspapers and magazines by such prominent economists as Gary Becker, Craig Roberts, Thomas Sowell, and Walter Williams. And, of course, Milton Friedman and Paul Samuelson were writing for *Newsweek* years ago. But despite these exceptions, I think it is fair to say that most economists eschew popular forums for their work; public policy application of economic thinking is just not something that most economists do.

Now, most people would love to lay upon economists all of the blame for the problem that I have been describing. That might be fun, but it would be misguided. R. Emmett Tyrrell (1992), in his recent and very interesting book *The Conservative Crack-Up*, observes that the media limelight seems to fall more favorably and more often upon those promoting causes that can be described crudely as liberal; market-oriented scholars receive such favorable press attention far less frequently (p. 319). Perhaps there is a media bias; perhaps advocates of greater government are more likely to utilize or are better at utilizing the media in the pursuit of popular support. Perhaps both of those conditions are present. Whatever the source, it is my view that poor economic understanding on the part of much of the media is a salient characteristic of U.S. political processes, one that infects the general population in perverse ways.

And let us not fail to consider the role of bad analysis. Almost any position—however self-serving, however inconsistent with economic growth and job and capital formation, however perverse—can be "proven" or supported with bad empirical analysis. I refer, of course, to the myriad "studies" put out by interest groups solely in efforts to influence thinking by the public and to provide cover for decisions by policymakers. And even good research often fails to identify crucial relationships, because of problems and biases inherent in data, because of econometric difficulties, and because of the other pitfalls with which all of this conference's participants are familiar.

Let me offer an example. One of my interests is the "litigation explosion" and its effects on economic growth. I came upon a paper by Charles R. Epps, a legal studies fellow at the Institute for Legal Studies at the University of Wisconsin; a short version of that paper appeared recently as an op-ed piece in the *Wall Street Journal* (see Epps, 1992a, 1992b). Epps examines the issue of whether various measures of the number of lawyers affect economic growth, and does so by comparing variables across the states. Using a methodology that I reject as fatally flawed for a number of reasons, Epps concludes that the "number of lawyer variables has no statistically significant effect on economic growth rates." The upshot is that the Trial Lawyers Association now has "hard data" to support its position. This "research"—I use that term very loosely—has elevated Epps to a prominent position in the national debate over the litigation explosion, and in my view has muddled the public discussion of the increasing activism of the courts, the attendant rise in the number of attorneys, and resulting effects upon national economic performance.

Another problem is the counterintuitive nature of even elementary implications of economic analysis. Many in Congress claim to believe that price controls on prescription drugs will make consumers in the medical market better off. During the presidential campaign, Mr. Clinton argued repeatedly that "cost controls"—meaning price controls—in medical care actually would reduce total resource costs. Others believe that high taxes on capital hurt only "the rich." The distinction between correlation and causation seemingly is one that public discourse will never discern. And one of my favorites is the implicit assumption so common in public debate that failure of a public program to achieve given ends automatically justifies expansion of the attendant bureaucracy's budget.

Has any journalist ever suffered a penalty for bad analysis or for a prediction that proved wildly inaccurate? Indeed, isn't bad analysis a *prerequisite* of receipt of a Pulitzer Prize? Well, perhaps I exaggerate—a little. Do the media demand *any* qualifications of its economics reporters? I don't believe that it is all that unusual for an economics journalist to have written for the society page the previous day. And here is a happy thought: Is it a similar process that produces my science and medical news?

Even those who purport to be economists, or who have some training in economics, may understand little about the actual operation of, say, financial markets. If the stock market rises on a given day, the journalists typically recite three reasons for that increase. If stocks fall the next day, three new rationales are offered. I honestly believe that were I to phone some business reporters and tell them that the market rose 100 points, they would offer three confident reasons; if I then told them that I had made a mistake—that the market actually had declined by 100 points— they would explain that in equally confident tones. One of my favorites came out of my television set five years ago, when the stock market took a nose dive: a television economics correspondent explained in quite serious tones that the market had declined because of "heavy selling pressure."

And do economics correspondents have a pathological need to be negative, or is it only bad news that sells? The gentleman who comes immediately to mind is the bow-tied economics maven of NBC television in the 1980s, Mr. Irving R. Levine. I maintain that he has never presented a story about good economic news without a "however," as in "The stock market rose 120 points today, however in Peoria two clerks were laid off by the local drug store due to oppressive competition from the giant Thrifty chain." I remember clearly a day several years ago when Mr. Levine reported a rise in the exchange value of the dollar, and commented that this would yield reduced employment; the very next day he reported a decline in the unemployment rate, and commented that this would lead to higher inflation.

And is there any way to deal with the sound-bite problem? Large sections of the press actually seem to believe that serious issues can be discussed in a serious way in 20 seconds. And 90 seconds of airtime—well, from their perspective, that is sufficient for an entire dissertation. I believe that this process is highly perverse, and that it increases substantially the ease with which utter disinformation can be injected into public discourse. To pick a somewhat parochial example: it is a matter of record that few S&Ls held any high-yield bonds at all, and that those that did held relatively small amounts. In 1989, the GAO issued a report saying high-yield bonds were the second most profitable investment for financial institutions, after credit cards. High-yield bond holdings created problems for some institutions only after new regulations in 1989 forced the liquidation of high-yield portfolios at fire-sale prices. It was the perverse incentives created by deposit insurance—and the large increase in deposit insurance, I might add—along with geographic restrictions on branching and other regulations, that yielded the S&L debacle. But a wholesale rewriting of history by politicians and part of the press—aided by an ability to make sound-bite assertions—has made "junk bonds" the culprit.

This sort of policymaking by sound bite, or by public opinion poll, in my view is highly perverse, and can only exacerbate the short time horizons already embedded in the incentives driving political behavior.

I believe that in some other nations, the population is better informed on economic matters. My casual observation leads me to believe, for example, that Canadians understand trade issues and the implications of protectionism and exchange rate shifts more fully than do Americans, probably because Canada historically has been more dependent on foreign trade than has the United States. The relative price of the Canadian and U.S. dollar is likely to be more important to Canadians, and so Canadians, I believe, do a better job of learning about them. Residents of Hong Kong follow exchange rate shifts on an hourly basis, not because all of them are engaged in currency arbitrage, but because their livelihoods depend so vitally on foreign trade. Perhaps, then, the first step toward improvement of the economic literacy of Americans is to get them to understand how closely their well-being is linked to the economic policies thrust upon them.

Thus, we should strive to increase the demand for economic literacy, and then we must be able to increase the quantity that we supply. More and more states have been mandating that high schools offer an economics course, and that may be the right way to start, if the course instructors themselves are literate in economics. If not, such efforts may be counterproductive. Too often, high school economics courses are little more than forums for the biases of economically illiterate teachers of history or English. My own sense is that more than a single course is necessary, and that sound economics education ought to start earlier. And it would be helpful if the press reinforced good economic thinking rather than confused it.

Finally, I believe that we should make efforts to identify and publicize poor or biased economics reporting. Perhaps a watchdog committee somehow can be established to serve that function. If we, as economists, do not hold economics and business reporters accountable, we are not fulfilling our professional responsibility. As things now stand, for perfectly understandable reasons, errors in economic analysis or business reporting, regardless of how egregious, simply become overlooked. Journalists simply are never held accountable; I am reminded of the headline in *Business Week* in 1982 to the effect that "Equities Are Dead"; this was just before the unprecedented surge in stock prices.

At one point I was thinking that perhaps we should require print and electronic media economics reporters to be certified as qualified to report on this subject. Lawyers, accountants, and tax specialists must be certified, and must take professional continuing education courses. Perhaps the business press should be held to the same standards. However, the First Amendment allows anyone to write almost anything—regardless of how misguided it is. And who would do the certifying: Chicago types, or Keynesians, or mathematical theorists? Obviously, there are many things about which economists do not agree. However, there are opinions and there are facts. Undisputed facts can and must be reported accurately.

This accountability process does not have to be wholly negative. Perhaps we can establish rewards for reporters doing outstanding work on economics issues. Indeed, we have been thinking about just such a recognition program at the Milken Institute; the Foundations of the Milken Families give awards to outstanding K-12 educators and to cancer and epilepsy researchers, and so we are considering a similar program to recognize and reward excellence in economics and business reporting. As this project evolves toward implementation, we will ask you for ideas and assistance.

Such a project would be a useful step in moving toward increased understanding of economics among journalists and the general public, a goal I believe is vital to attain.

Until the public and media become more literate economically, this nation will continue to be plagued by a national economic policy that satisfies the short-term needs of politicians for votes and of special interests for subsidies and protection from competition, instead of a policy that yields growing prosperity for all.

References

Bateman, B. W. (1992). "The Education of Economists: A Different Perspective." *Journal of Economic Literature*, 30, 1491–1495.

Epps, C. R. (1992a, July). "Do Lawyers Impair Economic Growth?" Institute for Legal Studies Working Paper DPRP 11–5, University of Wisconsin, Madison.

Epps, C. R. (1992b, July 9). "Let's Not Kill All the Lawyers." *Wall Street Journal*.

Princeton Survey Research Associates. (1992, June). "Milken Institute for Job and Capital Formation National Jobs Survey." Report of the findings of a study conducted for the Milken Institute for Job and Capital Formation.

Tyrell, R. E. (1992). *The Conservative Crack-Up*. New York: Simon & Schuster.

About the Book

The links between economic policy and economic growth are simultaneously obvious and obscure, with many factors interacting to influence the overall process. The list of relevant parameters affecting economic growth of interest to scholars and policymakers is lengthy and expanding. Although the importance of government policy is widely recognized, the effects of policy on economic growth, in terms of direction and of magnitude, are difficult to measure. In *Economic Policy, Financial Markets, and Economic Growth,* a group of distinguished scholars offers findings on this ongoing and crucial debate that will be of interest to both academic and policy audiences.

About the Contributors

Robert J. Barro is professor of economics at Harvard University and research associate at the National Bureau of Economic Research. A fellow of the American Academy of Arts and Sciences and of the Econometric Society, he has served as an officer of the American Economic Association and is a contributing editor of the *Wall Street Journal*. His books include *Modern Business Cycle Theory* (1989); *Money, Expectations, and Business Cycles* (1981); *Macroeconomic Policy* (1990); and the widely used textbook *Macroeconomics*, which will soon be in its fourth edition. He writes on economic fluctuation, taxation, inflation, and monetary economics and has published extensively in professional journals; he is currently working on a book on economic growth. He received his B.S. in physics from the California Institute of Technology in 1965 and his Ph.D. in economics from Harvard University in 1970.

George J. Benston is associate dean of the Emory Faculty Research and Development Center and is John H. Harland Professor of Finance, Accounting, and Economics at the Emory School of Business. Concurrently, he is professor of economics at Emory's College of Letters and Science and is honorary visiting professor at City University in London. He is coeditor and cofounder of the *Journal of Financial Services Research*, and he serves as associate editor of the *Journal of Money, Credit, and Banking*; *Research in Financial Services Annual*; *Contemporary Accounting Research*; and the *Journal of Accounting and Public Policy*. He has published more than a hundred books, monographs, and articles. His work examines such issues as SEC financial disclosures, economies of scale in banking, savings and loan failures, the regulation of banking and financial markets, and antitrust economics. His recent publications include *The Separation of Commercial and Investment Banking: The Glass-Steagall Act Revisited and Reconsidered* (1990) and "The Failure and Survival of Thrifts: Evidence from the Southeast" (1991). He graduated from Queens College with a B.A. in 1952, and received his M.B.A. from New York University in 1953, his C.P.A. from North Carolina in 1955, and his Ph.D. in economics from the University of Chicago in 1963.

Reuven Brenner holds the Repap Chair in Economics at McGill University's School of Management and is Associate Fellow at the Centre de Recherché et Development en Economique (CRDE), Universite de Montreal. He is a member of the Canadian Economic Policy Review Board, the Center for Research on Eastern & Central Europe, and also serves regularly as a consultant for EEC, a Montreal-based consulting firm. In 1991, he participated in discussions of reforms with Russia's Ministry of Finance, and in April 1992, with Thailand's government. He has authored articles for scholarly journals as well as five books: *History: The Human Gamble* (1983); *Betting on Ideas: Wars, Invention, Inflation* (1985); *Rivalry: In Business, Science, among Nations* (1987); *Gambling and Speculation* (with G. Brenner) (1990); and *Educating Economists* (with D. Colander). His books and articles have been translated into Spanish, French, and Italian. He is an occasional contributor to the *Wall Street Journal*, *Reason*, *Le Figaro* (in Paris), and the *Gazette*. In 1991, he was awarded the Killam Research Fellowship Award, being one of 15 selected from across Canada from a broad range of disciplines.

Jack L. Carr is professor of political economy at the University of Toronto and research associate at the University of Toronto's Institute for Policy Analysis. He is an expert in monetary economics, financial economics, and law and economics. His publications have appeared in the *Journal of Political Economy*; *American Economic Review*; *Journal of Finance*; *Journal of Money, Credit, and Banking*; *Journal of Monetary Economics*; *Journal of Law and Economics*; *Journal of Legal Studies*; and *Economic Inquiry*. His books include *Tax-Based Income Policies: A Cure for Inflation* (1982); *The Size of the Government Sector and Economic Growth* (1989); and *Monetary Anticipation and the Demand for Money* (with M. Darby and D. Thornton, Sept., 1985). He has received two Social Science and Humanities Research Council Grants totaling $65,000. He graduated from the University of Toronto in 1965, and took his Ph.D. in economics at the University of Chicago in 1971.

Michael R. Darby is professor of economics and vice chairman of the John E. Anderson Graduate School of Management at the University of California, Los Angeles. Concurrently, he holds appointments as chairman of the Dumbarton Group (Los Angeles and Washington), research associate with the National Bureau of Economic Research, economist with the Internal Revenue Service Statistics of Income, and adjunct scholar with the American Enterprise Institute. In 1990–1992 he was administrator of the Economics and Statistics Administration. He has written six books and monographs on macroeconomic theory and labor, employment, and productivity. He has also published extensively in numerous scholarly journals. His recent journal articles include "Economic Growth and Policy in the Nineties," "The Impact of Government Deficits on Personal and National Saving Rates," and "Buffer Stock Models of the Demand for Money and the Conduct of Monetary Policy."

He currently serves on the editorial boards of the *Journal of International Money and Finance*, *Contemporary Policy Issues*, and *International Report*. He has received many honors, including the Alexander Hamilton Award, the U.S. Treasury's highest honor, in 1989. He received his A.B. *summa cum laude* from Dartmouth College in 1967, and took his M.A. in 1968 and his Ph.D. in 1970 from the University of Chicago.

Robert Eisner is William R. Kenan Professor of Economics at Northwestern University, a fellow of the American Academy of Arts and Sciences and of the Econometric Society, and formerly president of the American Economic Association. He is the author of *Factors in Business Investment* (1978), *How Real Is the Federal Deficit?* (1986), and *The Total Income System of Accounts* (1989). He is currently working on recalculating the federal deficit and recently published an article that examines this issue in the Milken Institute's newsletter, *Jobs & Capital*. He received his B.S.S. from City College of New York in 1940, his M.A. from Columbia University in 1942, and his Ph.D. from Johns Hopkins University in 1952.

George Horwich is professor of economics and Burton D. Morgan Chair for the Study of Private Enterprise at Purdue University. Currently, he is teaching at the People's University of China in Beijing. He is also an adjunct scholar at the American Enterprise Institute, a collaborating scientist at the Oak Ridge National Laboratory, and a consultant to the Office of Foreign Disaster Assistance. He has written widely in the areas of monetary policy, energy economics, and the economics of natural disasters. His books and other publications include *Money, Capital, and Prices* (1964); *Responding to the International Oil Crises* (1988); "On Tax Policies for Encouraging Increased Energy Conservation;" and "The Role of the For-Profit Private Sector in Disaster Mitigation and Response." He received his A.M. in 1951 and his Ph.D. in economics in 1954 from the University of Chicago.

David I. Meiselman is professor of economics at Virginia Polytechnic Institute and State University. Concurrently, he is director of Virginia Polytechnic's Graduate Economics Program in Northern Virginia and associate director of Virginia Polytechnic's Center for the Study of Futures and Options. He is also an adjunct scholar at the Cato Institute, the American Enterprise Institute, and the Heritage Foundation, and serves as chairman of the editorial board of *Policy Review*. He has conducted extensive research in monetary economics, public finance, and the financial and futures markets, and has made important contributions and published widely in these and related public policy areas. His recent journal articles include "The Rational Expectation: New Classical Macroeconomics Revolution," "The Collapse of Deposit Insurance: From Apparent Success to Clear Disaster," and "The Stock Market Crash and the Economic Outlook." He received his A.B. in economics from Boston University in 1947 and his M.A. and Ph.D. in economics from the University of Chicago in 1951 and 1961, respectively.

Allan H. Meltzer, John M. Olin Professor of Political Economy and Public Policy at Carnegie Mellon University, is a founder and cochairman of the Shadow Open Market Committee and serves on the President's Economic Policy Advisory Board. His field of expertise is in monetary and capital markets. He has authored several books and more than 150 papers on economic theory and policy, including *Political Economy, Monetary Economics* (with K. Brunner; 1989), and *Monetarism and Contemporary Monetary Policy in the U.S.* (1985; in Japanese). He serves as coeditor of the *Carnegie-Rochester Conference Series on Public Policy* and as associate editor of several scholarly journals, including the *Journal of Monetary Economics.* His distinguished appointments include the positions of honorary adviser to the Institute for Monetary and Economic Studies of the Bank of Japan and director of the Cooper Tire and Rubber Company, the Sarah Scaife Foundation, and the Commonwealth Foundation. In 1983, he was awarded the UCLA medal for distinguished professional achievement. He received his A.B. in economics from Duke University before taking his M.A. and Ph.D. in economics from the University of California at Los Angeles in 1955 and 1958, respectively.

William A. Niskanen is chairman of the Cato Institute in Washington D.C. Formerly, he was a member of President Reagan's Council of Economic Advisers and a professor of economics at both the University of California at Berkeley and the University of California at Los Angeles. His expertise is in public finance, public choice, and tax policy. His publications include *Bureaucracy and Representative Government* (1971) and *Reaganomics: An Insider's Account of the Policies and the People* (1988), which was chosen as one of the 10 best books of 1988 by *Business Week.* As founder of the National Tax Limitation Committee, he has contributed to the drafting of several tax limitation amendments. He is also editor of *Dollars, Deficits, and Trade* as well as *Regulation* magazine. He graduated with an A.B. from Harvard College in 1955 and received his M.A. in 1955 and Ph.D. in 1962 in economics from the University of Chicago.

William Poole is Herbert M. Goldberger Professor of Economics at Brown University. Concurrently, he serves on advisory panels for the Federal Reserve Bank of New York and the Congressional Budget Office. He is a research associate at the National Bureau of Economic Research and an adjunct scholar at both the American Enterprise Institute and the Cato Institute. He is associate editor of the *Journal of Money, Credit, and Banking,* coauthor of *Principals of Economics* (1991), and author of *Money and the Economy: A Monetarist View* (1978). In addition, he has written numerous scholarly papers published in professional journals. In 1989, Swarthmore College awarded him the honorary degree of doctor of laws. He graduated Phi Beta Kappa from Swarthmore College and earned his M.B.A. and Ph.D. degrees from the University of Chicago.

Robert H. Rasche is professor of economics at Michigan State University, where he has been on the faculty since 1972. He serves as associate editor of the *Journal of Money, Credit, and Banking* and the *Journal of Economics and Banking*, and is a member of the Shadow Open Market Committee and of the Advisory Committee of the Carnegie-Rochester Conference on Public Policy. He has made several conference and seminar presentations and has authored numerous publications on fiscal and monetary policy. His recent publications include "Money Demand in the U.S. and Japan: Analysis of Stability and the Importance of Permanent and Transitory Shocks" (with D. Hoffman), and "Indicators of Inflation." He is also the author of *Controlling Growth of Monetary Aggregates* (with J. M. Johannes), published in 1987. In 1988, he was the recipient of a Distinguished Faculty Award from Michigan State University. He received his B.A. in economics and mathematics from Yale University in 1963 and his A.M. and Ph.D. in economics from the University of Michigan in 1965 and 1966, respectively.

Paul H. Rubin is professor of economics at Emory University in Atlanta and is an adjunct scholar at the American Enterprise Institute and the Cato Institute. He is also associated with Glassman-Oliver Economic Consultants, Inc., in Washington, where he was formerly vice president. He has written four books and more than 75 articles on the economics of law, advertising, product liability and safety, civil penalties, regulation, and antitrust issues. His recent publications include "Why Regulate Consumer Product Safety?" "Some Implications of Damage Payments for Nonpecuniary Losses" (with J. Calfee), and *Managing Business Transactions: Controlling the Costs of Coordinating, Communicating, and Decision Making (1990)*. He has addressed numerous business, professional, policy, and academic audiences, and his publications have appeared in economic journals, law reviews, and leading newspapers, including frequent contributions to the *Wall Street Journal*. He received his B.A. with honors from the University of Cincinnati in 1963 and his Ph.D. from Purdue University in 1970.

Lewis C. Solmon is president of the Milken Institute for Job and Capital Formation in Los Angeles. Prior to assuming this position in July 1991, he served as dean of UCLA's Graduate School of Education for six years. He has served on the faculties of UCLA, CUNY, and Purdue, and currently is a professor emeritus at UCLA. He has published two dozen books and monographs and more than 60 articles in scholarly and professional journals. His books include *From the Campus: Perspectives on the School Reform Movement* (1989), *The Costs of Evaluation* (1983), *Underemployed Ph.D.'s* (1981), and three editions of *Economics*, a basic text. He has written on teacher testing programs, foreign students, demographics of higher education, education and economic growth, the effects of educational quality, and the links between education and work. He is currently an associate editor of the *Economics of Education Review*. He has served as an adviser to the World Bank, UNESCO, various government agencies, and many universities. He received his A.M. in 1967 and his Ph.D. in economics in 1968, both from the University of Chicago.

Norman B. Ture is president of the Institute for Research on the Economics of Taxation, a nonprofit, nonpartisan public research institute in Washington, D.C. He served from early 1981 to June 1982 as under secretary of the treasury in the Reagan administration. An expert in tax policy, he has published several books and articles in this field. He is also a well-respected supply-side theoretician and is author of "Wealth Redistribution and the Income Tax" (1978), "Supply-Side Analysis and Public Policy" (1982), and "What Can We Learn from the United States' Experience?" (1989). These three publications are considered his most significant contributions to the understanding of supply-side economic analysis and its application to public policy. He received his M.A. in 1947 and his Ph.D. in economics in 1968 from the University of Chicago.

Glenn Yago is director of the Economic Research Bureau at the State University of New York—Stony Brook and faculty fellow of the Rockefeller Institute. He also serves as associate professor of management at Stony Brook's Harriman School for Management and Policy and as chairman of the New York State Network for Economic Research. He has conducted extensive analysis of public policy on industrial, transportation, capital markets, and public and private employment issues. Recently, he examined the transfer of new financial technologies developed in U.S. capital markets to Latin America and the former socialist countries. He is the author of reports on mergers and acquisitions, leveraged buyouts, high-yield securities, and initial public offerings, and his publications include *The Decline of Transit* (1984); *Junk Bonds: How High Yield Securities Restructured Corporate America* (1991); *The High Yield Debt Market: Investment Performance and Economic Impact* (1990); and *Corporate Restructuring* (1990). He has published articles in numerous scholarly journals and newspapers, including *Urban Affairs Quarterly, Journal of Commerce, Journal of Applied Corporate Finance*, the *Wall Street Journal*, and the *New York Times*. He received his B.A. from Tulane University in 1971, his M.A. from Hebrew University in Jerusalem in 1976, and his Ph.D. from the University of Wisconsin—Madison in 1980.

Benjamin Zycher is vice president for research at the Milken Institute for Job and Capital Formation and the editor of the Institute newsletter, *Jobs & Capital*. He is also a visiting professor of economics at the University of California at Los Angeles and an adjunct scholar at the Cato Institute. His area of expertise is the analysis of economic regulation and government behavior. He has published many articles and monographs in a wide range of subject areas, from defense economics and the analysis of Soviet economic conditions to the effects of government regulation on energy and environmental policy. Among his recent papers are "The Efficient Rise of Public and Private Debt," "Price Controls, Direct Democracy, and Taxation by Regulation," "Environmental Degradation under Eastern European Socialism," and "Military Dimensions of Communist Systems." He received his B.A. in political science from the University of California at Los Angeles in 1972, his M.P.P. from the Uni-versity of California at Berkeley in 1974, and his Ph.D. in economics from the University of California at Los Angeles in 1979.

Conference Participants

King Banaian, Pitzer College
Doug Bandow, Copley News Service
Richard A. Bergman, Bergman, Knox & Green
Richard J. Capalbo, Mitchum, Jones & Templeton, Inc.
Donald Chew, *Journal of Applied Corporate Finance*
Charles A. Cooper, RAND Corporation
Robert Davidow, private investor
Lance E. Davis, California Institute of Technology
Thomas E. Davis, Federal Reserve Bank of Kansas City
Laurence Dougharty, Manhattan Beach, CA
Catherine England, England Economics
Tim W. Ferguson, *Wall Street Journal*
Ralph Finerman, Goldstein, Golub & Kessler
Steve Fink, East/West Capital
Gerard B. Finneran, TCW Americas Development Association, L.P.
Penelope D. Foley, TCW Americas Development Association, L.P.
Frederick T. Furlong, Federal Reserve Bank of San Francisco
Robert E. Gallman, University of North Carolina at Chapel Hill
Michael E. Granfield, University of California at Los Angeles
Forest Hamilton, Fatburger
Ayse Imrohoroglu, University of Southern California
Selahattin Imrohoroglu, University of Southern California
Michael D. Intriligator, University of California at Los Angeles
Holman Jenkins, *Wall Street Journal*
Douglas H. Joines, University of Southern California
Nake M. Kamrany, University of Southern California
George G. Kaufman, Loyola University
Robert Kroll, California State University, Northridge
Mark Lacter, *Daily News*, Los Angeles
William W. Lang, Rutgers University
Edward E. Leamer, University of California at Los Angeles
Julius Lesner, Foundations of the Milken Families

Howard S. Marks, Trust Company of the West
Jonathan Marshall, *San Francisco Chronicle*
Richard B. McKenzie, University of California at Irvine
Lowell Milken, Foundations of the Milken Families
Aurelius (Bill) Morgner, University of Southern California
Charles I. Plosser, University of Rochester
Steve Postrel, University of California at Los Angeles
Virginia T. Postrel, Reason Foundation
Alan Reynolds, Hudson Institute
Patricia A. Reynolds, University of Southern California
Katherine A. Samolyk, Federal Reserve Bank of Cleveland
Richard Sandler, Victor & Sandler
Patrick Savin, Savin, Carlson Investment
Rodney Smith, Claremont McKenna College
Lorraine Spurge, Knowledge Exchange, Inc.
John F. Stehle, Villanova University
Shirley Svorny, California State University, Northridge
David J. Theroux, Independent Institute
Lewis K. Uhler, National Tax Limitation Committee
Albert Wohlstetter, Pan Heuristics
Roberta Wohlstetter, Pan Heuristics

Index